FOOTBALL WORLDS

FOOTBALL WORLDS

A Lifetime in Sport

•••

Sir Stanley Rous

with a Foreword by
Sir Walter Winterbottom

FABER AND FABER
London   Boston

First published in 1978
by Faber and Faber Limited
3 Queen Square London WC1
Printed in Great Britain by
Latimer Trend & Company Ltd, Plymouth

British Library Cataloguing in Publication Data
Rous, *Sir*, Stanley
  Football worlds.
  1. Rous, *Sir* Stanley 2. Soccer—Biography
  I. Title
  796.33'4'0924   GV942.7.R/

  ISBN 0-571-11194-7

Contents

Illustrations

(Between pages 128 and 129)

1. The Mutford village team in 1912. The author kneels *(second from left)* beside schoolmaster Cobb, who guards the loaned ball
2. The St Luke's College team with goalkeeper Rous in the back row
3. Serving in Egypt in 1916
4. Giving swimming instruction at Watford Grammar School
5. About to start the Hungary *v* Italy match in October 1933. Rous stands between the Hungarian captain Koranji *(left of picture)* and the Italian captain, Cesarini. Far right is the Hungarian linesman, Fryges Kann
6. Refereeing the 1934 Cup Final as nineteen-year-old Frank Swift gropes for a Portsmouth centre. Manchester City won 2–1 with two goals from centre-forward Tilson in the last fifteen minutes
7. Taking leave of Sir Frederick Wall as the FA secretaryship is handed over
8. A lesson in tactics for a sports journalist from Austria visiting the FA
9. Escorting the King to meet the players in a war-time International at Wembley. On the right is Eddie Hapgood (No. 3) with Stan Cullis (No. 5) next to him. Beyond Hapgood is Sergeant-Major Voysey, the Millwall trainer
10. Mrs Churchill at Lancaster Gate checks progress of her 'Aid to Russia' Fund. Watching from the left are Charles Wreford-Brown (FA Committee member), Lord Iliffe (Chairman Red Cross Committee), Lord Wigram (Chairman Red Cross Sports Committee), the author, Miss Holden (Secretary for Indoor Sports), and Ernest Miller (Secretary for Outdoor Sports)

11. Winston Churchill is introduced to the Newcastle team by Joe Harvey before they beat Arsenal 1–0 in the 1952 Cup Final. Bob Stokoe is on Harvey's left as Churchill shakes hands with Bobby Mitchell

12. The author with his wife after receiving his knighthood in 1949

13. FIFA's goalkeeper, Zenian of Austria, punches clear from Nat Lofthouse with Stan Mortensen lurking near as England draw 4–4 in the match at Wembley to celebrate the FA's ninetieth anniversary in 1953

14. Watching as Billy Wright and Joe Mears carry a wreath at a service for Eva Perón, who died as the England team was visiting Argentina in 1953

15. Leaving for Moscow with the Arsenal team in 1954. To the author's right are the manager, Tom Whittaker, Jimmy Joyce, Alec Forbes, and Chairman, Guy Bracewell Smith. On the steps are Tommy Lawton (*top right*), trainer Milne, and Don Roper; Peter Goring (*right*) and Jack Kelsey; Derek Tapscott (*right*) and Walley Barnes

16. All smiles as England beat Scotland 9–3 at Wembley in 1961 and the Queen presents the International trophy to Johnny Haynes, the England captain

17. Watching as Jimmy Adamson presents the Burnley team to the Duke of Edinburgh before the 1962 Cup Final, which Tottenham won for the second year running

18. Meeting the Pope as His Holiness gives audience to members of a UEFA Congress in Rome. Behind the Pope are Michel Daphinoff, Asst. Sec. UEFA (*left*); Gustav Wiederkehr, UEFA President (*facing, between the Pope and Sir Stanley*); Jose Crahay, Sec. Belgian FA; Sandor Barcs, Hungary; Herbert Powell, Wales; and Hans Bangerter, Gen. Sec. UEFA (*on the right of picture*)

19. Field Marshal Lord Montgomery of Alamein at the FA offices with Walter Winterbottom (*left*), Graham Doggart, and the author

20. In 1966 the Jules Rimet Cup is handed to Sir Stanley by Dr Luiz Murgel of Brazil, the holders. World Cup Organising Committee members in the background are from the left Gustav Wiederkehr (Switzerland), Lim Zee Sion (Malaysia), Harry Cavan (Northern Ireland), and Dr Ottorini Barassi (Italy)

21. The height of enthusiasm as some ticketless spectators are up the pole in their determination to see the 1964 final of the South American Youth Tournament in Bogota, Colombia
22. With Gillian Gilks and John Conteh receiving the first Manning awards in 1975. The author was the sports writers' first choice for outstanding services to sport
23. Receiving a decoration from the Senegalese Government on his eightieth birthday in April 1975
24. Watching the final of the first Gulf Cup staged in Kuwait
25. Watching football in Burma in the Asian zone pre-Olympic tournament
26. Organising the charity cricket match at Eastcote in 1955
27. Being entertained in Japan. Dr Käser, General Secretary of FIFA, is on the left; holding the chopsticks is Rosemarie Breitenstein, the author's secretary
28. Taking part in the activities at Plas-y-Brenin National Recreation Centre with Sir John Hunt (*at back*), and Prince Philip (*centre*), who talks to one of a group setting out on an exercise
29. Congratulations from Ernst Thommen of Switzerland after being elected President of FIFA in 1961

Foreword

It is a privilege and pleasure to write the foreword to the life story of
Stanley Rous—the great man of football—who is held in high esteem
the world over for his immense contribution to the organisation and
development of the game he so dearly loves.

Stanley came to football from a career in education with the qualification of being an outstanding referee. When I first met him at an FA
course just before the last war, he revealed his keen interest in teaching
method and his inspirational leadership. Throughout his life Stanley
has been encouraging others to busy themselves in improving and
developing the game of Association Football, and his sympathetic
understanding of people, and supporting interest in what they are keen
to do, is the source of much of his charm. There is also his abounding
sense of humour: his skill in using topical illustration or an amusing
tale to turn an awkward situation in meetings and to convey his message
more clearly. Like the big man he is, he will often poke fun at himself
and laugh heartily with others when a joke turns against him.

His zeal is reflected in everything he has done: he has never spared
himself. Stanley Rous was an accomplished Secretary of the FA:
methodical, clear and well-reasoned in his judgements, and ever on
the look-out for means of making progress. At the same time, he was
conservative in the sense of identifying and cherishing the best in the
present. Not for him the many proposals to alter the basic simplicity of
the game by fashioning more complicated laws and regulations. Anyone around him who has ideas was encouraged to give them tangible
expression—improvements to football boots and playing kit, flood-
lighting, training get-togethers for players, national courses for
groundsmen, managers and schoolboys, coaching qualifications,
publications (textbooks, annuals, diaries and the *FA News*), and the
use of television in promoting football.

When I left the Football Association to join the Central Council of
Physical Recreation as its General Secretary, Stanley was its Chair-

man. Working alongside him was fun, though you were ever conscious
of his drive and enterprise and his ability to respond to new challenges,
as when the Government decided to establish a Sports Council.

As President of FIFA his programme of engagements involving
extensive travel kept him a very busy man and brought him into contact with many heads of state and leaders in politics and industry, yet
he never lost his common touch. He still found time to talk to the
ordinary fellow and help him with his problems, and he always
maintained contact with his many friends. It is said that people who
give of their lives to others leave a rich inheritance upon which our
future depends. The work of Stanley Rous in football is a legend, but
I think Stanley would value most of all the warmth of the feeling of
friendship which his service to the game of football has helped to
spread throughout the world.

It is remarkable how much Stanley Rous has fitted into his life,
and it is characteristic of him to write of a career of such great achievement with simplicity and humour. As with all his work, he has fulfilled
this task with style, dignity and human understanding.

Walter Winterbottom

I

The Early Years

●●●

My home village of Mutford in Suffolk, where I was born on April
25th 1895, was an unlikely place to breed a soccer enthusiast. The
game was virtually unknown to this farming and fishing community
of some three hundred people, who had few shared amusements. For
us boys the main sport was chasing each other on our cycles round the
village, with one of us acting as timekeeper.

We also invented a kind of outdoor bagatelle. This involved gouging
out holes in the grassy verge of the main road, giving different values
to each hole and then trying to roll a makeshift ball into them. There
were hidden dangers in this game. A member of the Lowestoft branch
of the Suffolk Yeomanry was riding by when his horse trod in a hole,
broke its leg and had to be destroyed. My uncle, who was a Yeoman
himself, blamed me for the accident and I was nearly banned from the
game—the only time I have been given my marching orders in
any sport.

My football was learnt at a school in Beccles where I played in goal
for the students' XI. My own immediate enjoyment of the game made
me keen that others should share my pleasure in playing. I was fifteen
at the time and now marvel at my temerity in calling a meeting in the
village school and addressing the assembled farmhands and off-duty
fishermen. They responded well to a youngster, impressed by my own
fervent enthusiasm or the fortunate accident of my already being over
six foot tall, which gave me a certain air of authority beyond my age.

Organising a village side from scratch would have been a daunting
task, but for the splendid spirit of co-operation and self-help which is
such an admirable feature of these close communities. The local
carpenter-wheelwright, whose wife, Mrs Crouchen, was the efficient
headmistress of the village school, made us a set of goalposts. The

13

farmer, Frank Farman, at the Manor House, allowed us to use a meadow in the centre of Mutford, while the Beccles' teaching centre lent me the ball, which had to be carefully cherished.

There is such a natural urge to kick a football that once I had produced it there was no difficulty in getting a dozen young men interested in learning the game. After a few kick-abouts our scratch side felt confident enough to challenge nearby Kessingland, a seaside town some four miles distant. Other villages, like Barnby and Hulver, soon wanted to join in and within a season we had quite an extensive fixture list. The games were enjoyed and so was the opportunity to visit neighbouring villages, with competition also developing to provide the best teas for players after the games.

None of the teams we took on were more than four miles distant, but in 1912 our only means of travel was on foot or cycle, so you had to be keen to play. That was underlined when we raised enough money for a colourful set of jerseys. With a farm labourer's wage at 12s a week, they were not going to lay out a penny unless it mattered to them. I did, however, choose my time carefully to ask for this subscription for kit. During the harvest there was a special extra payment for farmworkers. The custom was for a 'handshake' contract, usually to work for a month for £5. After the handshake the bargain was always kept on both sides—more effectively perhaps than with all today's Contract of Employment statements and supporting legislation. So the farmworkers had a little spare pocket money at the end of the harvest. The fishermen's contributions were obtained when they had been paid off for their two-months' 'rest'. Their accumulated pay was always given them in sovereigns or half-sovereigns, so I had to have plenty of change.

My first appearance in a representative football match had been the year before, keeping goal for Beccles Schools against Lowestoft Schools. Crown Meadow, the Lowestoft Town ground, had an awe-inspiring atmosphere for a young boy aged fourteen and well aware of his lack of knowledge of the goalkeeping arts. Indeed, I had only been put there because of my size. There were quite a few spectators for this local derby and it was a depressing debut for me. We were beaten 9–0. I was so untutored in my duties that when a Lowestoft supporter behind the goal shouted 'leave it', I took his advice and the ball went straight into my net. The young, however, are not easily dispirited and we learned fast enough to have a creditable 2–2 draw in the return game.

When later I organised our Mutford team we soon had enough local success that I was invited to play for Kirkley in the Norfolk and Suffolk League and Suffolk Senior Cup. For a full season I was able to sample football of a higher standard. Playing with adults, I was impressed by the faster pace and the higher skills, particularly of the few county players in the sides. Ours was George Crisp, who had as many tricks off the field as on it. If you thought you had had a good game and sat back in the homeward train to read the expected complimentary comments in the 'Pink 'un', the *Eastern Football News*, you were apt to find the paper burst into flames before your face as George applied a match.

My most miserable game was against Cromer, played in thick fog since neither side could afford the expense of postponement. We lost 10–6, perhaps because I was more honest in telling the referee when the ball was in my net! It was so murky that you saw nothing until a player suddenly appeared a few yards away. At least no one else on the side could criticise my performance, as none of them could see me in action. My most lasting impression, however, was in another league match, at Great Yarmouth, when I dived to save and had some front teeth knocked back by a flailing boot. The dentist forced them straight, but said they would soon go black and have to be removed. In fact they served me well for another twenty-five years until I was told to have them out as they were too unsightly when invited to appear in TV programmes.

Playing in this league meant travelling farther afield to towns like King's Lynn, Gorlesham and Leiston. I was also fortunate enough to play in a friendly game on the 'Nest', the old Norwich City ground. And to that ground I took the keenest of my village boys to see the great players of the day and learn by example—still the best teaching method. To take them over one at a time I had an extra step fitted to the back axle of my bicycle on which they stood with their hands on my shoulders for the two-hour journey as I pedalled the twenty-five miles to Norwich. We had to push the bike up the 'hills', which seemed surprisingly frequent for such a flat countryside. We had to be keen to do that journey on a rainy day, but we thought it well worth the effort when any of the contemporary heroes was in form. A particular favourite whenever he visited the ground with Southampton was the remarkable Charles Fry, to whom nothing seemed impossible.

Fry was the epitome of the gifted amateur, a brilliant scholar, a scourge of the Australian cricketers and scorer of six successive first-class centuries, a cup finalist with Southampton. It was typical of Fry that after a good lunch he should go down to the Iffley Road ground at Oxford, change while smoking a cigar, put it down long enough to break the world long jump record at his first attempt, and return to his cigar without bothering to jump again.

To us Fry looked a fast and formidable right-back, much more constructive than the usual rugged destroyers of the time, with only his heading not up to the highest professional standards—but that was a normal weakness in amateurs. Harold Fleming of Swindon was another who excited us. He was inside to David Morris, scorer of almost three hundred League goals. Fleming was an imaginative player and a brilliant dribbler. It was his intuitive sense which made so many goals for Morris. In the Norwich team there were also some memorable players. Naturally I made a special study of their famous goalkeeper, Bobby Beal, who was exceptionally agile and kicked vast distances down the 'Nest's' noticeable slope. From watching him I learnt more about positional play, but I know now how much faster I could have improved had more direct coaching been available.

Billy McCracken was another Norwich player before he joined the outstanding team of the pre-war years, Newcastle, and became so adept at playing forwards offside that the law had eventually to be changed. He was an intelligent interceptor and tactician, but rough and rugged in his tackling. So durable and dedicated has been McCracken's passion for the game that he is still scouting for Watford though over ninety years old. Willie Hampson was the other, more versatile back, a poised and clever player who used the ball well. That no doubt was what attracted Newcastle United when they acquired him, as this formidable Norwich defence was broken up by transfers.

But it was not only the footballers who caught my eye. For the first time I became aware of the influence a good referee can have in controlling a game and keep it flowing. The man who especially impressed me was Johnny Talks from Lincoln, a small gnome of a man with a hunched back, but with personality which gave him absolute authority over the players. He was noted as the loudest and most decisive whistler among all the referees. And the crowd was put in instant good humour, laughing as he came out flanked by two tall linesmen whose chests overshadowed his head.

In those days the shoulder charge was an essential part of the game, and all except the most skilful dribblers expected to be bowled over if they held the ball too long. It is a pity the genuine shoulder charge has almost disappeared now, and is even penalised by some referees, though it is still legal.

There was a high concrete wall so close behind one end that the ball would even come flying back out of goal if there was any give in the net. So disputed goals were not unknown. It was also typical of the ground that the turnstiles were so rickety that those who knew the secret could get in free by pressing against the wooden partition and squeezing through.

Before football became an interest in my life I had been absorbed by the railways, which then held a special place in our society. My father was a grocer and provision merchant, dealing also in coal and glass. His business was not very prosperous and never appealed to me. I never considered it as a possible career, but from an early age I had a passion for railways and might well have tried for a job on them. Many boys then thought of being an engine driver as the height of ambition, but it was the running of railways that concerned me. It was an odd attraction, since the nearest line, from Lowestoft to Beccles, was at least four miles from Mutford. Yet I knew the times of every train which passed and of those to Norwich, Yarmouth and London. When I daydreamed it was always of railways. I made a mock signal box in the upper room of our warehouse and imagined the road as the line down which trains rushed under my control. There were few cars passing to represent the trains, but in my mind our house was a busy station with constant activity all organised by me.

Nevertheless, daydreams a railway career remained. Both my elder sisters, Hilda and Ruth, were teachers at schools in Lowestoft and Oulton Broad and my father thought that would also be a suitable career for me. He interviewed 'Pedlar' Palmer, Headmaster of the Beccles School to which I cycled daily, and they agreed that I should move on to the Teacher Training Centre in that town. There I studied three days a week and spent two more in practical training at the Yarmouth Road School in Oulton Broad. In the lunch hours and after school I organised football in the open space opposite the school. The surface was rough, but that never dampened the enthusiasm of the boys and students, about twenty in number, who came to the practices. Two regular teachers became interested enough in these to carry them on when I was at Beccles. An echo of my teaching at Oulton Broad, the first I had attempted, came when I was FA Secretary. Arthur Oldham, a fish merchant of Lowestoft, wrote to me offering to send me a 'good fry' fresh from his boat and asking, like thousands of others, for a Cup Final ticket. He added that he hoped I remembered him as well as he remembered me since 'you was the best English master what ever taught me.'

My football activities had to be undertaken without interfering with other studies, and inevitably this involved an arduous routine. On Wednesday afternoons I played for the 'Centre' team against mid-week sides ranging from Bungay to Diss to Harlesden. On Saturdays I played in the afternoons for Kirkley, which involved travelling considerable distances by train after leaving my cycle at Beccles or Lowestoft station. In between I kept the Mutford matches and practices going. So much of my school work had to be done early or late. A boy next door worked on a farm and left punctually at 5.30 every morning. He acted as my alarm clock, pulling as he passed on a rope I left dangling from the window and secured to my wrist. The body soon settled to this regular routine and I woke seconds before I felt the tug.

After my silent awakening I crept down without waking my parents and fitted in two hours' homework before breakfast. Then it was a twenty-minute cycle ride to Beccles or Oulton, pedalling back home by 6 o'clock. The twelve-hour day was further extended by more homework in the winter, or by joining in the village cricket, which I had also introduced, or other games on the long summer evenings.

So I was able to have my fill of sport and still qualify as an un-certificated teacher in two years. Just as I took up my first appointment the war crept up on us.

In the midst of peace we were suddenly at war. Or that was how it seemed to me on that hot August day in 1914. There had been none of today's ceaseless barrage of radio and television comment to prepare us. And it had been the sports pages of newspapers which focused my attention, not the distant events at Sarajevo.

Perhaps the suddenness heightened the atmosphere of excitement and expectancy when we read of Belgium invaded and war declared. There was no conscription, and I had no special feelings of outrage with the Germans over events all too dimly understood. But I had been brought up in a world of simple responses with the emphasis on duty and responsibility, rather than individual rights. So the natural reaction of myself and three fellow teachers of the Beccles Primary School was to attend a recruitment meeting that same week in Beccles Town Hall. The main speakers were the Mayor, and the Lord Lieutenant and a Territorial Army recruiting Sergeant-Major. There was nothing said to arouse passionate excitement, but duty seemed to dictate that we volunteered—so we stepped forward and did so.

We had been involuntary volunteers and now we expected some months to elapse before the Army called us up. The meeting had been on the Saturday, but to our surprise the recruiting Sergeant was round at the school on Monday, with our travel warrants made out and requiring our instant departure for Ipswich. What upset me was not the abrupt break in a teaching career barely begun, but that I had no chance now to accept an offer to play for Lowestoft Town, who had just amalgamated with the Kirkley club. But not even war could interfere for long with football. Having gone through the formality of being presented with the King's shilling, as token that I was an enlisted man in the East Anglian Royal Field Artillery Brigade, I found that our training ground was the Portman Road ground, home of Ipswich soccer. Our artillery training did no damage to that fine pitch, for the guns and horses were all imaginary. For weeks we spent endless hours of drill loading notional shells into non-existent breeches and waiting for the chance to break off to play football. That was the only relief in a life of boredom and discomfort, as we slept on the bare boards of cold huts with only one blanket apiece and spent our days in ceaseless repetition of gun drill without guns. The outlet of my energies was to get together a brigade football team and arrange fixtures with the local amateur clubs. We collected a most successful side built round a formidable centre-half. George Tuthill claimed to have been a professional footballer and we assumed him to be a Norwich player, although he never told us his club. Certainly he played like a good professional and gave our team a touch of class that was too good for the locals. Playing behind a man such as Tuthill gave me further lessons in goalkeeping. His calling was clear and confident and he taught me what balls to go for, what to leave to him. Goalkeepers then were not meant to stray more than a yard or two from their line and it certainly never occurred to me how much more difficult it could be made for forwards to score if we came out to intercept through balls or to narrow the shooting angle as current keepers do. Obviously this improvement in goalkeeping technique is a major reason for the decline in scoring in the modern game.

Our real soldiering only started when we were posted away to villages like Mildenhall and Cuddenham. At last we had horses and eighteen-pounder guns to keep us busy, and to add to the variety I spent a fortnight as a battery clerk. That brought me in touch with Colonel Lord Stradbroke, who was instantly intrigued by my name. Rous was his family name also and he knew my grandfather, the Reverend Thomas Warrell Rous, who had been born near his estate in the village of Westleton. With so many Rouses living in that district I could not trace my direct kinship with Earl Rous, but at least I had a name so far as the officers were concerned and was no longer just a number.

By October we had been shipped to France, supporting our troops in the St Omer-Amiens area. The mud and slush of this static warfare was such that we could never get clean, never stay warm. We slept in barns which seemed to be entirely surrounded by chill wastes of water and slime. And when the guns had to be shifted it was a nightmare of hauling and heaving for us and the horses. With advances or retreats measured in hundreds of yards, such moves of the battery position were rare enough except when enemy guns ranged on our position. It is the mud and the cold which are still the indelible impressions in my mind, not the danger and the deaths.

What a pleasant contrast it was when we were sent in the spring to Marseilles to re-equip and prepare for service in Egypt and Palestine. But the hotter climate in Egypt, which we had anticipated with such pleasure, had its own hazards. Instead of the blight of a French winter we now had dust storms which swept away the tents, and instead of the slime we had plagues of locusts, mosquitoes and sandflies. I had never credited the destructive capacity of locusts until I saw a swarm settle like a black enveloping cloud on a Cairo garden and in minutes strip it bare of all fruit and vegetation. For us the worst pest was the scorpion. The warmth of our sleeping bags attracted them and on some mornings we would find a score underneath as we rolled up the bag. And they did not always stay underneath. One night a scorpion crawled across my face and stung me between the eyes. The poisoned area at once became swollen like an oak apple and the medical officer had to lance it. That was one war scar which stayed visible for half a century. A Turkish shell exploding close to our gun pit in Palestine was later to fracture my wrist and my foot was badly injured when the wheel of a gun ran over it; yet it was the discomfort of our conditions which was to leave the deepest impression on me, not the dangers of the action. Indeed my luckiest escape was when someone called my name just as I was putting my water bottle to my lips having filled it at the water cart. When I looked back a large hornet was just crawling out of the bottle, and if I had swallowed it I would no doubt have died from the sting in the throat, as had another gunner just before.

The camels, which were later to be my responsibility when acting as Quartermaster, could also turn awkward. One Australian drover, a cheerful self-sufficient man, seemed to have a special affinity with his camel, which he fed by hand with the 'loofa' or clover-like grass they especially liked. One day he forgot to give the camel his special *hors d'oeuvre* and as he led it along in front of me it retaliated by suddenly stretching down that long neck and biting a pound of flesh from his calf. The wound was so deep and so quickly turned septic that the drover died.

Marching or moving guns in the desert was never easy. When we moved to Palestine and Lebanon we had a rough ride round the long curve of the Bay of Acre. The land sloped gently down to the sea, tilting the wheels of the gun carriages. This so strained the harness that it chafed the flanks of the horses until they were skinned and raw before we were back on the level.

Wire matting was an essential of our existence. Many roads were of wire matting laid on sand, and it was wire matting that made us tracks even over the Bitter Lakes. But the lingering memory is of a march without any such aid. Arriving at Cairo from Port Said we went on a twelve-mile route march to our camp at the Pyramids. That was no great distance for us, but in one way it was the longest and most frustrating of my army life. After half an hour the Pyramids loomed so large we seemed to be almost touching them. And at each regulation halt, on the hour for ten minutes' rest, we were always sure that there were only a few hundred yards left to go. Yet always the Pyramids seemed to stay out of reach.

In a Cairo YMCA I met Miss Roffe, who had once tried to teach me Latin at Beccles Student Teacher Centre. With her I studied Arabic and could soon speak it well enough for most conventional needs, though I later found that the camel drivers attached to our battery to collect rations and water seemed to speak a somewhat different language from that of Miss Roffe. I was offered a posting to the Officer Training Corps at Heliopolis, but declined as I did not yet feel experienced enough for such command. So it was as an NCO that I continued for the next three years. At first I was in charge of the railhead office at Lydda in Palestine. My most perplexing experience was the arrival of a brisk young man who announced he was 'up down from India. Name of Major up down Walker. Want to go up down up the line.' It was some time before I realised that some bright quack had tried to cure his stammer by making him say 'up down' whenever he was struggling for a word. So my attempt to tell him how to get up the line and back down to HQ produced five minutes of farce worthy of Morecambe and Wise. And if I had problems they were nothing to the bewilderment he was later to cause the troops unlucky enough to have to unravel his orders.

Three years' service in Palestine was not too demanding by the standards of the Great War, and I was fortunate to escape the privations and the holocaust of the major fronts. There were still some testing and unusual experiences: long periods of boredom were quickly succeeded by the bizarre or the unexpected. As the battle of Gaza wavered to and fro I found myself riding up to the town one night with the guns. But when we entered Gaza in the dark we suddenly found ourselves surrounded by the shadowy figures of Turkish soldiers and our cheerful greeting died in the menacing silence. The tension was broken by a Cockney voice informing us that these were his prisoners, he the minimal escort.

One of our pleasantest pastimes was bathing in the clear blue of the Mediterranean off the coast of Jaffa. For the horses too this was a good conditioner and a break they obviously enjoyed. But one afternoon as we all swam happily in the sea a sudden barrage of shells turned the playtime to shambles.

A bad bout of malaria had me sent back to Cairo to convalesce and though my recovery was rapid, this recurred for many years afterwards. In the Gardens at Cairo we were entertained by the Co-optimists concert party. They had been going home from India when they were stranded in Cairo, to our great pleasure if not theirs. The man who impressed me most was the singer and composer, Wolsey Charles, best known for his 'wheel-tapper' song, whom I often met afterwards. But inevitably my main recreation was football. The wound in the wrist prevented me from playing, so I took up refereeing in the well-organised fixture list which the Egyptian FA ran there during the war, since the nearest war front was far away in Palestine. There were the 'Egyptian League' games and the 'Sultan Cup' matches.

To find where I was meant to officiate I had to buy a copy of the *Egyptian Mail*, which was rather eccentrically advertised by the local vendors. We used to collect it in the evening coming out of the cinema and the newsboys' cry was '*Egyptian Mail* tomorrow', as it was really the next day's paper. They served as their own posters, once introducing an edition with the shout, 'Buy paper, very good news, Lord Kitchener dead.'

There was a number of top-class players serving out there, so the standard of play was good. Hegazi, a Cambridge blue who had played for Dulwich Hamlet and Fulham, was particularly impressive.

The Gezira Sporting Club was the most exclusive sign of the British presence in Cairo. The beautiful lawns there were ideal for cricket, and I was also involved in organising matches on a pitch where international teams were later to play. On one of the few occasions I was invited into the Club I was fascinated watching the barman work. The bar was lined with branded bottles of whisky, but he was refilling some twenty differently labelled empty bottles all from the same long ewer, which was no doubt well watered. In 1976 I was back at the Gezira Club assisting with a referees' training course, and was not surprised to find that the whisky was now sold only in bottles with the seal unbroken. There were other striking changes too. The Club is now a recreation centre open to the public, and with a wide range of sporting facilities. The lawns and gardens are as well tended as ever and come under the care of the Minister of Agriculture. Fahmy, Secretary of the Egyptian FA, worked for the Ministry and was responsible for ensuring that all flower gardens in the cities were kept in good order. He also took a special interest in the National Football Stadium, which is the equivalent of our Wembley.

In Nasser's day I was once present to watch a game there when the Sudan played Egypt in the final of a competition. My host was General Mostafa, later Vice-President of FIFA, and an enthusiastic crowd of 110,000 worked themselves to a pitch of excitement when the winner had to be drawn by lot after the game had ended with the scores level. The referee was blindfolded before making the draw, and a great roar of cheers greeted his pulling out the slip with Egypt on it.

When the General returned from the field I congratulated him on the luck of the draw. He replied that there was no luck involved as, by agreement, both pieces of paper had Egypt written on them. He may have been joking, but the Sudanese officials showed no sign of disappointment and the result made the day for Nasser and the spectators.

To me that was typical of the friendly and hospitable approach which I have experienced in this area. There is so often a delightful mixture of the casual and the courteous. When FIFA met in Cairo in 1963 we were treated to a fascinating tour up the Nile to Aswan and Luxor. So full was the programme that it was impressed on us we must all be at the domestic airport punctually at six in the morning for the start. But this was the first day after the Ramadan festival, and our pilot did not arrive until after nine. He was so profuse in apology, so helpful as a guide, that his lateness was at once forgiven and forgotten by us all.

That stay in Cairo in 1918 was all too short and I was serving in Beirut when I was finally drafted to the Officer Training Corps back at Heliopolis. Shortly after my arrival came the Armistice and the need to rethink one's life. I was offered a choice of jobs in Cairo as schoolmaster or stationmaster, but my intention was to go to Emmanuel College, Cambridge, so I declined them all and was put with Group 43, made up of intended students. We were told that this gave us priority for demobilisation, but as so often in the Army practice proved the reverse of precept. Three weeks, we were told, was our estimated sailing time as our group put its tents on the edge of the Suez Canal. Each few days some new group arrived and we were nudged farther and farther out into the desert. 'To your tents, O Israel' would declaim one of our party as we saw the dust of a new squad approaching. And it was over three months before we were finally remembered and sent to embark at Port Said.

My father, who had been arranging for me to go to Cambridge, had died before I could get back home, and it was to St Luke's College at Exeter that I went on return.

2

Work and Play

●●

While studying at St Luke's College I took my first serious steps towards becoming a referee. Again it was an injury to my wrist which
prompted the decision. I had been keeping goal regularly for the St
Luke's team, and I fractured it again as I dived for the ball at a forward's feet. Rather than be kept out of a game I so much enjoyed, I
decided that I had had enough experience of refereeing to take my exam
after a little further study. Refereeing itself had always appealed to me,
having started on it young. My first effort had been at the age of
fourteen. When holidaying in Norwich with some cousins I was
asked to referee a match in default of any adults being available.
Knowing little of the laws and nothing of my duties I asked with some
trepidation when I should blow the whistle. 'When I tell you,' said the
captain of the Norwich side who had recruited me. It was not sur-
prising that they won comfortably.

Refereeing good-quality games in Egypt had given me the necessary
confidence, and it was not long before I was able to take the examination. Unfortunately it was held in the evening, and so I had to sneak
out of College through a side window; we were not allowed out after
6 pm. I had considered asking permission, but the odds seemed
against it, as there was a strict and almost monastic regime in the
College and any outside activities were not encouraged. In these freer
days it is perhaps surprising to reflect on the restraints we were prepared to accept without too much concern, even though we had just
spent five years helping to win a war.

The exam itself was a mixture of written questions and practical
tests that were elementary by today's sterner standards. So I passed
without difficulty and was soon refereeing matches throughout Devonshire, including the semi-final of the Devon Senior Cup and the final
played at St James's Ground, Exeter.

St Luke's College was the ideal place to foster the love of football. Theirs is the fourth oldest Association Football club in the world, having been founded in 1866. At the turn of the century they shared the Devon Senior Cup with Plymouth Argyle, drawing 0–0 in the final. The tradition of good football persisted and shortly before the First World War the captain of the college club was Evelyn H. Lintott, later to play for England. I was pleased to follow him and to have as my vice-captain another fine soccer player in George Reader. Reader was a dashing forward with an eye for goal who later played for Exeter and Southampton, the club of which he was Chairman when they won the FA Cup in 1976.

Oddly, Reader was also to take to refereeing, inspired perhaps by my own enthusiasm. And it was as an international referee that he won a fine reputation when appointed to take charge of the emotional World Cup final in 1950. The host nation, Brazil, lost to Uruguay before an excitable crowd of 200,000 but his firm control ensured there were no incidents, no recriminations and no favoured party.

My own goalkeeping was improving all the time until my wrist injury and I benefited by seeing Dick Pym in action. This Devon fisherman was one of the best goalkeepers of the period, and his skill helped Bolton Wanderers to a run of Cup Final victories. He was a frequent visitor to the College and a very helpful coach. With Reader in the forward line we were never short of goals and he had unexpected reinforcement from two Thai students at the College. They were lodged at an old rectory where all the floorboards creaked to the step and the door hinges grated. Yet the vicar, Prebendary Thompson, a lecturer at the College, told us they moved so silently he was always being startled by their soft voices at his ear when he thought the room empty. He also told us they had played football for Thailand and were keen to try over here. He had fitted them out with full kit including boots, but they were accustomed to play barefooted and soon limped off in their first match with cramp. Throwing aside the boots, they came back to show remarkable skill in dribbling and one of them proved a very effective partner for George.

That incident made such an impression on me that when I became Secretary of the FA I early suggested an amendment to the rules, which were so positively written in relation to the type of boot to be worn that no allowance was made for being without any. My proposal was thought too far-fetched to be pressed, but by an odd coincidence the point was forcefully underlined in the 1938 World Cup game between Brazil and Poland. It was a remarkable match, with Brazil winning 6–5 as two players each scored four goals. There could hardly have been a greater contrast between the elegant blonde Willimowski and the elemental 'Black Diamond', Leonidas da Silva, Brazil's exciting centre-forward. The two swapped goals, with Leonidas scoring a first-half hat trick. Then, feeling constricted by the mud, the small, supple Leonidas took off his boots and tossed them dramatically away over the touchline. At once the referee ordered him to put them on again or go off himself as he was in breach of the rules.

It was at St Luke's that I first tried my hand at journalism, writing a column for the local paper on the week's sporting events entitled 'Up College'. The articles appeared under a pseudonym and there was speculation—particularly by those criticised—as to which tutor was writing them. To keep my anonymity I had to be careful to be critical of my own performances as well.

When I returned to refereeing I covered games in many Devonshire villages and continued to take on matches in the vacations. My holidays were spent at Hemel Hempstead, where I had been billetted in the war, with the family of Adrienne, who was later to be my wife. As I returned so frequently to be with her, I began to referee Hertfordshire games as well. My first was not a happy introduction. It was at Apsley, where the home side was playing Leavesden Mental Hospital. Leavesden were one of the best sides in the Herts County League since they recruited as staff a number of leading players such as 'Skilly' Williams, the former Watford goalkeeper. This was something of a needle match and in the first half I sent a man off for kicking an opponent. It was the first time I had had to do this and I was not well briefed in the procedure. During the interval the club officials said they would like to remind me that it was quite all right for him to come on again in the second half and in my innocence I let myself be conned by them. As a result of allowing him back I was up before the Herts FA Disciplinary Committee.

That depressing start proved an unexpected gain. After dealing with the case the secretary, George Newbury, went out of his way to be helpful and established himself as my guide and mentor. I owed much to his advice in improving my refereeing, and it was he who involved me with FA affairs. He took me to the Annual General Meet-of the West Herts FA at the Fishery Inn, Boxmoor, and I found myself elected Secretary. That automatically gave me representation on the Hertfordshire County FA and brought me in close touch with Football Association personalities and methods. I had much help from two football enthusiasts, Bill Ling and Percy Poulter, who both sub-sequently became Football League referees themselves.

My first Chairman of Hertfordshire was Wagstaffe Simmonds, a powerful figure on the FA. He was, however, summarily dismissed by them after a disagreement over expenses. Simmonds continued to be a considerable influence in football as a Tottenham director and a very able sporting journalist. He was the Sports Editor of the *Sporting Life*, and for us referees that was a very important publication. The draw for Cup games was on Mondays and the *Sporting Life*, out on Tuesdays, was the only paper which gave the refereeing appointments.

I still have the notebook in which I recorded all my matches, fees and expenses from 1926. Taking the line at Millwall in the Southern League, I was paid 10s 6d. For refereeing Isthmian League games I received 15s and for Football League matches 1 guinea. The first FA Cup tie I controlled was Notts County against Sheffield United. But I felt none of the excitement of the spectators at that 'local Derby', for a referee is so concentrated on the flow of play that the result is of little concern to him. Noel Watson of the Notts FA, himself a former Cup Final referee, was kind enough to come to my changing room before the game with welcome advice and with congratulations after it.

On Sunday March 13th 1927 I refereed my first International match, the Belgium *v* Holland game at Antwerp. The fee was 5 guineas and my expenses for the trip £6 11s. The last International I refereed was also a Belgium *v* Holland game at Antwerp in April 1934. The fee was unchanged, but the expenses had crept up to £7 5s. They were paid without comment, and in that I was more fortunate than John Langenus, the tall, thin Belgian referee. He came over to two Internationals in England within a year or so of each other. The eagle-eyed treasurer of the FA, Harry Huband, noted his expenses had increased by a few shillings and promptly disallowed the differ-ence. 'But the fares have gone up,' said Langenus. 'The value of the English pound never changes,' said Huband firmly, paying over the same as before. What would poor Huband have to say about the pound in our pocket today?

Langenus, looking like an animated lamp post, was the referee in the 'Battle of Highbury' in 1934 when England defeated World Champions Italy 3–2 in a hard, angry game. The Italians fought back ferociously after being three down early on, and the bitterness was blamed on the huge bonuses offered to them by Mussolini if they won. But I could appreciate there were other factors which may have roused them. Ted Drake, that bravest and most dashing of centre-forwards, was ever ready to shoulder-charge the goalkeeper in a way common in our game, but not relished on the Continent. And the iron man of English soccer, Arsenal's Wilf Copping, would have stopped a bulldozer with his crushing tackles. Copping was always absolutely fair—I checked his record and was not surprised to find he had never even been cautioned—but he was devastatingly hard.

I was running the line for that match, but may have an unbalanced view of the game. It was the custom for the English linesman to lunch with the officials before the match and travel to the ground with them. So great was the interest, however, that our coach became jammed in the press of cars. Although I changed on the way I was still twenty minutes' late and a deputy had had to be recruited by megaphone from the crowd. My arrival abruptly changed England's luck. We were already three up with the Italians down to ten men, and yet at the end England appeared somewhat fortunate to hold on to win after Meazza, the Italian centre-forward, had scored twice.

Another famous match at which I was linesman was the 1928 game against Scotland at Wembley—the year of the 'Wee Blue Devils'. Scotland had four skilful little midgets in the forward line, together with the long-striding Alex Jackson. On a greasy pitch they had England slithering to a 5–1 defeat.

I was too busy watching the pattern of play to appreciate fully the talents of that wonderful forward line of Morton, Dunn, Gallacher, James and Jackson. Towards the end the left-winger, Alan Morton, kept sidling up near me and making comments. His broad Glaswegian dialect made it hard for me to interpret and when he kept repeating them with growing force I was close to reprimanding him for making critical remarks. However, I finally deciphered his words as a simple request: 'Wi' ye get me the ba', ref?' He had played so well, his crosses 'hanging' invitingly for his opposite winger Jackson to score three goals, that I was glad to secure the ball for him at the finish.

Another problem for me came in the Hungary *v* Italy match in Budapest in 1933. This, incidentally, was the first ever International to be broadcast, as Mussolini had a transmission specially relayed to the stadium in Rome where he was watching Primo Carnera, that formidable giant of a heavyweight boxer. I was the referee and there was soon plenty of action to keep me busy. The Hungarian centre-half was Gustav Sebes, who was later to manage the 'Magical Magyars', the team with Puskas and Kocsis which massacred England at Wembley in 1953. Early in the game the Hungarian right-back, Koranyi, had his leg broken in a hard tackle and the Italian responsible became a marked man. I kept a close eye on him but he too was injured before long—and such was the feeling against him that I had to fetch the bucket and sponge and attend to him myself; neither team's trainer would do it.

When I came to the ground I had been surprised to see thousands of triangular-shaped pieces of cardboard being given away. A small slice was cut off the top and they appeared to be an advertisement for some brand of coffee. Their real purpose became apparent as soon as the Hungarian player was injured, and whenever I gave a decision they did not like. By pressing on the side they converted into a makeshift megaphone and the blast of noise as thousands made their anger known through them was frightening in its intensity.

Afterwards a young sports journalist interviewed me for the paper *Nemzeti Sport*. He was Sandor Barcs, later to be a valued colleague in FIFA and UEFA. He tells me my comments were that it was a very good and exciting game marred only by the serious injury and by the handicap to the Hungarian side which influenced their 0–1 defeat. And that I expressed my gratitude to the two Hungarian linesmen, Frigyes Kann and Mihaly Ivancsics, for their excellent support. Barcs also reminded me that he saw me referee the first European Champion's Cup final in 1930 in Geneva when the Hungarian champions, Ujpest, beat the Czech club Slavia of Prague 3–0. The competition then was called 'Coupe des Nations' and was played soley in Switzerland.

The journey to Budapest was an experience for me, travelling on the Orient Express and seeing the floodlit city for the first time with the Citadel of Buda standing out on the skyline. 'Be a referee and see the world' might have been my slogan.

Zurich, along with Geneva, has always been a favourite city of mine and I was fortunate to referee there on many occasions. But in one game I saw another side of life. With the scores level the Swiss back, Minelli, fouled a Belgian in the final minute and I awarded a penalty. The Swiss goalkeeper flung himself forward and saved to the joy of the crowd. As he had moved before the kick I had to order it to be taken again. That was too much for the spectators, some of whom streamed on to the pitch to argue, with the linesmen joining in as well. When order was restored the Belgian scored and I had to be escorted off by the police with alsatian dogs. The Secretary of the Swiss FA at once made every player come to my dressing-room and apologise personally to me and we ended the best of friends—but I still had to be smuggled out the back way.

It so happened that a high percentage of the International matches I refereed involved Switzerland, and in later years I was much moved by this tribute in the *Swiss Referee* of 1974, on the occasion of my being awarded the Grand Cross of Merit by the German Federal Republic.

During thirteen years as President Sir **Stanley Rous** directed FIFA with wide experience and great success.... We Swiss, friends of football, wholeheartedly congratulate Sir Stanley on this high honour and sincerely wish him many years of good health and continued pleasure of football, his great life hobby.

The Editor of the *Swiss Referee* joins with the expression of the above congratulations. With his retirement from the official activities of FIFA Sir Stanley also retires as *spiritus rector* of questions and decisions in the laws of the game, a resort of eminent importance to world-wide football. He is well known here in Switzerland for his outstanding performance as a former International Referee.... Sir Stanley holds the rare record of twelve appointments in International matches involving the Swiss team with foreign opponents.

My League refereeing had started in 1927. At that time the list of League referees was made up from League club nominations and it was one of the Queen's Park Rangers' directors who put my name forward.

Much of my League refereeing was in the Second and Third Division games and I seemed to be assigned in particular to local Derby matches. These can be inflammatory affairs and it was always important to avoid incidents which might stir the passions. In one such clash between Millwall and Charlton Athletic an error of mine might have roused angry protests. At a crucial point in the game I saw a defender's hand fist the ball away in a goalmouth melee. As I blew the whistle for a penalty the players untangled themselves and looked at me in surprise. It was then I realised that it was the goalkeeper, not a full-back, who had punched the ball. So I walked on past the penalty spot, past the goalposts, to the edge of the crowd and called at the top of my voice: 'If the man with the whistle blows it again I will have him removed.' Then I restarted the game by dropping the ball and the mistake was retrieved without disaster.

In my refereeing career there were two significant changes which I pioneered. The first was in the style of the University soccer match. Popular mythology tended to represent Oxford and Cambridge undergraduates as languid and effete, but the University match was in fact a good deal harder and rougher than most professional games. When rugby and soccer first split it was over the question of hacking, not handling. The rugby followers claimed that the end of hacking would mean the end of 'all the pluck and courage of the game'. So far as university football was concerned they need not have worried, for this remained an example of the philosophy 'Don't worry about the ball. Let's go on with the game.' Or, as it was more simply put to me, 'Fouls have to be intentional. Gentlemen don't foul intentionally. So there are no fouls.' Before the first match I refereed, the two captains, Howard Fabian and John Hazledean, told me, 'We don't want you to referee as you do in professional games. We like to get on with the match without interruption.' And I was indeed to see the Oxford goalkeeper with an ear half torn off shouting, 'Don't mind me. Get on with the game.' But I told the captains the following year that I would referee as strictly as in a professional game, since it was important that they learnt to play skilfully as well as physically. Geoffrey Green, whose writing on football was to win him a well-deserved OBE, was in the Cambridge side that day and has since told me how fortunate it was that I did not take the usual permissive line: 'My instructions had been to put the Oxford insides out of action in the first twenty minutes.'

Proper refereeing of the University match did indeed help to improve the standards of skill. So it was with real pleasure that I saw the combined University team, Pegasus, win the Amateur Cup twice in the fifties before capacity 100,000 crowds at Wembley. The importance of this was in encouraging Association football in the schools, since so many of the masters were apt to take a lead from the universities.

A more revolutionary change was to introduce the diagonal system of refereeing, with linesmen keeping mainly to one side of the half-way line instead of trying to cover the whole touchline. There was considerable criticism when I instructed my linesmen to operate in this way in 1933. But particularly on muddy grounds, I had found that the referee might still be struggling through the central morass and the linesmen also trailing behind the play when a difficult offside decision had to be made from a distance. So on such grounds I asked my linesmen each to keep in line with one set of forwards while the three of us kept in the diagonal line. This proved so effective that I began to use it in all my matches. It put more responsibility on the linesmen, many of whom welcomed it while others were apprehensive about this new method.

There was considerable criticism at first, but in time there was to be universal acceptance after I had submitted it to the FA Referees' Committee backed by a detailed memorandum and diagrams. That memo was to be included thereafter in the FA's Referees' Chart and FIFA's Universal Guide for Referees. The system has stood the test of time and still operates in every country in the world. Indeed the linesmen are now more strictly controlled to their own alternate halves whereas I thought—and still think—it is better if they use their own initiative in going several yards into the other half when this would be helpful.

For me first approval for the system was my appointment to referee the 1934 Cup Final and the ready acceptance by my linesmen that they would operate at Wembley to my direction in this diagonal method.

There was of course a tradition that no one was sent off in a Cup Final, but this was as much due to the players' sense of occasion as to any leniency in the refereeing. In those days it would have shamed a footballer beyond endurance to be sent off in such a match. But certainly I was not prepared to compromise. Portsmouth were struggling against Manchester City in that match and their right-back, Mackie, was using threatening language to Eric Brook, an elusive winger with a cannonball shot. I warned Mackie that he would be sent off if he carried out his threats and he answered me back, 'Sure, you'll never send me off at Wembley, Mr Rous.' 'Try it once more and you will find I will,' I told him in a tone that seemed to convince him. Certainly he gave no more trouble, and certainly I would have sent him off if he had.

Apart from taking charge of an International in Belgium the following day, that Final was to end my refereeing career, as a new prospect opened for me in football.

3

Refereeing Reminiscence

●●

A football referee has to be regarded as a judge. His main job is indeed to judge the situations occurring in play and interpret them correctly in relation to the laws of the game. So it is apt that the motto of the Referees' Association in England is taken from a judge's description of himself in a book of Ovid as 'a man, who, though heavens may fall, will remain just and unafraid'. That is even more essential today than when I was refereeing, because the heavens are that much more likely to fall on him. There are greater pressures from crowds, more criticism of his decisions by Press and TV commentators or by players, more gamesmanship to cover up offences, more explosive reaction to his judgements.

As well as being scrupulously honest and impartial, a referee needs also to be a person of authority and a disciplinarian. He has not only to judge but to control; and in the modern game the emphasis has tended to switch from judgement to control as the most important and onerous of his duties. Handling of players has become as vital a part of his task as knowing, and sensibly applying, the laws.

There was more respect for authority in the twenties and thirties, with the players creating fewer problems and putting less pressure on referees. So in that sense it was easier for me. But there were still difficulties from time to time, and I found certain principles invaluable in dealing with them. The most important part of a referee's reputation is that he is accepted as being both honest and impartial. To ensure giving this impression it is essential to be aloof. 'Talk to players as little as possible' is therefore a good maxim. Once you become embroiled in argument and disagreement your authority and impartiality will soon be challenged. The dangers are magnified in International matches, with language problems to complicate any discussion. In a match between France and Switzerland in Paris I disallowed a goal because the ball had been over the line before being centred. The angry French forward demanded of me 'Bloody pourquoi?', and had I attempted to explain why in the same pidgin French and English, total incomprehension or an unprofitable altercation would have been the likely outcome.

Even using interpreters after the match there can be misunderstanding. After a game in Genoa, the interpreter assigned to me informed me that there was a complaint against me: 'They say you are not good-looking. They say some are better-looking than you.' I was antagonised by these personal comments until I discovered later that they were merely disagreeing with one of my decisions on the grounds that they had been better placed than me to see the incident. That impressed on me how easy it can be to misinterpret a remark in translation and be unnecessarily riled by it.

It is always the case of the less said the better, even when there is no language barrier. If you are giving a warning it has to be clear, simple and direct, and if you are threatening action for a repeat offence then your manner must make it clear that action will indeed follow. But when a tense situation is building it is often better defused by a humorous or understanding comment than by an angry lecture.

My dislike of much talk by referees was reinforced by the unfortunate and short-lived practice introduced a few seasons ago of referees giving a pre-match dressing-room lecture. Not only was this quite contrary to the principle of aloofness, but it showed a distressing insensitivity to players' and managers' feelings. Just before a match players are certain to be tense and nervous and in no mental condition to absorb a lot of instruction. Inevitably all such talks tend to be repetitive and therefore disregarded, undermining, not reinforcing, a referee's authority. And for managers the final word with their players can be very important and they naturally resented the referee having it rather than them.

Apart from keeping talk to a minimum the referee needs to keep interference with play to a minimum. The more petty or niggling stoppages which are enforced, the less the advantage rule is applied to keep play moving, the more exasperated players become, and the more difficult they are to control. In my first International in Antwerp in 1927 I was watched by the eight members of the FIFA Referees' Committee. Fortunately, my handling was commended, especially because I refereed 'in a large manner'. When I later enquired what that phrase meant I was told that the feature which appealed to them most was that I kept play flowing without continual minor interruptions. To me that remains one of the most desirable aims for a referee.

Refereeing so much abroad, I was always interested in the problems caused by language and by different interpretation of laws in different countries. In later years at one of the Olympic Games matches, I was struck by the fact that in most of the games the referee and linesman would be unable to communicate with each other or with the players because of language difficulty. Following this up I was attracted to the idea of coloured cards—yellow for a caution, red for dismissal—to show beyond doubt that a player had been warned or dismissed from the field. This was tried out in the Olympic Games of 1968 and the World Cup of 1970, and soon accepted as standard practice by FIFA for Internationals, Olympics and World Cup matches. But whatever the rule books may lay down, referees still have to use initiative in dealing with unexpected situations not covered in their instructions. I much admired the inventiveness of one referee faced with the problem of warning six players at the same time when a defensive wall refused to retreat to the correct distance and ignored his order to do so. Having held up the yellow card he then tore it in six pieces before giving one piece to each player.

The yellow and red card system was designed specifically to get over language problems and for use where referees could not be sure of communicating with a player in a way he was certain to understand. I regret its extension to domestic matches where no such problem exists. This unnecessary flourishing of the card in such matches serves only publicly to emphasise guilt. It can humiliate the player and provoke his supporters in the crowd, something the good referee should always try to avoid.

As a referee travelling abroad I was always on the look-out for new ideas which might improve the game. In Italy I first saw a pitch marked with an arc on the edge of the area to ensure players kept far enough away when a penalty was taken. I at once reported to the FA that this was an excellent innovation which ought to be more widely used, and as a result it was—within two years—incorporated by the International Board in their 'plan of the field'. With football now such a world-wide attraction sensible developments often start in countries where the game is relatively new. It was in a youth tournament in Malaysia, for instance, that I first saw the system of holding up a card with the number of the player to be substituted. Koe Ewe Teik, former Secretary of the Asian Football Confederation, had introduced it and I passed it on to the FIFA Referees' Committee for adoption.

That has been a considerable help to referees and managers, since the player concerned is often reluctant to be taken off. Dave Mackay, when managing Swindon, wanted to make a substitution, but despite all his gesticulation the player concerned continued to avoid his eye. He then called to the referee to tell No. 6 to come off. No. 6's response to the message was to say 'You can't substitute me, ref. Only my manager can', after which he kept as far away from the infuriated Mackay as he could, delaying his substitution by some minutes. I had a very different experience when I was asked to referee a club match in Le Touquet. It was necessary to award a number of free kicks against one particular French player, who began to complain to me in perfect English that he was being victimised. 'If you don't like my refereeing you are free to leave the field,' I told him. That was just what he did, stalking off to be seen no more.

To be fit, fast and fair are the main requirements of a referee and, in general, British referees have fulfilled these requirements. Certainly they were much in demand on the Continent in my time and that may have accounted for the high number of European Internationals entrusted to me. There was a feeling, generally justified in practice, that British referees were less dramatic in gesture, but more daring in judgement. Too many European referees in the twenties and thirties would shy away from an awkward decision by giving a free kick just outside the penalty area when the offence was clearly just inside it. We, however, had a deserved reputation for applying the laws without fear or favour and for dealing with every situation exactly as we saw it. As a result even quite ordinary referees by home standards had considerable reputations abroad. There was a Captain Prince Cox for instance, who was without great honour at home but was much requested abroad. He was very firm in his handling of incidents, and that too was part of our reputation which appealed to Europeans. In my own case there was an invasion of the pitch at half-time in an International in Amsterdam. Determined not to be intimidated or distracted by it, I immediately stopped the players from going back to the dressing room, turned them round and restarted the match. The demonstration at once subsided and the game was completed without further incident, for which I was afterwards congratulated.

A difficulty English referees—and players—then had to overcome was that without much interchange of refereeing experience and ideas, European football tended to develop in some respects in different ways to the English version. Shoulder-charging of goalkeepers for instance was accepted here, but frowned on there. And in Europe it was not always appreciated that we only permitted a fair shoulder charge according to the existing laws. Before one International the captain of Holland asked me: 'Is it true you permit charging of the goalkeeper?' I confirmed that fair charging was allowed. Within minutes he had hurled the opposing goalkeeper into the back of his net and was incensed to find me awarding a free kick because his assault had been far from a fair shoulder-to-shoulder charge.

Sliding tackles were another source of trouble. In muddy English conditions the sliding tackle was much practised by English defenders and, by the laws, was quite fair if the tackler played the ball and not the man. Most expert English defenders would tackle this way by instinct and were used to being allowed to do so. On the harder grounds of the Continent such a tackle tended to be regarded as dangerous and was penalised whether the ball was played or not. I can remember seeing that fine centre-half, Bernard Joy, put off his game in Olympic matches and in an International in Belgium when he was penalised for tackles we regard as quite fair within the existing laws.

Apart from problems of interpretation, there were occasional problems from overcrowding at Continental matches. For one game in the Parc des Princes in Paris the conditions were much like the famous Wembley Final of 1923 when the game had to be played within a solid square of people cleared from the pitch by Constable Scorey on his white horse, Billie. The touchlines in Paris were lined with spectators as if this was a village match. Indeed at one point I was about to award a goal when I realised just in time that a spectator had diverted a shot at goal into the net, not a player.

But despite the differences English referees maintained their reputation abroad, while we regarded many of the Continentals as outstanding in their handling of our games. Langenus of Belgium was undoubtedly the best with whom I officiated as linesman, and he was a most popular referee of his day. There were many other excellent European referees then, such as Dr Bauwens of Germany and Mutters of Holland, who were as good as any Englishman. Italy also had an outstanding performer in 'The Cardinal', a referee given to dramatic gesture, but, as his nickname implied, contriving to be dignified and authoritative as well as theatrical.

In my time as referee there was never any attempt to 'influence' me before Internationals or any thought that this might later become a danger, with a referee being 'fixed' before one notorious European final. But I was aware of the problem of accepting gifts from any country and my own rule was only to accept a present if given *after* a match. The first time I refereed in Italy was in an International at Bologna which was played in an atmosphere of frenzied emotion and nationalist fervour. Thousands were locked out of the ground and, before the start, a real Cardinal gave the crowd and the game his blessing and sprinkled holy water on the pitch. Not even Anfield could have given the impression of more fevered dedication to winning, and it required some effort to remain aloof and unaffected by the emotive pressure. After the game I was presented by Mussolini with a gold watch of new and unusual design, prized until stolen. Had it been offered before the game an embarrassing situation would have been unavoidable.

With that experience to guide me, I later at FIFA tried to ensure that no presents were given in advance of a game. On one occasion in Holland the club President reported to me his concern that the visiting Italian club officers had just left presents in the room in which the match officials were changing. I at once went in and removed the parcels only returning them after the match was over. In fact these were no grand presents, only key rings in club colours, rather than gold watches, but the principle seemed important. On a more recent occasion one national Association offered free places on a special course, in luxurious surroundings, to active referees from neighbouring countries. Having pointed out to them the danger of appearing to put referees under any 'obligation' I was glad they accepted that invitations to foreigners should be confined to Chairmen of Referees' Committees who no longer officiated.

How desirable it is for referees not only to be just but to be seen to be just was well illustrated in the 1966 World Cup. The pool of referees for the final was heavily weighted with Europeans. There were also British referees on the panel, and though we are used to regarding the Scots, Welsh and Irish as different from the English it may not look that way to South Americans. It would clearly have been better to have had the bulk of the referees from countries not represented in the finals, but this proved impossible because of the difficulty of nominating referees of high enough standard. So we had the unfortunate situation in the quarter-finals in which an English referee sent off two Uruguayans in the game against Germany while a German sent off an Argentinian in England's match at Wembley. Inevitably the South Americans felt hardly done by, particularly when England and Germany met in the final.

With hindsight this may appear an obvious error. But who was to know in advance that there would be such controversial incidents in both matches, or that England and Germany would meet in the final? The final might so easily have been Portugal against Russia—or indeed any combination of the last eight teams. As President of FIFA I had emphasised that our priority must be to avoid anyone refereeing in a group in which his own country took part or refereeing a game which included a country for which he might have a special sympathy. To have a Scotsman refereeing an England game, for instance, might be interpreted as 'British' bias, even though he would be unlikely to show favours to the 'auld enemy'. Similarly, a Russian referee might be vulnerable to allegations of bias in relation to 'Iron Curtain' countries. Even wives had to be considered. This, for instance, has always been a point on which the French are very sensitive. On one occasion the French wrote to the FA requesting that I did not referee one of their Internationals, as I had a French wife and might be suspected of bias. In that case they got short shrift from Sir Frederick Wall, who told them they could have me or no one. But I recognised the genuine concern and was therefore not surprised when I read recently of the French rugby authorities refusing to accept a Scottish referee on the grounds that he lived in the South of England and might be biased towards their English opponents.

We considered first, therefore, all the possible exclusions on grounds of national sympathy, whether in the referee himself or through his wife or home location. One other prime principle re-stricted the permutations possible. Selection of officials from the quarter-finals onwards had to be from those referees who had proved themselves the best in the earlier matches. That was an essential, but it did mean that we could not have so cosmopolitan a final group that we could avoid every possibility of suspected prejudice, however remote. And as that final group was weighted with Europeans there was no way of evening it out, so that a 'Continental' bias as well as a 'national' bias could be totally eliminated.

It was unfortunate that the sending-off of Rattin largely determined England's victory over Argentina, and that Jim Finney's dismissal of Troche and Silva sped Uruguay to 4–0 defeat against Germany. But it was difficult to question the correctness of the decisions, even though the Argentinians spent some eight minutes arguing on the field about referee Kreitlein's action before play could be resumed. One could understand their disappointment while not appreciating their behaviour. Even one short they looked better than England in the final twenty minutes, and my view accords with several good judges of the game who felt that they would have won the World Cup had they controlled their tempers. When the competition was over it was easy to suggest that this pairing of referees and teams might have been avoided. But in prospect it looked no more undesirable than the several other combinations our limited choice allowed.

The Russians however did their best to make political capital out of my being President of FIFA when England won the World Cup. The attacks did not start until some years later, when Russia had been angered by FIFA's refusal to grant them the special privilege of playing their return World Cup qualifying match against Chile on neutral ground after a o–o draw in Moscow. In 1974 the official news agency Tass culminated the attacks by announcing that their officials would support João Havelange as President, rather than the 'notorious' Rous, as 'Rous had gathered round him a group of officials who put the interests of the Anglo-Saxon countries, and above all Britain, in the first place.' The commentator, Allan Starodub, added for good measure that I had helped England to win the World Cup in 1966. 'The English side was granted privileges by Rous while all kinds of obstacles were created for its most dangerous rivals, such as biased refereeing, and inconvenient schedules for matches and training sessions.' I wasn't surprised it took them so long to think that up! Perhaps it was a case of imputing to others what you might do yourself.

Granted that it is vital to select only outstanding referees for the World Cup finals, it is difficult to produce a national mix in which they not only are impartial, but are seen by all to be impartial. In the previous World Cup in Chile for instance, Ken Aston, who was head of the Referees' Committee in 1966, was himself appointed to referee a group whose winner was likely to play England. He found that an embarrassing sequence, though no one questioned his impartiality or competence even when he had to deal with an inflamatory match between Italy and Chile. That violent game, and the explosive matches in 1966 between England and Argentina, and Germany and Uruguay pointed to a new problem.

Once we had worried about the differing styles and interpretations between British and European soccer. Now we were seeing the same gulf between Europe and South America, and the same annoyances when what was accepted or barred at home was questioned or allowed by a foreign referee. Reflecting on this before the next World Cup in Mexico in 1970, I felt the situation could be improved by developing further the pre-match conference of referees started in

1966 to ensure that so far as possible all had the same interpretation of offences and dealt with them equally firmly. As Chairman of the Referees' Committee Professor Andrejevic with his deputy Ken Aston did everything possible to ensure not only a fair, but a uniform approach, and their arrangements certainly helped to improve standards in these respects. I was well aware of the difficulties in getting all countries to interpret laws in the same way. I had already, on a South American tour, experienced the amusing sight of Ken Aston making mock shoulder charges on Uruguay's able administrator, José Codesal, as they attempted to reconcile their views of this controversial law. So I did not expect too much at first; but in Mexico the refereeing was firm and yet no one had to be sent off.

The idea was so successful, indeed, that it has been steadily extended and developed. Before the next finals in West Germany the conferences began four days in advance of the first match. There were then a series of daily meetings throughout the tournament with videotape replays of various incidents. In all cases these 'inquests' were conducted in a helpful way designed to point out the best solutions and not to criticise. Though we focussed on past action we were looking only to the future, and the referees themselves seemed not only to get valuable ideas in the exchange, but to enjoy the sessions as well.

The standards of refereeing in that 1974 World Cup were at least as high as the standard of play. It was a pleasure to find an Englishman, Jack Taylor, put in charge of the final and living up to the referee's motto. He was indeed fearless enough to award a deserved penalty against the host nation in the first minute, impartial enough to award another against the Netherlands when they too transgressed. More important was the depth of refereeing talent available from the football world, including the developing nations, and their readiness to move towards a common interpretation of the laws. There is no longer a handful of nations giving the lead. We are all learning from each other in a truly international spirit.

One advantage of today's television replays is that in disputed decisions they show how much more frequently the referee is right than those who dispute his decision. But some mistakes are inevitable, particularly now that gamesmanship is rife and players are skilled in the art of misleading the referee. When there appears to be a mistaken decision in a vital match, the cry is raised for full-time professional referees. From my experience this would be a most undesirable development, not just because it would be a costly one. The essential is that there is a highly professional system for training and testing referees, and *that* we already have.

By the time a referee has served his apprenticeship and made the long trek to the top through 'feeder' leagues, his ability is well tried and his experience thorough and varied. It is a much more demanding and professional training than in my day, and it weeds out any weaklings. Indeed it is so demanding that few professional players ever take up refereeing in the way county cricketers turn to umpiring. And even though he is not a full-time professional, the referee is kept in constant practice with two and sometimes three games a week. And there the analogy with cricket is apt, because in the days of cricketing amateurs who played regularly, a Cowdrey, a May or a Dexter were as good as any full-time professional. It is match practice that keeps player or referee in tune, and the top-class referees get enough of that without being full-time. Indeed being full-time might well prove a disadvantage. Their living would depend on their continuing to be acceptable and might make them hesitate over unpopular decisions. There would be greater pressure on a full-time referee without any compensating advantages.

Our part-time referees are still held in the highest regard abroad. When watching a 1974 World Cup match beside Prince Rainier of Monaco he commented to me that the referee handling that game was rarely in the correct position to judge and added that the best refereeing he had seen was by Clive Thomas. That is typical of the many compliments still being paid our referees.

What kind of person makes the best referee? Knowing the laws is not enough, for he has to have the instant judgement to apply them and to do so with common sense where interpretation is difficult. Above all he has to command respect and maintain discipline with the players. In my experience this comes most easily to those who have been used to instruct, for instance in the Forces, or as a schoolmaster. A love of the game is essential, but it can be taken for granted in those who take up refereeing and persist on the long trail to the League list. There is an adequate fee for League games, but it is certainly not the money that is an attraction for anyone. And that is good because it helps ensure that only those are recruited who have a genuine dedication to football and to refereeing. It would be helpful if they were reinforced with more players with League experience, well versed in footballers' current attitudes. But few players are prepared for the grind of starting at the bottom and working through to get the right experience and qualification. Those that are can become outstanding like Bob Matthewson, who refereed the 1977 Cup Final. And they will appreciate that even the best referee, like the best player, will make the occasional mistake. When I gave a foul once against Joe Devine of Burnley and Queen's Park Rangers, he said, 'You made a mistake then, Ref.' I replied, 'Do you mind if I tell you when you make one?' 'No,' Joe said, 'but I shall make more than you, I expect.' Referees are only human like the players. They will make mistakes too, whether they are part-time or full-time professionals.

4

Schoolmaster to Secretary

●●

Soccer, sport, and schoolmastering have been the three main strands
in my life, and all three came together in my thirteen years at Watford
Grammar School. This was a good posting for me, as it was near my
home in Hemel Hempstead and also near to the girl I was to marry.
Adrienne was French and herself very keen on sport, being an excellent tennis player. She came to many of the games where I was
refereeing, and while we were engaged she was unwise enough to
bring her mother to watch a match at Apsley. Some of my decisions
did not please the crowd and there were loud comments about my
parentage—or presumed lack of it. This her mother took rather too
literally, urging Adrienne to break off her engagement with such an
apparently unsuitable man whose lineage was as suspect as his popularity. Fortunately her mother's advice had as little effect on her as the
crowd's criticism on me, and it was not long before we were married.
That was in 1924, and since our understanding reached back to the
early war days we had not skimped on the long engagement fashionable
at the time.

When I started at Watford Grammar School in 1921 I was soon
asked to take charge of all sport, including physical training. I found
the gym covered with instructional notices, all forbidding or warning
about this, that or the other and with illustrations showing the *wrong*
way to perform, not the right. I cleared them out at once, as I have
always had as a guiding principle that sports instruction should be
positive and helpful, not negative and inhibiting. As I commented to
the Headmaster, 'Even the Ten Commandments have one "Do"
among the "Don'ts".'

Watford was then a soccer school, but I soon changed it to playing
rugby. In view of my own interest that may seem an odd decision.

Certainly in later years it was greeted with cheers when I mentioned it at rugby club dinners. The atmosphere would alter quickly when I added that the reason for the change was that the boys in the school were not skilful enough to play soccer.

In fact, the reason was a simple case of expediency. Games had not been well organised at Watford and the standard of football was too low to get a good fixture list. The schools in the area we would like to have played, such as Haberdashers, Berkhampstead or St Albans, were out of our class. It was much better for morale to start again with rugby and play the many schools around which were of much the same standard as us beginners, and which we were quickly able to equal or surpass.

It always seemed important to me that masters should sensibly decide the games a school plays on considerations such as these rather than on their own personal preference for a particular one. I was well aware that several secondary schools were then changing to rugby for the wrong reasons. With Burnham salary scales making teaching more attractive, many graduate teachers were looking for posts in state education instead of aiming solely at public or private schools. Most of them had been brought up in the strong rugby traditions of the universities and it was easier to make their mark by changing to a game they understood and enjoyed, than by learning to coach one in which they were not themselves interested or proficient.

They would cover up with the defeatist argument that it made better use of available space to have thirty playing on one field, rather than twenty-two. To judge how spurious that reasoning is you have only to try the same logic on classroom teaching. There are not many who hold that it is educationally desirable to have classes of thirty or more because that makes better use of available classroom space. It may sometimes have to be accepted as a necessary evil, but is never preached as a positive virtue.

My own view was, and is, that soccer is for a number of reasons marginally the better game for schoolboys. All the twenty-two tend to be more involved than the thirty at rugby, many of whom in my experience were frustrated at so rarely touching the ball. Then soccer puts a greater emphasis on skill and less of a premium on strength. That must be a gain, except for those who think you can only build character through suffering. And for those who dislike games or are fearful of physical contact, soccer puts less pressure on them than the maul of rugby.

But the decision should always rest on such dispassionate judgements—and in particular on factors such as the sporting tradition of the school's environment—rather than on an individual's personal preference. So I made the change with considerable regret, but at least for me practice has matched precept. The fixture list was the overriding reason, more important in my view even than the environment, which was soccer-oriented. Indeed many of the boys were keen followers of Watford or the strong St Albans City team. But I ensured they were properly coached in rugby and with a good programme of fixtures were soon enjoying the game and performing creditably.

About this time Sir Frederick Wall, the FA Secretary, tried to deal with the growing problem of conversion to rugby by sending a circular letter to schools extolling the virtues of soccer and requesting that it be given a fair chance. That drew the responses to be expected. When the file was available to me later I was amused to find that most of the replies had been aggressively worded, from the Headmaster of Rugby's predictable 'If Winchester College starts playing rugby, we might consider giving soccer a trial', to the more frequent variants of 'When you are Minister of Education you can try and direct us what games to play, but not now.'

From my own experience as a schoolmaster I knew that the only approach with any hope of success was a dual effort to raise the status of soccer—particularly at Oxford, Cambridge and London Universities which all had a major influence on educational policy—and to provide a proper instructional and coaching back-up. Only when this was available could schools develop well at the game, even if no master had a natural expertise in it. When appointed to the Football Association this was to be my first priority with the start of an instructional network which now covers the country, and with a number of new youth competitions to give encouragement to schools.

The only handicap now for soccer is the self-inflicted wound of the public display of bad temper and bad sportsmanship. That was a very infrequent problem in the thirties, but sadly is a real threat to the game in the present. The situation must be equally confusing to these psychologists and politicians who relate behaviour to poverty and to the geneticists who relate it to heredity. There was no hint in the pre-war days of how far standards would fall with a new generation despite a more affluent society. It was easy enough then to quote the comment of that splendid nineteenth-century footballer, John Goodall of Preston and Derby, who gave this as the attitude of professionals of his time:

One great point in football that cannot be too strongly urged is the maintenance of good temper. I do not say this merely because of the desire to keep the game pure and honourable, but because an even temper is essential to good play. There is no game more calculated to arouse the evil passions, and therefore a great deal of restraint and self-control are necessary.

The enemies of football argue that the game rouses the combative instincts in one; the friends reply that therefore there is all the more reason why the game should be played, because a golden attribute is curbing one's temper, and long experience of football tends to this.

That dates him, of course, because you would not expect this emphasis from a modern professional, although the words express a fundamental truth. Sadly I have found myself having to sympathise in recent years with a comment made to me in 1965 by Nils Middleboe, the Dane who was such a fine player for Chelsea in the twenties. He wrote: 'How pleased I am to see that English referees have been giving marching orders in much greater numbers than ever before. Presumably the English League player has now realised he has to "watch his step", but it is necessary that the reckless tackler in the Continental teams should learn to do the same, and you know better than anyone that the person who is up to mischief (be it in the classroom or the football field) only fears one thing, "stern handling".'

It was indeed a sign of the deterioration of manners and sportsmanship (noticeable also in rugby, incidentally) that he should use the word 'stern' when 'firm' gave better results in my days as teacher and referee.

For a games master a school term tended to be a seven-day working week. The condition of the grounds was also my responsibility, as Edward Reynolds, the Headmaster, took as keen an interest in them as in the standard of play. Indeed he was not too happy to permit my Saturday refereeing, particularly when distant travelling was involved. So mid-week matches were something of a problem and on occasions I slipped away to them rather than ask, and risk a refusal. This was easier once we got a new playing field some distance from the main field, which was next to the school. My colleagues were good in covering for me, saying in surprise when asked my whereabouts, 'He's up at the "new" field, I think, or perhaps its the School field'. It was too far away for the Headmaster to look in on both.

Trouble could still blow up out of the blue. One evening the Headmaster had the vicar in to play bridge and he unfortunately commented on my handling of a mid-week match at Highbury, in which Arsenal played the Corinthians and which I had neglected to mention. Another tall, well-built referee of the day was Rudd, so when queried I said I was sure the vicar must be confusing him with me, and the matter was not pursued.

Cricket was the Headmaster's passion, and another game which appealed to me. We built up a strong side, so that the school even gave a good account of itself against an MCC team which included the Compton brothers, Denis and Leslie, and other notable players. That was a great day for the Headmaster whose mind in the summer term was more often on cricket than anything else. The Captain of the School XI at the time was Eric Robinson, who was later to become such an outstanding musician at the BBC. He was an enthusiastic cricketer who bowled spinners with a curiously round-arm action. Later, when I was telling Reynolds of Eric's growing musical reputation, I added that his speciality was playing the violin. 'Does he do it underarm or overarm?' enquired Reynolds, whose thoughts never strayed far from cricket.

One development we pioneered at Watford was allowing the sporting facilities to be used by boys from the local schools in the holidays. During one vacation early in my career there, I saw some of the boys from the school playing on the local recreation ground with their friends, on a pitch too rough for cricket and with only a minimum of equipment. With the Headmaster's ready approval we collected twelve bags of cricket kit and then prepared a dozen pitches—all fortunately with matting wickets which would suffer no damage—available for organised parties of boys from the school or the community. All we required was that there was a responsible adult in charge of each group. It was the same with the splendid swimming bath. For the bath we had the more stringent requirement that the party be supervised by an experienced adult who was not only a competent person but a good swimmer. When that requirement was met we loaned the bath readily, and even set a special period aside for the nurses from the local hospital.

It has been a matter of concern and regret to me how slow others have been to develop this idea, not solely in the use of school playing fields, but in the sharing of facilities between different sports.

At the Football Association we made a major effort to help in this way. In 1951, as part of the Festival of Britain celebrations, we sent a letter to all clubs asking what facilities they had which could be made available to other sports. Many League clubs have running tracks round the ground (as is standard practice in most Continental countries) and several were willing for these to be used by athletes, together with the excellent changing facilities. The idea was stillborn because of the reaction of the Amateur Athletics Association. The Marquis of Exeter spurned the offer on the weird ground that 'amateurs must not be contaminated by using professional facilities'. That was not untypical of the isolationist attitude within British sport which has hindered full use even of such facilities as are available.

The Central Council of Physical Recreation has also done its best to encourage shared use of school and club grounds. Prince Philip, the President, has taken a personal interest in this. Once as I flew with him in his helicopter from North Wales to Bisham Abbey and on to Buckingham Palace he pointed out the acres of empty playing field round Oxford and along the A40. 'What a waste', he kept saying, and his urging at least has produced some action.

The CCPR also took the step of setting up the Wolfenden Committee on sport and its recommendations in 1960 gave a further push towards maximum use of school and club facilities and the spread of multi-sports centres. But in the main, school authorities, governing bodies, and sports clubs have been less than enthusiastic in implementing such schemes, which are of obvious benefit to the country as a whole. In our cramped island with its current economic problems, such co-operation is a clear necessity, but progress has been disappointingly slow.

These were a very happy thirteen years for me at Watford, but my interest in football grew stronger all the time, nurtured not least by the excitement of the many International matches which came my way to referee. I was also finding as the representative of the Herts FA that I had wide contacts in the Association, a growing understanding of its work, and a feeling that I could contribute to it. So I made instant application when at Ross-on-Wye, on my way to referee the Welsh Cup final in April 1934, I saw this advertisement in the *Daily News*: 'The Football Association invites applications for the position of Secretary. Candidates should state age, qualification and experience. The commencing salary will be £800 per annum with residence.'

It was a pleasant surprise for me to find that I was on a short-list of six to be interviewed on a Friday in May at 22 Lancaster Gate. That was a momentous few days for me. The previous Thursday I refereed the Welsh Cup final. On the Saturday I refereed the FA Cup Final. On the Sunday I was in Antwerp refereeing the Belgium and Holland International. At the dinner afterwards it was something of a shock to hear Mr Seeldrayers, then the Belgian President, say he hoped I would never referee another international match! Fortunately, this proved to be no slur on my refereeing in that game, only an optimistic guess that I might be appointed Secretary of the FA. And my international refereeing career did in fact end as it had begun, with the Belgium–Holland match.

I arrived in good time for my Friday interview, though I was the last to be interviewed. So I saw two of my rivals, the Fulham Secretary, whom I recognised, and an unknown man wearing lavender gloves and a high-wing collar.

Since I had little hope of winning the job, I was determined to be relaxed and not to be overawed by the interviewing Board. Although naturally apprehensive, at least I had the advantage that I did know the members of the panel, including Harry Huband, the Treasurer, Billy Heard of Middlesex, Mark Frowde of Dorset and Arthur Hines of Notts. As Referee's Secretary to the Isthmian League and as a member of the Council of the Hertfordshire FA I had met them all, as well as the President, Sir Charles Clegg, and the Chairman, William Pickford.

Mr Pickford's opening comments hardly put me at my ease: 'The President is deaf and unlikely to hear your answers, but may ask you questions. Direct your replies to me, but don't shout as I have a heart condition and must not be upset.'

By good fortune my Headmaster at Watford had allowed me to teach games once a week at a private Deaf and Dumb School nearby in Bushey. So I had learnt to lip-read and to make myself intelligible to those who had to read my lips. Sir Charles suddenly asked me if I had any questions. 'Is this post pensionable?' I asked, framing the words carefully. To the surprise of the panel Sir Charles at once answered, with that alternating pitch which characterises the voices of the deaf, 'Your predecessor was well rewarded for his services.' 'My predecessor, sir? Am I appointed then?' 'Not so fast, young man, that was a slip of the tongue.'

Two years later a lady introduced herself at London airport, saying 'You will not know me, but I am Sir Charles Clegg's sister. I well remember him coming back home and saying "We've appointed a new Secretary today. A nice young fellow who was the only one of the candidates who could converse with me."' I had not realised that lip-reading would be the key qualification in winning the post of Secretary to the Football Association.

After the interview Charles Sutcliffe, who had been one of the main critics of my new style of refereeing came up and congratulated me on my handling of the Final. Previously he had written in his syndicated newspaper column that one Football League referee was asking his linesmen to co-operate with him in an unusual manner and might soon find himself without refereeing appointments. So I could not refrain from saying, 'I am glad you have seen the diagonal system working well.' He took it in good humour, but I wondered if the remark would weigh against me. I began to think it had when I heard nothing more for over two months.

After so long a silence I had written off my chances and had not bothered to inform Reynolds of my application. One day in July he bustled up and said: 'The place is swarming with photographers and newsmen saying you are Secretary of the FA. That's not so, is it?' 'Not so far as I know,' I cautiously replied. 'Come and play tennis to get away from them,' said Reynolds. After the game we went to his drawing-room where he turned on the news. The final item broadcast was the announcement that a Watford Grammar School master, Rous by name, had that afternoon been appointed Secretary to the FA.

Reynolds always had a menacing sniff and it was twice as pronounced as he said 'So it was true then!' The photographers had duly followed us after the game and we were posed for a number of pictures. They were not so fortunate when I went to Lancaster Gate for confirmation of the appointment. They asked Sir Frederick Wall to pose shaking hands with me. 'Why should I?' he said testily, leaving me to be photographed open-mouthed and with hand held haltingly forward.

The *Fullerian*, the magazine of Watford Grammar School, summed up my teaching career with the tribute it is customary to pay the departing. Issue No. 81 for the winter term 1934 recorded:

Men may come and men must go and even Schoolmasters must go when the Fates decree. Mr Rous became a Master at Watford in September 1921 and his position amongst us was so peculiarly his own that it is difficult to think of living our ordinary lives in the School without him. This is not an attempt to enumerate the many activities that Mr Rous initiated and looked after nor to place on record the great service he rendered to many generations of boys. It is rather an effort in a few brief sentences to say what Mr Rous really meant to the school. A good Schoolmaster, a wise and thoughtful teacher in the classroom, he will be remembered more for his skilful training of boys in the Gymnasium and more still for his indefatigable work as 'Games Master'. Yet he will be remembered most of all for his own personality, his deep unfailing kindness to all with whom he lived, his love of his 'neighbour', his untiring energy to do a good turn to somebody, no matter at what cost of time and trouble to himself. For thirteen years he worked and lived with us; he has left us to take up, as Secretary to the Football Association, work of national and international importance. We cannot grudge his giving his great services to other causes than our own. The work he did here bears its own reward on the help he has given to many boys, particularly with regard to their future when they themselves become men.

The grateful thanks of those for whom he strove, with whom he lived and worked will ever be his and the love of what will always be his old School can never be taken away.

What better thing can man ask for in this world?

What indeed! 'De mortuis nil nisi bonum' is the standard instruction to record nothing but good of the departed. But I felt I had indeed established a special relationship with the school and the bond has continued, as indeed it has done with St Luke's, throughout my life. It was with this sense of having already achieved something worthwhile that I was able to face the new challenge with confident expectation.

What was this Football Association of which I had become Secretary? Its structure has changed little over the past forty years, although the scope of its work has vastly increased. In 1934 the FA was not in membership with FIFA, but otherwise it was in essence much the same as today. The FA was even then a pyramid with numerous schools and small clubs as its base. Above them came the layers of local and county Associations with their leagues and cup competitions. Then came the big amateur clubs and leagues and the professional leagues with the Football League at the apex of them all. At the top, in overall control of these activities, was the Council of the Football Association.

The Council consisted of the officers and representatives of the leading clubs, the county associations, the universities, public schools, Army, Navy and Air Forces, the Football League, and of the then Dominions of Australia, Canada, New Zealand, and South Africa, the

Football Alliance, and the English Schools Football Association. The Council numbered some eighty in all. All those clubs in membership or affiliated to the FA played under the same laws of the game. Only for schools football and for the Dominions, who had their own local requirements, were some relaxations of rules permitted.

Britain was recognised as the founder of the game and our methods and principles had been largely followed elsewhere. So even though we were not members of FIFA, the international body which was then mainly oriented to Europe, we recognised each other's decisions and registrations subject to their reasonable conformity with our own practice.

The FA was a limited liability company with a capital of £100 divided into 2,000 shares of 1s. It was itself in membership with the International Football Association Board, which included the Scottish, Welsh, and Irish Associations. The International Board decided the Laws which governed the game and made the decisions on any special regulations to govern International matches and the Home Championship. The system for control of the game was well established, but the services to clubs in membership were then very limited. And it was in the expansion of services to improve and develop the game, and in the expansion of clubs in membership that there was scope for progress.

Twenty-two Lancaster Gate was in many ways a quiet backwater when I arrived on August 4th 1934 to start my work at the headquarters of the English FA. There was no problem parking my Hillman Minx, as there was rarely another car in the road. That was in striking contrast to today's constant bustle, and the pace of work was as leisurely. Some London offices did not open until 10 o'clock, and indeed some even had it written into their leases that they would not begin work before then. And that was the standard starting time for the five staff who worked at Lancaster Gate, so arriving before nine, I had the place to myself for an hour or more until I had converted them to my own way of working.

My senior assistant was Charles Earl; George Neale was in charge of accounts; Ernest Miller, who had been secretary to Sir Frederick Wall, continued as administrative assistant to me, while Stanley Whitehorn looked after match arrangements and Mansell was the office junior. We were able to cope with such limited numbers, compared to today's fifty, because the pressures and range of work were so much less. Disciplinary cases for instance were very rare, not more than five or six cases a year needing personal hearings, as most were dealt with by post by the General Purposes Committee of three. Many matters were ignored, however, in which the Association ought to have been taking an active part, and it was their failure to do so which kept the work level down so low. But before any changes could be introduced it was necessary for me first to become established and accepted in the job.

Being Secretary to the FA puts one in much the same position as being clerk to the Magistrates' Court. Most of the main decisions are finally taken by the part-time amateur officials, but the full-time professional expert is relied upon to guide and direct and, often, initiate those decisions. He cannot expect to force his views through, but if he has foresight and is reasonably adroit in his relationships with people he should be the chief influence on development. Two other factors gave the Secretary further opportunity to play a major role. So far as the public and players were concerned he was the spokesman for the FA, and was seen by them as having a more significant part even than the Chairman. I was only the third FA Secretary in sixty-four years, and my two immediate predecessors had both been men of stature in the game.

The first was Charles Alcock, who pioneered Association Football, took a leading role in forming the FA in 1863 and was responsible for starting nine years later the Cup competition which did so much to popularise football. Alcock was Secretary from 1870 to 1895 after the office had been briefly held by Morley, Willis, and Graham, who covered the first seven years. Frederick Wall then served for thirty-nine years until I took over from him. So he too had been a major influence on football. But he was very much the inside man, with few direct contacts outside Lancaster Gate or the Association.

Despite his long experience, Sir Frederick gave me little help. After my appointment I was invited to attend the FA summer meeting at Scarborough. Unfortunately the school was unable to release me that week-end, as Parents' Day and the School *v* Old Boys game made it impossible for me to be spared. Pickford then suggested that I visit Wall two or three times to get briefed before starting the job. The first time I looked in all Wall said was 'The job's straightforward. You can read up the files. There is nothing much I can tell you.' So I didn't return until my start date.

At least Wall had left me the legacy that the Secretary's job was given high prominence and was of prime importance in the development of the game. This was both an inspiring and a humbling thought for me and I saw the first year as of vital importance in establishing myself so that I could maintain that tradition of excellence.

My first Council meeting began badly. Item 5 on the agenda had been submitted by the Surrey representative, and Sir Charles Clegg had asked to speak to the proposal. As it involved a complex legal point and Sir Charles was a lawyer of repute, the Chairman readily agreed. Sadly, the Surrey representative died a few days before the meeting and we had to start with a minute's silence in his memory.

At Item 1 Sir Charles rose to his feet and I had to mouth 'Not yet, Sir Charles', hoping he could read my lips. At Item 3 he was up again and again I had to say 'Not yet, Sir Charles.' At Item 5 he at last delivered his impressive fifteen-minute speech, but then called on the Surrey representative to reply. 'He can't. He's not here,' we chorused. 'He must be here to reply,' said Sir Charles, 'the item *must* be adjourned until he is present.' 'He's dead!' the members shouted. 'He *must* be here,' said Sir Charles, who still had not heard properly. At last I managed to draw his attention to the note I had written on his agenda: 'One minute's silence for the Surrey representative who died last week.' 'Why didn't someone tell me?' said Sir Charles crossly.

It was not long before I was in trouble with Sir Charles again. For the first match which I attended as Secretary of the FA I sported a dashing pair of plus-fours, which were then very popular with sportsmen, particularly golfers. At once I received a letter from Sir Charles saying he had seen a picture of me in the paper apparently inappropriately attired: 'I would remind you that Sir Frederick Wall would go to matches in a top hat and frock coat.' Thereafter I compromised with a sober lounge suit and bowler.

Before Council meetings the tradition apparently had been for £20 to be given to Sir Frederick Wall so that he and his wife could do the catering. They cut sandwiches the night before, provided the coffee, saved what they could, and sent out to a nearby café for more cakes if the food ran out. That did not appeal to me as part of the Secretary's job, and I arranged instead for members to eat in the Merchant Navy Club restaurant which adjoined the FA. A full meal there cost only 7s 6d a head, so they ate better for less money and trouble.

The Secretary's job demands a basis of order and method so that the routine work is effectively and expeditiously dealt with and time left for the fundamental thinking, which may be of even greater importance. My first priority therefore was to get the right system of work. I had been advised in my very limited 'job induction' from Pickford to pay careful attention to the way letters had been so competently dealt with in the past. I found that all outgoing letters were copied in leather-bound books by a water process, and these became smudged and often indecipherable. The style, too, was autocratic and unhelpful, as if to give the writer the least trouble and the enquirer the least information. A typical sample was an exchange of correspondence with a man from Cornwall enquiring about a complex point on the interpretation of a regulation. His answer from Wall simply stated: 'I direct your attention to para 6 subsection (iv) in the handbook. I find the ruling very clear. I suggest you follow the instructions as set out.' So the poor man was as much in the dark on the right interpretation as when he wrote.

As a simple start in reorganisation I had carbon copies kept of all letters instead of the peculiar wet copying process which had left such poor records. More important, I trained the staff in an entirely different approach to drafting letters, trying to eliminate their thinking and writing solely from the 'I' position. Instead they were asked to imagine they were the writers of the original letters, and then to consider what answers they would like and how they would like them expressed. In that way the replies could both be enlightening and give the impression that there was a genuine desire to help.

It seemed to me equally important that all correspondence was swiftly handled, and I tried to ensure that letters were answered the same day if possible. To achieve this my method was to read all the post on arrival and sort it into departmental trays for the straightforward answers to be drafted. Whenever the letter involved a complex point which needed further discussion, or a decision at my level, I put a red star on the letter and kept an hour free from 9.30 for departmental heads to come and see me about these letters. And since I read all drafts before signing, the staff had soon become so familiar with my views that correction was kept to a minimum.

Relationships with the League and with the FAs of the other home countries was then a simple matter and there were few of today's problems of conflict of interest and power. But I was aware that the Association was in many respects giving a more limited service to football than it could and should. So I began cautiously to propose some reforms, and was much encouraged when the first three suggestions were all accepted by the Council.

As a schoolmaster I had seen how little was done to encourage youth or to provide any training and coaching facilities. Now a knock-out competition was agreed for juniors and a County Youth Championship started.

The next and most important step was to develop training courses for coaches and referees. So far as coaches were concerned, this was a new idea for any sport. Indeed in rugby football some quarter of a century later, being professionally coached could imperil one's amateur status!

The initial course in 1935 was of the utmost importance, as it was likely to determine the response to a project which had not yet gained wholehearted backing. It was held at the Duke of York's Head-quarters in London, and for the lecturers in this three-day programme I was careful to choose some outstanding managerial and coaching figures of the day. There was Tom Whittaker of Arsenal and Arthur Grimsdell of Tottenham, together with Jimmy Hogan, just returned to manage Fulham after building a great reputation in Europe as national coach for Austria's 'Wunderteam'.

This was not the success I had hoped, for none of them proved expert in putting over their subject. However, it did serve to emphasise the need for such training, since the 'masters' of the day were obviously in need of some instruction themselves. Hogan was the most forceful and interesting of the three, although he had been unwilling to submit advance notes of his sessions in case too much might be learnt about his methods. So he at least was not totally in sympathy with the course aim of passing on the best in coaching method!

What alarmed us was how ill organised Hogan was when it came to taking the practical periods, which should have been his forte. We had made it clear that the timetable for so short a course had to be inflexible, with no overrunning of any periods. Yet for his three-quarters of an hour on tactics and skills he took the class to the furthest pitch, wasting five minutes walking there. On arrival we found he had forgotten to arrange for the balls to be there and Joe Edelston was despatched to get them. I had to suggest to him exercises which might keep the course occupied while we waited. When the balls did come he talked and demonstrated so long that there was no time for practice. And he stood with his back to a strong sun shining into the eyes of his class, so that they saw very little of the expert demonstration. Hogan's party piece was a wonderful demonstration of eighteen different ways to trap a ball with the outside or inside of either foot, with toe, heel, instep, chest and many other parts. But the demonstration was too fast to be assimilated and too advanced for a class wanting to know first the best way to bring a ball quickly under control.

Afterwards I was to get to know Hogan well. When Fulham dismissed him he appealed to me at the FA to get him compensation. We had no powers to do this, but it was always one of my principles that the FA had a responsibility to try and help all footballers. By asking

Fulham to consider whether they had treated him fairly I did persuade them to make a payment to him. In discussion with Hogan on coaching matters I came to realise that his great reputation abroad was in part fortuitous. Because he could not speak the Austrian players' language he had to content himself with endless demonstration of his own high skills. He would for instance have a board put up with a hole in the middle barely larger than a football. From fifteen yards' range he would slot eight shots out of ten through that hole. Hogan himself was content with the demonstration. It would interest the players too, who would try themselves but soon became disillusioned and bored when hardly a ball went through the hole. It was then that Hugo Meisl, the Austrian manager, would take over and compel the players to go on practising that skill until they were as proficient as Hogan. They were an effective team, but on the course it was clear that Hogan on his own lacked many of the organisational skills a coach requires.

The deficiencies of the first course pointed the method for the second, held at Carnegie Physical Training College in Leeds. Many managers, coaches, and some senior players came to the residential week, where the emphasis was on the proper organisation of coaching and the pooling of ideas and methods. Facilities at Carnegie were perfect for our purpose and we relied mainly on the expert staff of the College, all highly qualified teachers of games and physical education. Major Major, the Principal, took a leading part, as did Walter Winterbottom. And while Hogan again taught tactics he was supported by a College tutor, Wilson, who had great success in teaching 'small' games as training for skills, stamina, and alertness.

The trial run had allowed us to strike the right balance for this well attended and publicised course. A number of club directors, including Arsenal's George Allison, came to assess it. And the verdict as reported in the Press was 'Those who came to scoff left to praise.'

That was an encouraging launch for a project which was of special interest to me, and which I felt to be vital to the healthy development of the game. Success and acceptance at Carnegie won approval for the courses to continue annually, attended by senior players who had an aptitude for teaching. Soon we were taking it farther, issuing certificates to those who passed the terminal examination and appointing them to a panel of coaches available to clubs, or for work with schools, colleges and youth clubs. There was adequate support now to ensure that the game could be properly taught in schools and that there was no need on this account for a continuing drift to rugby.

In these early years at the FA there were a couple of routine engagements which were to stir my Suffolk memories. On a visit to Norwich, who had just been promoted, I had the unhappy task of declaring unfit for League football the 'Nest' ground where I had spent so many hours watching the heroes of my youth. On the inspection I was accompanied by Chief Constable Scott of Norwich, and we were in reluctant agreement that the ground was too small and the facilities too poor for Second Division football. A new ground, Carrow Road, was obtained and made ready in three months. A happier occasion was at Portman Road ground, where I had done my Army training. Captain Cobbold, father of Ipswich's present Chairman, invited me to their first League game there against Southend in 1938. Ipswich had been admitted to Third Division (South) in place of Gillingham and I was pleased to find them quickly established as a team of character, finishing seventh that first season.

It was a main principle with me to see as much as I could at first hand rather than remain remote in my office. And it was from days such as this that I derived much of the fun and satisfaction of my job as I renewed old acquaintances or made an ever widening circle of new friends. But there was one annual event which was in many ways the climax of the football year.

At my first Cup Final as Secretary in 1935 I had a nervous day wondering if all would go according to plan—because as far as I could find there was no plan. Certainly there were no guide lines left for me and I could not help worrying that something might have been overlooked which I had assumed was Wembley's responsibility and they presumed to be the FA's. Who was responsible for the guests, the officials, the balls? From past experience in refereeing a Cup Final I knew that some of the arrangements were haphazard. No one had met my linesmen or me, or told us where to find the dressing-rooms. We found we had to change in an office used by Sir Arthur Elvin's secretary. At the game's end we were left on the field to watch the presentations to the players and as there was no bath for us we begged one off the winning team. It seemed wiser to use their dressing-room than that of the losers!

All went off all right on that Cup Final day, but immediately afterwards I sat down to write a comprehensive guide for future years. This covered all the timings of this complex operation and the responsibilities of everyone taking part. So at Lancaster Gate it became known colloquially as 'from ball boys to the king', and this guide has remained a standard part of the tradition of the day.

The plan for seating in the Royal Box had to be submitted for Palace approval. For the rest however I was told that the booklet made everything so clear for the King and Queen that there was no need for consultation, since it covered every detail from arrival to presentations to departure. The booklet also covered the responsibilities of all the FA Cup Committee, such as who should receive the guests and who was responsible for the lunch.

I determined that the referees should be properly looked after in future and made Nigel Bird, my staff member who dealt with refereeing affairs, responsible for meeting the referee and linesmen and taking them to Wembley. And instead of their having to slip away to the Secretary's office, I made sure there was proper accommodation in future and that they would follow the teams to the Royal Box to receive their medal from the guest of honour. The day should belong to all who take part on the field.

5

Tours with England

●●

Innovation was an important part of the job, but day-to-day matters consumed most of my time. None of these was more important than the International match programme, and none gave me more pleasure. The England team in the thirties was very powerful, and we were the side every country wanted to play and beat. Mussolini's offer of huge bonuses to his team for the Highbury game in 1934 was only a reflection of the immense prestige which accrued to any country beating England. Italy at least clearly regarded this as just as important as winning the World Cup!

The Dictators saw success in sport as a political weapon, and it was not long before Hitler's Germany was reflecting this attitude. 'Strength Through Joy' was a part of his regime's philosophy, and to him winning at games was another means of impressing the world with Aryan supremacy. The Berlin Olympics of 1936 were staged with this very much in mind. This was most noticeable in the extravagant displays which heralded the athletics in the great stadium, as well as in Hitler's fury when it was an American—and a Negro at that—who dominated the Games as Jesse Owens set three world records.

The football was not given quite such prominence, for Germany was not then a great force in amateur soccer. But Hitler had another tantrum when he came to watch Germany play—only to see them beaten by Norway. The German manager Otto Nerz was the main object of his wrath and was dismissed the following year.

During the Olympic march-past we gave the customary 'eyes right' as we passed in front of Hitler. The French contingent however, held their arms out sideways to the body in the old Olympic salute. The French gesture pleased the crowd, as it was so close to the Nazis' own salute. Ours, however, was not felt to be respectful enough, and as a result the French were given the best changing-room in the stadium, while we were banished to the farthest and smallest.

The football did not bring us much joy either. Although none of the home countries was then a member of FIFA, Great Britain had permission to enter as a team. This was the first joint venture and resulted in our party including more selectors than players. Each country had four, who sought to get their own men in the side. So the matches themselves were tame affairs compared with the selection battles which preceded them.

Bernard Joy, who was shortly to win a full International cap against Belgium when still an amateur, was the natural choice as stopper centre-half. But his left-back, Fulton, was an Irishman who was more used to playing in the centre, rather than staying wide to watch his winger. Even the Chinese were therefore able to put severe pressure on our defence, having been given the freedom of the wing. After beating off one fierce attack Joy was heard to comment acidly to Fulton, 'Don't you feel safe outside the penalty area?'

Not surprisingly we did not reach the late stages of the competition, losing 4–5 to Poland after beating China 2–0, and it has always proved a more satisfactory arrangement to select as Great Britain's representative the winning side in the home championship, rather than have a mixed team.

Games against Germany gave me problems early in my career at the FA. Germany have always been a strong soccer nation, and in 1930 held England to a 3–3 draw in Berlin. It needed a late equaliser from Arsenal's David Jack to prevent defeat after Hofmann, one of the best inside-forwards of his day, had completed a hat trick.

When in 1935 Germany came over to play England at White Hart Lane, feelings had run high against Hitler's intervention in Spain. The TUC in particular were incensed that German and Italian support for General Franco had enabled him to get the better of the Republicans and their Russian allies. So demonstrations were organised by them at the match, and some fourteen people were arrested for insulting behaviour.

The FA Council view was that politics should be kept out of sport, and that so long as the Government approved the match the visitors should have all the normal courtesies. The German spectators were particularly well behaved and the newspaper comment ran, 'Exemplary conduct by 10,000 visitors' or 'Almost an affair of friendship rather than football.'

Sir Charles Clegg was upset by the contrasting demonstration and, as usual, was prepared to make forthright comment. At the banquet after the match, which England won 3–0, he apologised to the German officials and went on, 'This TUC have thought fit to interfere in a matter which was none of their business. This is the first time the TUC has interfered in football and I hope it will be the last. Before they start to tell a sporting organisation what to do and how their members should behave, they should see that their own members responsible for rowdyism are kept under control. The TUC seems to forget that this is a sport free of all political interference.'

Sir Walter Citrine replied later for the TUC: 'The TUC has never given any of its members any encouragement to rowdyism. So far as the remarks about perverting football into politics are concerned, the trouble is that Sir Charles Clegg does not bother to inform himself of the nature of sport in Germany. If he did so he would realise that football there is nothing more nor less than part of the Nazi German regime.'

For me this was an object lesson in the dangers of taking political standpoints about sport. If the Government of the day does not stop a match, how can sporting bodies grade the character and politics of another country? By a nice historical inversion, Russia is now the country that looks on sport as a means of furthering its political aims, and is often blatant in its political manipulation of sport. Yet the TUC is hardly likely to take the same view about Russia as it did about Germany. And once you involve sport in political judgements you are soon in a morass of special pleading, double standards, and biased thinking.

Sadly the administrators of sport now find themselves unavoidably embroiled in politics as more and more countries and organisations find they can use sport for their own political ends—a disastrous development for sport and for international goodwill.

The return match in Berlin in 1938 certainly embroiled me in politics. When we arrived we were told that the Germans would stand to attention for our National Anthem and were asked to return the compliment by giving the Hitler salute during the playing of theirs. Together with Charles Wreford Brown, the FA official in charge of the team, I had an interview with the British Ambassador, Sir Neville Henderson, and asked what we should do. 'When I go in to see Herr Hitler I give him the Nazi salute because that is the normal courtesy expected. It carries no hint of approval of anything Hitler or his regime may do. And if I do it, why should you or your team object?' was Henderson's advice.

So I put that view to the players, leaving the choice to them, but pointing out that on the decision depended whether the game was held in a friendly or hostile atmosphere. All agreed they had no objection, and no doubt saw it as a bit of fun rather than of any political significance. Inevitably, however, there was heavy criticism of the action in some of the press. Ivan Sharpe, himself a leading player, was the man who best expressed my own view: 'Abroad there is generally a ceremony of greeting from teams to onlookers, so I could never understand the fuss that was made because the Football Association allowed the English players to return the Nazi salute. It was just a friendly gesture ... "When in Rome" style ... there was no appeasement about it. And after all we were friendly enough to be playing them at football.'

Sir Neville Henderson had in fact warned that we should be cautious in advocating contests between British and German teams, as the Nazis were looking for easy victories to boost the idea that the regime had produced a super-race. This game did nothing to help that theory. The terraces were packed with shirt-sleeved spectators sweltering in the sunshine while below, the velvety green pitch, surrounded by its rich red running tracks, was in perfect condition. And it was the British forwards who won the cheers and proved the only supermen on view. Two fine wingers started the goal rush as Cliff Bastin volleyed home Matthews' centre. Two expert strikers continued it as Aston Villa's Broome and Sheffield Wednesday's Robinson scored a couple each. And Chelsea's Len Goulden finished it with the sixth and best goal, driven home from twenty-five yards, to leave us 6–3 winners.

Hitler did not come to the game. I was amused, however, at the contrast between Sir Neville Henderson, sitting there wearing a shooting-hat with a hawk's feather and an old pullover, and Hermann Goering beside him glistening with medals and military magnificence. Henderson had a large pair of binoculars slung round his neck and each time we scored he would proffer them to the unsmiling Goering, saying, 'What wonderful goals. You really ought to get a closer look at them.' Perhaps there was a hint here of how British humour and improvisation would win out in a more important contest against the disciplined efficiency of the Germans.

One of my earliest tours abroad was to Scandinavia, where we played Norway, Sweden and Finland. All these teams were amateur, but the Swedes in particular showed a natural aptitude for the game. We won all the matches easily enough and beat Finland 8–0. That was an interesting game for me as Joe Payne, playing in his only International, scored twice. Payne had become something of a legend by setting two scoring records which still stand. On April 13th 1934, playing in his first game at centre-forward for Luton, he scored ten goals out of twelve against Bristol Rovers. To prove that was no freak performance Payne next season set a Third Division (South) scoring record with 55 goals. Oddly in the same season Ted Harston of Mansfield Town set the Third Division (North) record—also with 55 goals. How the game has changed in forty years, with the emphasis shifting from attack to defence! When attack was our natural game in the thirties we bred such a succession of great centre-forwards that even the incomparable 'Dixie' Dean had a struggle to hold his place against the likes of 'Pongo' Waring of Villa, Vic Watson of West Ham, Ted Harper, who set scoring records for Preston, Blackburn and Spurs, or George Camsell of Middlesbrough with his career record of 346 League goals mainly in the First Division, his 59 goals in a season and his 18 goals in only nine Internationals.

Joe Payne was forceful and athletic, too skilled and powerful for the Finns. He was lithe and swift like Jackie Milburn and ran leaning forward, crouched over the ball so that he was hard to dispossess and able to ride the shoulder charges. But he was still not talented enough to hold his place then in the England team. At international level he proved just another centre-forward, no match for Freddie Steele of Stoke or Tommy Lawton of Everton, when we had such an embarrassment of riches for the position.

The Scandinavian tour in 1937 was a particularly happy one, with the matches not too demanding and the boat travel a relaxing interlude. In those days the relations with the Press were also much more free and easy. The reporting then was mainly of a factual nature, with little of today's hunt for exclusive angles, 'inside' stories, or scandalous gossip. That may have made for duller reading, but it put less pressure on the players themselves. The interchanges too were less guarded because the star players had no agents then, no bargaining ambitions over the price of a 'quote'. And since the writing was rarely critical and had less of the know-all attitude, there was less friction with those who really did know and did perform.

The close relationship then existing was characterised on that Finnish trip when our comfortable Swedish Lloyd ship was becalmed for more than forty-eight hours in thick fog. With the boat full of Finnish girl students going back on holiday from Stockholm and Uppsala Universities, it was a merry time for all with a number of

impromptu dances. And the great entertainer proved to be one of the
Press party, Vernon Morgan, of Reuters, who had been an Oxford
soccer blue. His stories and jokes were a constant source of amusement to all. So too were his attempts to improve the Finnish students'
English, since he suffered from our usual failing of assuming that if
you speak slowly enough and loud enough everyone *must* understand,
even when the languages have nothing in common.

The friendly relationships established with Scandinavia on that trip
had an important sequel after the war. In 1946, as these countries
tried to re-establish the game after their bleak football-less years, they
turned to the Football Association for assistance with coaching. We
readily agreed and some fifteen coaches went to Norway and Sweden
in the close season. So successful was this experiment that the Swedish
FA asked us to find them a national coach. The man I proposed was
something of a surprise to them, since George Raynor was an almost
unknown Third Division footballer.

As our courses had shown, however, the best players are not
always the best instructors, and I was well aware how dedicated and
intelligent a coach George had made himself. The Swedes accepted
my recommendation, but were shaken when a First Division side
touring there claimed never to have heard of Raynor and laughed at
the idea of his being national coach. Raynor was undeterred. At a
time when most English coaches tended to emphasise physical fitness
and have comparatively few sessions on ball skills, George was ini-
tially greeted with the remark 'You will teach us the English way and
make us hungry for the ball by denying it to us?' But George was soon
cartooned with a sack of balls on his back as he built on the Swedish
strength of skilful control. To that he added some of the robustness of
the English game, and he now figures in the *Guinness Book of Records*
as the most successful national team manager ever. Certainly he
helped raise Swedish football to a continuously high standard, even
though so many of the country's amateur players were tempted
abroad. Raynor had another asset for a national team manager. He
was open and competent in his dealings with the Press. Before his
first International game he told the reporters exactly what tactics he
would employ and the reasons he expected to get goals. And when
Sweden scored seven, his reputation was established. Perhaps I was
too helpful. In 1949 Sweden beat us 3-1 in Stockholm with Tom
Finney scoring our only goal, and in 1959 they became only the second
overseas team to beat us at Wembley—much to Raynor's joy.

But in the forties there were many memorable successes to enjoy.

There was the 10-0 win in Lisbon with the Portuguese devastated by Finney, Matthews, Mortensen, and Lawton. So dejected were their team that none of them came to the banquet afterwards.

Yet the most notable victory to me was our 4-0 win in Milan in 1948 against the powerful Italian side. This match was refereed impeccably by my old friend Pedro Escartin of Madrid. And keen though the Italians were to win they generously recognised the English skills—particularly those of Lawton, Finney, and Mortensen, whose remarkable early goal from the acutest of angles gave us the confidence to win. Before the match all the shop windows displayed a photograph of our team with the caption 'Made in Britain', and in those days that was still a hallmark of quality.

The most thrilling goal on these tours was the one which earned Lofthouse the nickname 'the Lion of Vienna'. It was in 1952, when Austria were one of the best sides in Europe. With the score 2-2 Finney sent Nat Lofthouse racing through the centre with characteristic dash and determination. As the goalkeeper challenged, Lofthouse slid the ball accurately home, though crippled in the collision.

We had travelled to Vienna by Swissair and the crew stayed on to bring us back. They regarded themselves as mascots for our success, especially the chief hostess of Swissair, Margaret Faust, who always managed to get posted to any aircraft carrying the England team. She was delighted by that goal, as were the many British troops watching. Others were not so enthusiastic. Vienna was still divided into four sectors and the game was played in the Russian sector. Two thousand seats had therefore been reserved for the Russians, but none came to watch.

Dr Josef Gero, the President of the Austrian Football Federation, was so anxious for his team to win that he could not sit out the last fifteen minutes, walking up and down behind the stand unable to watch. But he was delightfully generous in acknowledging our success, despite his disappointment.

I knew just how he felt, having myself sat through an agonising ninety minutes watching our defeat by America in the World Cup of 1950. I had had a premonition that was how it would go. Arthur Drewry was in sole charge of selection, though advised by Walter Winterbottom, and it seemed there was a danger of his taking America too lightly after we had won our first match 2-0 against Chile.

The United States' team had already shown its quality by giving the strong Spanish side a fright, holding them at 1-1 until two second-half goals gave Spain an uneasy victory. Stanley Matthews seemed to me the ideal man to undermine a team like theirs, which was clearly long on spirit and short on skill. Special arrangements had had to be made for him to join the party and it seemed sense to put him in for this game. That I thought also to be the view of team manager Walter Winterbottom, so I went to see Drewry to urge some changes and especially Matthews' inclusion. Drewry was adamant, however, that we should not change the team that had beaten Chile 2–0. 'Never change a winning team' was his philosophy. But I felt that we were also regarding the USA as a pushover when in fact they had a fair record in the World Cup, having once reached the semi-final in 1930, which we were not to do for another sixteen years.

My fears grew when I saw the stadium. There are magnificent facilities now at Belo Horizonte, but then there was not even changing accommodation of any standard. Our players had to come down in the bus already changed to a ground which was walled in on three sides like a fives court. The atmosphere was steamy, the pitch bumpy and suddenly we were a goal down as Gaetjens headed past Bert Williams. That shattered our confidence and with the luck running against us we could find no way past a side that from then on contained a goal-keeper and ten full-backs. It was a shattering result, which was still an agonising memory when many years later I was invited back to Belo Horizonte to open the new stadium there, one of the best equipped I have ever seen.

The *Daily Express* correspondent was sitting near me and I saw he had made a note 'Knock Drewry' which he did at length. Yet whatever the selection errors, or whatever the failure of the players to take the game seriously enough, this was a match we should have won with the likes of Finney and Mortensen in the side. But this was a Cup game and the bigger they are the harder they can fall in Cup football. That's its charm—unless you are with the England team which has just been beaten by the United States of America.

The team for that 1950 World Cup was weakened by the loss of one of the best centre-halves to play for England, Neil Franklin. In those days of a maximum League wage of £20 per week it was not sur-prising that lucrative overseas offers should be particularly attractive. And Franklin had accepted just such an offer from Bogota in Colombia after secret negotiations.

This might not have affected his future career had this club been affiliated to the Colombian Football Federation. Since, however, he broke his contract with Stoke to play for a club outside either FIFA or FA jurisdiction we had no alternative but to suspend him from our football. Before the Disciplinary Committee was forced to take this step I contacted the Bogota officials to see if conflict could be avoided, explaining to them the long-term damage to Franklin's prospects. When no compromise proved possible Franklin was suspended on the grounds that 'he gave untrue reasons to the FA for not wishing to be considered for international matches; deceived his club and broke his contract and made statements to the Press and allowed articles to appear in his name likely to bring the game into disrepute.'

The suspension was lifted just over a year later on January 31st 1951, but his international career was in ruins. It was particularly unfortunate that Neil Franklin should be at the centre of this tug of war, for he was the nicest of men and a fine player, vital to the England team of the time. When I saw Neil recently at a Highbury match he was as pleasant as ever and with no rancour over the past. He recognised that in preserving a principle England's loss had been as great as his own.

From my own and the FA viewpoint there was no bar to movement within clubs affiliated to national football associations, although the League was naturally resistant to depredations from Europe as well as South America. Gigi Peronace, the smooth-talking Italian who fixed up so many deals, was a *bête noire* for them. But the FA made no objections to the trickle of players abroad to clubs within FIFA's orbit. John Charles, Denis Law, Gerry Hitchens, Eddie Firmani, or Jimmy Greaves were free to make a name and money in Italian football after Franklin had pointed the way. Some, however, found the money too hardly earned and were soon homesick for English football. When Greaves fell out with Milan the club inhibited his return by setting an impossibly high transfer fee when Tottenham first enquired. I saw Gigi privately about this, suggesting it was in his interest to use his influence to get it reduced to reasonable levels because otherwise the adverse publicity might prevent future transfers. Fortunately, Tottenham were able to settle and our greatest goalscorer of a generation came home.

How we should have played in that World Cup match in Belo Horizonte became apparent when we met the United States team again three years later in America. At half-time in the Yankee Stadium we were struggling again to penetrate a massed defence. Then Walter Winterbottom told Finney, Broadis and Lofthouse: 'Forget the team play and the passing. Run at them yourselves and go through on your own.' And their individual skills then brought a deluge of goals as England won 6–3.

That World Cup defeat underlined the stupidity of divorcing the team manager from team selection or giving him such limited powers that the side he fielded was rarely one of his own choosing. At least there was one man, Arthur Drewry, who took responsibility in this instance and had the opportunity to pick a team as a team. At home the established system was too deep-rooted for early change and was even more chaotic in concept, with the whole committee responsible for the choice.

They say of the camel that it looks so weird it could only have been designed by a committee, and some of our international teams were just as ill-balanced as a result of the system. The committee of up to twelve would discuss each position in turn and vote on it if necessary. Inevitably personal preferences intruded and positions were considered in isolation rather than thought being given to the team as an entity. A typical exchange might start with Major Keys saying 'But you cannot include Ronnie Clayton. The last time I saw him play, our own half-back looked much more impressive.' Then another would add, 'Yes. When we played Blackburn he wasn't in the same class as ours.' Walter would point out that they were judging Clayton on one away game, and in away games there is a disadvantage for individuals as well as teams. He would add: 'The real reason I want Clayton is that he and Bryan Douglas understand each other so well that we are much stronger down the right when those two play together, even if two other individuals may be as good or better—as individuals.' But within a few minutes the committee might have ruled out Clayton and be considering the other players of their own nomination. By the time the process was repeated with four or five other players it was a hybrid side that was finally announced to the Press.

Selection problems were the one cross Walter had to bear as England's first team manager. In other respects he was perhaps more fortunate than Ramsey and Revie. For he also held the post of Director of Coaching, playing the lead part in building up a system which became a model for many other countries and for many other major sports in this country. That meant he was always occupied in exciting developments and not totally reliant on England's success for job satisfaction. It can be a very frustrating experience to change from the bustle of League management to the isolation of national team manager, where a couple of bad results may be followed by months without a match or a squad to train. The long periods of waiting can then ferment too many new ideas and encourage excessive change. It needed a man of Ramsey's iron determination to stick to a consistent basic plan, with a success for which he did not always receive full recognition from the public, or those who are more concerned with entertaining quotes or fanciful ideas than with solid results.

One advantage of keeping closely in touch with the national team was that I could better appreciate the ideas being put forward in Europe which might be of value to us. It was at a conference in Split in Jugoslavia that a number of European Associations first proposed a competition for 'under-23' teams. This was an idea I welcomed, since it seemed to me highly desirable to have 'feeder' arrangements which would prepare young players for the national team, test them out in international competition, and get them used to combining with players of different styles, rather than just following their own club tactics. Tom Finney, for instance, often told me how much he enjoyed playing for England, as he was allowed to lie deep with the full-back not daring to follow him under the old marking system. This gave Finney all the space he needed to confuse the defenders. But back at his club he was always told, 'I don't want any England tactics here.' And he was instructed to play well forward like a normal winger. So it was not Preston, but Alf Ramsey at Ipswich, who finally confounded the club tacticians by just that strategem, as his left-winger, Jimmy Leadbeater held back much as Finney used to do for England. The confusion that move caused helped to take Ipswich from the Third Division to the First Division Championship in three years.

Clearly it had to be valuable for promising young players to have the wider training of international competition and of the different styles at that level rather than be kept to the narrow confines of their club. But though I had little difficulty in getting support to start a few friendly 'under-23' matches, the League tended to oppose any extension of international games which might make frequent calls on their players. The then Chairman of Newcastle was also antagonistic to any such step, fearing young players would be the targets for club scouts encouraging them to transfer. I had overcome similar opposition before when we introduced youth tournaments and got the League's agreement to an extra International in mid-season to help pay for them. And while appreciating the League's problem, I eventually won acceptance of the idea that there has to be a coherent development plan for the national side, so 'under-23' games became an important part of the system which was soon copied by a number of other sports, such as hockey and rugby.

Sadly, in recent years, instead of extending arrangements which would allow a consistent development plan for the national team, there have been more restrictions on the use of League players. And after our second successive failure to qualify for the World Cup final round it was clear there must soon be greater co-operation in producing a worthy national side. When England's performances are depressing, all soccer suffers from the disillusion, so poor national performances cannot be shrugged off as no concern of the League. Following Ron Greenwood's appointment as England team manager it was good to see evidence that all concerned are co-operating to ensure improvements in team building, with some old concepts revived and given new life.

6

Losing the Pools

●●●

The International team and the tours abroad were inevitably a centre of attraction. But much of my work and my interest was concerned with the base of the pyramid rather than its peak. It remained my conviction that the game could only be healthy if it was well supported and well taught in the schools. To assist in this I personally produced in 1936 an instructional booklet for youngsters for use in schools entitled *First Steps in Playing Football*. It is essential that the basic principles are learnt correctly before the youth adds his own frills to them. Good or bad habits are drilled in early and become instinctive thereafter. So it's best to start right, and at the time there was a need for a few simple hints to make sure the first steps were the correct ones. Though the booklet is more than forty years old, the essentials haven't changed much. The opening paragraphs, for instance are:

To be of maximum service to your side you must fully understand the following and be able to put them into practice.

I. Kicking

One-footed players are of little use as they waste time in manoeuvring the ball to their *one* foot. The ball must be kicked with the instep. For example: if you are kicking with the *left foot* the following points must be observed:

1. The right foot must be level with the ball.
2. The left knee must be directly above the ball.
3. The left toe must be kept down in order to get the left instep to the ball.
4. The body must be leant to the right.

In the same elementary way ball control, heading, passing, shooting, marking and covering, throwing-in and goalkeeping were also covered. At the end was a list of 'do's' and 'don'ts' with, of course, the 'do's' first:

1. DO know the rules.
2. DO keep your eye on the ball.
3. DO learn to kick with both feet.
4. DO learn to head.
5. DO tackle firmly.
6. DO make use of practice to improve your weaknesses.

Then the 'don'ts':

1. DON'T keep on yelling during a game.
2. DON'T give up hope when you are losing.
3. DON'T assume the ball is going over the line. Always chase it.
4. DON'T 'toe' the ball.
5. DON'T dribble in circles. Once is enough to beat an opponent.
6. DON'T tackle with your back (your eyes are at the front), and DON'T tackle like a 'bull at a gate'.

Already it was clear to me that however much I enjoyed producing such guides we needed expert coaching staff at Lancaster Gate, capable not only of giving basic or advanced instruction for schools but also of advising and instructing at any level. This was not a readily acceptable idea to the Council, and needed much preparatory discussion before I could launch the proposal with hope of acceptance. Indeed, it was another ten years before I was finally able to get Walter Winterbottom appointed Director of Coaching.

By that time it was in my own mind a double-edged appointment. On tours abroad I had become well aware of the weakness of having alternating Council members in charge of the team selection and tour management. It meant for instance that each one would take the trainer of his choice, usually the trainer from his own club. With the tour manager and trainer constantly changing there was no continuity for the players. But unless there was an obviously better solution immediately available, the Council members were unlikely to abandon of their own choice a system they personally enjoyed and with which they were quite happy. But as soon as Walter had made his expected mark in organising coaching on a much more systematic and professional basis, it was simple for me to suggest that this job could easily be combined with that of manager of the England team and that Walter was in any case the ideal man to help improve our International match preparations. And so it proved.

Walter had come to us in 1946. It was one of the best appointments ever made for football, and we were fortunate to get him. He was in his early thirties and had already made such a mark in physical education that he was being considered for the post of Principal at Carnegie College. That would have been a better-paid position, but Walter was never one to think in terms of short-term gain or immediate cash advantage. He had been raised in Oldham and from the grammar school there had gone to Carnegie College on a physical education course, which he paid for from his earnings as a mid-field player for Manchester United. Winterbottom was such an outstanding student that he was invited onto the staff. During the war he became a Wing Commander, organising PT at the Air Ministry and playing football for Chelsea until a back injury ended his playing career.

Walter had an abiding enthusiasm for football and was attracted by the challenge of developing a great national coaching scheme from such small beginnings. He had also the vision to see the possibilities that might develop. It was soon clear that Winterbottom had brought an entirely new concept to the game. He had the analytical mind of a detached scientific observer and the practical experience to translate that into tactical or coaching methods, which achieved remarkable results. Walter is a big man in every sense, impressive in presence but with an engaging personality and an attractive boyish smile which communicates the youthful zest he still retains. To some he appeared donnish in approach, or too businesslike in subjecting football to a time-and-motion-study-type analysis. Yet his results disarmed criticism and he had the happy knack of gaining professional players' trust and of understanding them. A 'natural' like Jimmy Greaves, who could not abide coaching or tactical talks, he let go his own instinctive way. He recognised that Greaves was blessed with exceptional 'peripheral vision' and did not worry that he had no idea what the words or the theory meant. But there were many players for whom his combination of the scholarly and the practical opened up new horizons, so that the likes of Ron Greenwood, Dave Sexton, or Jimmy Armfield were inspired by him to develop into a new breed of manager. And that ability was so early apparent that I was soon able to get him appointed the national team manager.

Only by tacking the duties on to an existing job, which incidentally is a more satisfactory arrangement in any case, could I get approval. Apart from other obstacles, any new and independent appointment would have run into difficulties on the question of cost. My own salary for instance remained unchanged for twelve years until Amos

Brookhirst, the Chairman, happened to ask me when I had last had an increase. When Graham Doggart became Chairman he raised it again to £3,000, which remained the salary until I left my paid position with the FA.

My own relatively low salary was not a cause of worry as I was allowed to live rent-free in the flat at Lancaster Gate 'above the shop'. This meant I was never 'off duty', but it also meant the benefit was tax-free, since I was required to live there as part of the job. My concern was more with my own staff. They too had suffered from having no regular review and from expenditure on staff salaries being kept to a minimum. Indeed it irked me to find that the only 'system' was for them to come to me when they felt the pinch and ask for an extra 5s a week, or whatever. As early as 1935 I dealt with this by arranging incremental scales for them, and also a contributory pension scheme. Although none of them qualified for a pension, only one would join. That changed dramatically when the accountant, George Neale, died suddenly when on holiday. He had had the sense to join the scheme and as he was a widower his daughter received the large sum for the time of £4,000. Once that news got round the office all the rest rushed down to the solicitor's to sign the necessary contract.

But I had had considerable difficulty in getting agreement to the new scales and pension scheme. And how necessary it was to get it can be appreciated from the salary list at the time. The Council were right to watch the pennies, but my staff of six cost them a mere £2,004 10s. The salary list read:

Earl, C. (Married, age 51, service 33 yrs)	£546 pa
Neale, G. H. (Married, age 46, service 31 yrs)	£390 pa
Miller, E. M. (Married, age 30, service 13 yrs)	£260 pa
Whitehorn, S. L. (Married, age 28, service 8 yrs)	£260 pa
Mansell, L. M. (Single, age 20, service 3 yrs)	£117 pa
Battersby, C. J. (Single, age 19, newly started)	£71 10s pa

Miller's salary had advanced from £3 per week in 1915 to £10 10s per week in 1935, Neale's from £1 15s per week in 1914 to £7 10s. Yet in those pre-inflationary days that allowed a passable standard of living, and at least the pensions they now built up were not quickly eroded into worthlessness when they received them. Still, these were not generous payments from a reasonably financed organisation; the Council however, were never easy to persuade that further money be spent on staffing.

One possible source of income they resolutely denied themselves.

The FA had been opposed to gambling on football because of the dangers of abuse and the possibility of players being involved in fixing matches. That these were no empty fears was underlined in the sixties, when England players Swann and Kay were found to have taken bribes to lose matches and were promptly banned from the game. The Association's attitude was defined in 1908 when a Consultative Committee passed a resolution the first sentence of which read 'The Football Association, having endeavoured for many years past to prevent betting in connection with football, consider it desirable to call attention to the fact that betting is prohibited by the rules of the Association upon all football grounds and have reason to believe the rules are generally observed.'

Five years later, as a result of the spread of coupon betting, a Commission was appointed which made two main recommendations:

1. That rule 42 be amended to provide that an Official of an Association or Club, Referee, Linesman, or Player, proved to have taken part in Coupon Football Betting, shall be permanently suspended from taking part in football or football management.
2. That clubs be required to insert a Clause in their Agreements with Players providing that the Agreement be terminated upon it being proved that a player has taken any part in Coupon Football Betting.

So seriously indeed did the FA regard the spread of coupon football betting that the same year a Bill was presented in Parliament by the Rt Hon Hayes Fisher at the instigation of the Association and aimed to prevent 'Ready Money Football Betting'. Shortly before he retired, Sir Frederick Wall gave evidence to the Royal Commission on Lotteries and Betting and I was also involved soon after my appointment. The FA was preparing a Report on football pools betting to support a new betting Bill, and their attitude was still one of total opposition to pools. The President, Charles Clegg, had always had strong views about betting, and the Report summed up the official FA view.

While I was a signatory to the Report and had to accept the Council's view on pools, I was privately concerned that we were merely fighting a losing battle against something which had already won popular support and approval. It seemed more sensible that we should aim at controlling the pools and partake in the profits rather than ineffectually try to outlaw them. The first chance came with the outbreak of war.

Without the normal football programmes or any need for constant monitoring of the game, there was no need for formal Council meetings during the war. It was possible for me then to act as an individual following my own inclination rather than majority rulings. It was then that I came close to establishing a pool, which in my view would have done much to benefit English football. There was hope that something could be introduced as an exceptional war-time measure and so be free of the traditional prejudice against it. Once established and the benefits seen, the pool would have in all probability continued without too much opposition.

Arthur Elvin and I therefore concocted a scheme to run a 'National' or 'Wembley' pool in the interests of football, as well as of Elvin's business interest. Elvin was a brilliant entrepreneur who had on his own initiative progressed from running a tobacco kiosk to running Wembley and a whole range of successful commercial enterprises. He had a restless energy in driving ideas through to practical reality, a good judgement of what was a winner, and an inventive mind in promoting his schemes.

With established pools temporarily stopped when normal fixtures were abandoned, Elvin aimed to set up a pool company which would share its profits fifty-fifty with football. He used the break to work out details and finance for the scheme.

To save labour and materials the Government arranged for all pools to be combined in one centrally authorised 'Unity Pool' when they restarted after a few weeks. We felt that we could get permission to run in opposition to this consortium of pools, or the Government might even agree to give us the sole agency for the duration, as this would build up needed funds for the sport in the post-war period. I therefore approached Ernest Bevin, whom I had often met at Wembley to see if the idea was practical. He was instantly interested and undertook to promote it with the War Cabinet. Unfortunately the proposal died, and of course no explanation needed to be given to us in war-time.

Despite this setback I included a more positive approach to pools in a memorandum for the FA which tried to chart the future development of football once hostilities were over. In a long and complex document the pools section attracted most comment, as for instance this piece by Ivan Sharpe in the *Athletic and Football Annual* of 1943:

The memorandum on problems confronting the resumption of the game after the war is a commendable attempt to cover the whole front and fear no controversy. The many suggestions have yet to be considered by the committees probing these revolutionary proposals. The pools plan has caused such comment that the reference should be quoted in full: 'The use of pools is so firmly established with such a large proportion of this population that it is suggested that the FA should approach the appropriate Government departments with a view to their devising a scheme whereby part of the proceeds of pools should form a central fund from which the costs of grounds gymnasia, recreation rooms, sports centres, and clubs might be made. A scheme of this type has been in operation in Sweden under government control and it resulted in no less than eight million pounds being made available for health and recreation services in three years.'

Participation in pools proceeds would involve a drastic change in FA policy and the secretary of the Pools' Promoters Association, Mr Holland Hughes, indicated that his Association would be willing to cooperate with the FA in a post-war scheme designed to benefit players and the game of football. Influential members of the FA evidently take a different view from their predecessors of the effect of pools on the game—a welcome development. My own view is that they have never been a menace and indeed are a safety-valve.

Sadly this was the one proposal in my memorandum which has never been implemented—though I keep hoping it is never too late as climates of opinion change—and I was one of the very few 'influential members' with this different view.

So pools proved a recurring theme of lost opportunity as one chance after another was spurned. My memorandum achieved no change in the FA attitude at the war's end, since the Council adopted a number of recommendations beginning:

1. That the Football Association shall not under any circumstances, be a party to the promotion of Football Pools.
2. That clubs and organisations under the jurisdiction of the FA shall not be allowed directly or indirectly to associate themselves with the conduct of Football Pools.

However, there was a slight change of mood apparent in discussions and I was glad to find Sir Leslie Bowker of the London FA with support from Maurice Love of Berks and Bucks putting forward a counter-proposal which began:

That the Football Association should approach the Government for the purpose of securing some statutory control of Pools by the appointment of a Football Pools Control Board with powers similar to those conferred upon the Race Course Betting Control Board.

This was not successful but it did give me hope that progress could be made. There was an attempt in 1947 to start a new National Football Pools organisation, which involved me both in relation to the FA and the Central Council of Physical Recreation. A consortium of businessmen, whose spokesman was Mr J. Carter of Reading FC, approached us on the basis of sport taking 80 per cent or more of the net profits. As their memorandum set it out:

1. A Committee of several businessmen has had under consideration for some time a scheme which would render much needed and substantial financial assistance to professional footballers, football Clubs, and Physical Education Associations. . . .
2. It is therefore proposed that a Company be formed called the 'National Football Pools Ltd' to carry on business as football pool promoters, and that 80 per cent or more of the nett profits of the Company be paid into three Trust Funds . . . In this connection it is proposed to send an invitation to the following persons asking if they would be willing to serve on the various Boards:
A. Players' Trust Fund: Messrs James Guthrie and James Fay, Chairman and Secretary of the Association of Football Players Union and others.
B. Clubs Trust Fund: P. Harper Esq, Crystal Palace Football Club, and Mr Sargantson, Southampton Football Club and others.
C. Central Council of Physical Recreation: Lord Portal, Lord Burghley, H. M. Abrahams and others.

The aim was to help football players and clubs in financial difficulty and to assist the CCPR to construct stadiums, provide coaches, establish holiday camps, provide training camps and finance the Olympic Games team. Had the pool materialised many of these very desirable objects might have been achieved. But the pool was consequent on 'the majority of clubs and players giving wholehearted support and this undertaking being given full publicity in the national Press'. The support was not forthcoming either from these or from the CCPR.

Elvin and I returned to the attack some years later. Elvin set out his proposals to me in a letter dated April 2nd 1952 after I had reopened the matter with him:

Some time ago I put forward to you a proposal something on the following lines: That this Company, or a subsidiary Company, formed by us, should organise a football pool in competition with the existing pools, to be conducted from here at Wembley, and to be called 'The Wembley Pool', or 'The National Pool', or some similar title, which would convey the fact that the pool was being conducted from the headquarters of football. I had in mind, as you will remember, that this venture would be approved by your Association and by the Football League.

The financial arrangement visualised was that we should raise the capital to commence operations, and that after the deduction of the expenses of running the pool, any profit should be divided as to 50 per cent to this Company, or to any other Company which might be formed under the auspices of this Company to take over the business, and the other 50 per cent of the profits to be set aside for charitable and other similar purposes.

I had in mind that a Board of responsible and independent people would be gathered together to deal with and allocate any amounts which became available from time to time for the distribution for these charitable purposes, and that the Football League and the Football Association should be represented on this Board. In order to secure the co-operation of the Football Clubs, it was my idea that the Football Benevolent Fund and/or some other such object specifically connected with the welfare of football, should participate in the share-out of any profits which might be handled by this independent Board, and in return the Football Clubs and the Associations should co-operate in ensuring the success of this new pool, by giving it sole publicity in the various football programmes and on the football grounds throughout the country. . . .

When this idea was first discussed between us, you will remember there was no tax on football pools; now there is a 30 per cent tax which, of course, makes it rather less attractive, but if you feel there is any chance of reviving the idea and of getting official backing even under present-day conditions, I could make arrangements to launch such a scheme and that when launched it is still my view that it would only be a matter of time before we attracted the bulk of the football pools business which now goes elsewhere.

Sadly, I could get no backing from Executive Committee members for Elvin's proposal and the League members on the Executive were as strongly opposed as any. There is no doubt that Elvin would have made a financial success of this, as of all his commercial ventures. His pool could have removed all the money worries which so frequently beset the League and its smaller clubs. But many both in the League and in the FA continued to regard pool money as the root of all evil. This was in line with the League's negative attitude expressed in this rejection of the pools promoters' offer at the end of the war in a letter from Holland Hughes to the League:

It has come to the notice of the members of my Association that at the meeting of the Football League Limited to be held in Manchester on October 22nd, it is intended to raise the question of receiving financial assistance from the football pools.

At this stage, I feel I should make it clear that the members of the Unity Pool who are the members of my Association have always been willing to make a contribution towards the encouragement of football and the furtherance of the interests of those engaged in sport.

You will recollect that as recently as April last, my Association submitted to the Management Committee of the Football League a written offer to assist the sport by a substantial contribution, subject to arrangements being concluded with the Inland Revenue. Since that date, Unity Pool have been in consultation with the Inland Revenue authorities, following which it is now proposed to the Management Committee of the Football League that a contribution of 1 per cent be deducted from the winnings payable to the football pool clients, which contribution Unity Pool will hand over on their behalf to the Management Committee.

It is appreciated that the proposed method of assistance to the League is one on which football pool investors might hold varied opinions, but in view of the fact that my members have decided, should their proposal be accepted by the League, to reduce their commission from 5 per cent to 4 per cent, this question can no longer arise, since it ensures that the dividends payable to the winning clients will in no way be affected.

At present, it is anticipated that in this way the Unity Pool will be able to hand over the sum of £100,000, increasing as times become normal. The members of the Football Pool Promoters Association are prepared to enter into an Agreement with the Football League Ltd, to give effect to these proposals for a period of at least three years. The members of my Association will be glad if you will communicate these proposals to the Football League at their Meeting.

This drew the following response from the League Secretary, Fred Howarth, on October 23rd 1945.

Further to the proposal of a grant from your Association to the League, as contained in your letter of the 18th inst, I have now to inform you that at a meeting of the shareholders of the Football League Ltd, held in Manchester yesterday, your proposal was fully discussed and the vote was taken on the question 'Should the League accept the offer or not?' The result of the vote showed that of the 48 shareholders present (only one was absent), 39 were against accepting the offer and 9 only were in favour. Accordingly it is my duty to inform you that the League rejects the offer of any financial payment from your Association.

The League had indeed stared the gift horse in the mouth and rejected it. They must contemplate sadly now the vast sum that decision has cost them over the years.

After Alan Hardaker became League Secretary he took a more businesslike approach, realising the importance of this source of funds and persuading the League to let him negotiate with the pools on the basis of their making a payment for the use of the copyright fixture list. The previous attitude of rejection even of offered gifts hardly helped him; nor did the knowledge that legally the copyright argument was of doubtful validity. But his forceful negotiation succeeded in getting agreement to a reasonable payment to the League and to the FA. By the seventies English football was receiving £700,000 from the pools and Scottish football £225,000. But that was still under 1 per cent of a turnover of £150,000,000 and less than 2½ per cent of profits of over £40,000,000.

A different outlook would have brought much more much earlier, had any of the proposals for a pool for football been followed up. There is a more liberal attitude now to pools money, but the ingrained prejudice is getting another airing in the attack on sponsorship money for sport coming from tobacco companies.

The basis of the reaction against pools of any type being used to fund sport was a distaste for being associated with 'betting' and a feeling that this was tainted money. That attitude persisted into the sixties when Norman McDermott interested a number of us in the idea of starting 'Portland Pools Ltd' from which 1d in every 11d would go to a Trust for sport and the young. Details of this were passed to me by Rear-Admiral Christopher Bonham-Carter, Treasurer to the Duke of Edinburgh. But his final dismissive letter to

McDermott summed up what we all found to be the insuperable obstacle—a general antagonism to sport being involved with, or benefiting from, pools:

> I have given the question of the Youth Aid Trust much serious thought and have consulted a number of people including 'Boy' Browning [General Browning, later Treasurer to HRH]. I am, very genuinely, sorry that I have found it necessary to recommend to the Duke of Edinburgh, who has agreed, that the Duke of Edinburgh's Award Scheme should not take advantage of this potential source of income.
>
> There is nothing new in the argument 'for' and 'against', with which I am sure you are fully familiar after our talk together. The fact is that those 'against' are, in our country and at the present time, more cogent.
>
> I personally greatly regret that this should be so and have done all I can to find a way round which would be acceptable, but I have to confess failure.
>
> I am sending a copy of this letter to Sir John Hunt and to Sir Stanley Rous, to both of whom I have talked on this matter.

7

The Laws and I

●●●

In my early days at the FA I also drew on my own past experience to try and improve the codification of football's laws. As a referee I knew some of the problems of learning and interpreting laws which were set out in such a way that they appeared complex and disjointed. Even though there were then, as now, only seventeen laws, you had to examine three or four of these to find all the references to offside. Punishments for certain offences were not clearly defined. There was no logical sequence: for instance Law 1 covered among other matters some provisions about equipment, but not until Law 12 was there reference to the condition of football boots. Perhaps because the laws were something of a jumble as set out, there were no proper headings even in the 'Referees' Chart and Players' Guide to the Laws of the Game' which the FA issued annually.

It was necessary to tread as warily as Agag in putting forward my suggestions for revision. For my Vice President, William Pickford, regarded himself as the supreme arbiter on the laws. He had been a prolific writer on the game and the four-volume work he produced with Gibson, *Football—and the Men who made it*, is still a major reference work for the game's early history. But he did not readily appreciate that there is a difference between the style required of an author—and flowery writing was the vogue then—and that needed to draft regulations for which brevity, clarity, and order are the main requirements. When I broached my project to him his reply was 'Don't you dare tinker with *my* laws. Don't dare alter the meaning of one of them.'

It was not my intention to alter the laws, merely to set them out more intelligibly. So the lengthy work proceeded and I crystallised them into the exact form which survives and remains universally accepted as I write more than forty years later. My final draft was passed to the Referees' Committee and welcomed by them. It was still another year before our International Board adopted them in their present form.

There have been numerous attempts to redraft the laws since, but none has won approval, as the suggested changes have been referred through this long chain. No doubt this is because those aiming to redraft usually end by making the laws sound more complex. I have always felt that it is one of the great advantages of football over most other games, such as cricket with its bookful of ever changing laws, that our laws are few, easily understood and rarely altered.

The only real change that was made in the substance of 'Pickford's' laws was at the request of the Scottish FA. They required only one small alteration, wanting an indirect free kick for tackling when the ball was not within striking distance. So in the main it was a redraft rather than an alteration, and I did retain in full the excellent offside diagrams designed by Pickford to explain that difficult law. Looking at the last Referees' Chart which I approved under the old layout of laws in 1937/8 I am struck by how apposite the end of the final section—the memorandum for guidance of referees—is today:

The attention of referees is especially directed to the instructions given by Law 17 that they may refrain from putting the provisions of the law into effect in cases where they are satisfied that by enforcing them they would be giving an advantage to the offending side. For instance, if a goal is deliberately prevented by the improper use of his hand by a defender, and an attacker immediately receives the ball and scores, the referee should award a goal and not a penalty kick. When a penalty kick is taken and a goal scored therefrom it must only be retaken in case of an infringement by the attacking side. The spirit of the law and the power to refrain, is that wrongdoers should not benefit from their wrongdoing.

The duty of referees is to administer justice fairly and fearlessly. A firm controlling hand in the opening minutes of a game will prove invaluable to all concerned. It will indicate that a rigid control is possible by the officials; be apparent to players that unfair play will not be tolerated and obtain from them and spectators the respect which is due.

Referees must always punish the more serious of two offences committed simultaneously. Referees must keep physically fit. They should always conduct and control games in such a manner as will win respect of players and spectators. Only well trained and athletic officials can do this.

My new codification of the laws had been aimed at making them easier for referees to learn and administer, simpler for players and spectators to understand. An intelligent member of the FA staff arranged to copyright the new laws in my name. 'It is *your* draft and they are *your* laws, if accepted, as much as the old ones were Pickford's.'

Had I charged a fee for my copyright laws their widespread use for the forty years or so before my copyright lapsed would have provided a profitable income for me. But my object was simply to ensure they could not be tampered with without my being consulted. I was amused, therefore, when I heard my successor as FA Secretary, Denis Follows, tell FIFA that the Football Association ought to charge a fee for the use of *their* laws. Privately I warned him off a course which would have lined no pocket but my own.

Another development which I was able to influence was the acceptance of broadcasting and, later, television. Council members were at first greatly opposed to the idea, fearing that the games would be misreported or that crowds would stay at home for the broadcast rather than come to watch. My own feeling was that if football was to remain a sport of the people we should accept all the current means of keeping the sport in the public eye. This was not only desirable to give the football enthusiast the best available service, but was in the game's interest as if the spotlight focused on other sports because of our reluctance, then those sports might gain in popularity at football's expense.

The main objections came from League representatives and were based on fear of the unknown. In discussion with the BBC I suggested therefore that one way to overcome this was to invite William Pickford to give a broadcast in the south, and Charles Sutcliffe, the League President, to do the same in the north. The BBC representatives were Gerald Cock and S. J. 'Lobby' de Lotbinière, one of the few men who could look down on me from his 6ft 7in eminence. Both were enthusiastic and helpful, readily agreeing on the plan which quickly converted these two key figures and so gave broadcasting a fair wind. The early commentaries were stilted and formalistic with the *Radio Times* including a diagram of the field divided into numbered squares and the commentators spending much of their time identifying the square in which play then was. But at least it was a start. This breakthrough followed on from the broadcast Pickford undertook in 1937. He was well pleased to have been invited and commented to me in surprise that the producers were 'real gentlemen'. Clearly their attitude disarmed his opposition.

Pickford's broadcast was on the control of the game and in his introduction he looked back at the vast changes in his lifetime:

> When I first fell in love with and played football nearly sixty years ago, there was very little control. The clubs were few in number and our match lists were small. We did not begin until October and it was all over in March. The rules we played under were few and not too definite, but certain things were not done. We were rough and banged each other about like skittles. Occasionally human nature flared up and there was an angry moment, but on the whole the game controlled itself. If we disagreed with our opponents about the validity of a goal we reported it as 'disputed'. There were no hectic Cup-ties and no exacting League battles, and at the close of a vigorous game we gave three cheers for each other, and rubbed our bruises with somebody's embrocation. I only remember one occasion when our captain took the law into his own hands and administered the knockout to an opponent who had deliberately tripped one of his men. Incidents did occur, as when an artilleryman was unable to stop the career of W. H. Ainger, a Cambridge blue, and hit him in the back with his fist. But he disarmed the wrath of the Cantab by saying: 'Sorry, sir, but it's so bloody exciting.'
>
> This game of Association Football is now remarkably well organised. It is computed that there are in this country over 35,000 clubs playing Association Football.

Pickford's own pleasure in giving his talk ensured that regular broadcasting of football soon followed.

There were to be many later arguments, particularly over TV, as to how much exposure could be permitted. But at least the principle of allowing radio and TV was sensibly and swiftly resolved, and soon the Cup Final was to be designated as one of those great sporting events, like the Grand National, which must be televised live because of the important place they have in the nation's affection.

Presentation by sound and vision have become ever more expert and sophisticated. But there is one principle of those starting days which might be more profitably retained now. We were asked to put forward a few possible candidates as commentators. The final tests were for Walter Winterbottom, Norman Creek, and Jimmy Jewel. As real experts on the game, Walter and Norman interpreted every move and added enlightening technical comment. Jewel, who had been a referee and later manager of Norwich City, could not match them in football knowledge or fluency. Yet he was chosen. 'Jewel simply gives a picture of the play and a clear, precise description of what is happening' was the reason given for the selection. That still seems a proper appreciation of the requirement of a commentator on a game in play, rather than to overlay it with technical jargon and irrelevant comments.

Some technical skill was however required. George Allison was another to broadcast, seeming a natural because of his beautifully modulated voice and his commanding reputation as Arsenal's manager. He was however a somewhat careless watcher of a game. After one International between England and Italy at Highbury he commented dogmatically to us in the Board room 'The outstanding player, as I kept telling the listeners, was the Italian centre-half.' 'Before or after he was sent off?' was the amused query, to which George had no answer, having failed to notice the dismissal and having focused on the wrong man throughout.

Britain in the thirties was still a self-sufficient, self-confident country with a sublime belief that British was best. How else could this small island have pioneered the industrial revolution and built the Empire on which the sun never set? There was a sense of natural superiority, a smug feeling that all was right in our enclosed world and others had nothing to teach us. *We* could tell *them* how to organise parliamentary democracy, or an empire, or a football team. And so we were largely unaware of our need to learn and develop and to be part of the mainstream of European life.

This attitude was certainly reflected in our football administration. In my early days at Lancaster Gate, England and the three other home countries took no part in FIFA, the International Football Federation. We could have been the leading influence within FIFA when it started. Instead we had preferred to stay aloof, now in, now out whenever we objected to their approach. Our recent haverings about joining the European Economic Community, and having joined about whether to remain in, follow the pattern set by football, except that the politicians were slower to decide and had less influence on the shaping of the Community. For even when not in FIFA, Britain's special position as the game's founder allowed us to guide events.

It was in 1902 that the Dutch FA wrote to the Football Association asking for matches and suggesting the founding of an International Association to promote football in Europe; to arrange an International

Championship, and to secure uniformity in the laws of the game for all countries.

After leisurely discussions with Scotland, Ireland and Wales it became clear the British wished to preserve their insularity. France, however, followed up with another approach in the next year, only for the Union des Sociétés Français des Sports Athlétiques to be informed that the FA could see no good purpose in forming a Federation of European Football Associations, but would be prepared to confer if joint action was desirable.

France went ahead anyway, and the Fédération Internationale de Football Association was born in Paris on May 21st 1904 without the British Associations. So the founder members were France, Belgium, Denmark, Netherlands, Spain, Sweden and Switzerland. But already Britain was finding the need to confer as more and more teams went abroad to play—an FA XI to Germany, the Corinthians to South Africa, Sunderland to America, Surrey Wanderers to Germany, and Southampton to Austria. Clearly some overall control was needed and the FA agreed to organise a FIFA conference at Crystal Palace in April 1905. We also participated in another Congress at Berne the following year when an Englishman, D. B. Woolfall, was appointed FIFA President, an office he held until October 1918. Woolfall was also elected to the Committee to draft articles of constitution for the Federation. Indeed he played a decisive part in giving FIFA a harmonious start and ensuring that the British and European game developed in concert, not in opposition. It was Woolfall who was responsible for the two FIFA members joining the International Board along with England, Scotland, Ireland and Wales. He then got agreement that FIFA members should play according to laws promulgated by that Board.

This was typical of European willingness to accept guidance and to acknowledge that Britain was then the 'master' of the game. Had we not been so aloof in attitude we could from the start have been leaders of this new movement. But we were slow to appreciate its importance, and only the efforts of individuals like Woolfall gave us a somewhat undeserved prominence in FIFA's early developments. And after the First World War we left FIFA again in 1920 in a dispute over the Central Powers, Germany, Austria, and Hungary, re-entering international competition so soon.

Europe remained eager to secure our full co-operation, and in 1924 the British Associations were re-elected to FIFA. Yet still our insular attitude persisted. No sooner was some joint decision taken which we disliked, such as broken-time payments to amateurs, or separate membership for Eire—or the Republic of Ireland as it later became—than we withdrew once more into ourselves. FIFA had started up as a European Federation and was still dominated by Europe, although several South American countries and the USA had joined between 1912 and 1921 with Egypt, Siam, and Japan soon following. But once Jules Rimet had started his World Cup in 1930 FIFA rapidly expanded to become a truly international organisation, though still without Britain, the African Associations and some other important groupings.

That was the position which I inherited and I certainly had no thought that this was splendid isolation. To me it was a matter of regret and a constant cause of difficulty that we were not more closely associated with FIFA. It was ridiculous, for instance, that special arrangements had to be made to allow us to enter the Olympics. So my endeavours were always for a new integration when the chance came. Meanwhile I established my own close links with leading FIFA personalities to ensure as far as possible that we worked to a common goal, even though we were not officially members.

In 1938, the seventy-fifth anniversary year of the Football Association gave me the opportunity to further the close relationship with FIFA. The FA was concerned at the cost of the celebration banquet, so I proposed that we stage a match against a European XI as an added attraction, and also to cover the cost of the dinner and other expenses. This was readily agreed, and as it was the first time ever that a FIFA team had played in Great Britain the match was a centre of interest.

With a forward line of Matthews, Hall, Lawton, Goulden, and Boyes we won that Highbury match 3–0, which no doubt reinforced our complacency about the unbeatable standards of English football. But indeed this had been a golden decade for the attacking English style of forward play, with the great William Ralph ('Dixie') Dean, the finest centre-forward I have ever seen, always having to fight for his England place against the likes of George Camsell, who averaged two goals a game in his nine Internationals, Vic Watson, 'Pongo' Waring, and a dozen others. As Dean faded Tommy Lawton took over with such outstanding players as Freddie Steele to challenge him. Our forward line then had not only great skill, but the finishing power which gave us the edge over Continental teams as in that Highbury match. What a change there has been in recent years, with the 'masters' having to relearn from their 'pupils' how to take chances.

If the match did nothing to make us aware of the dangers of being so inward-looking, the occasion at least helped those of us who were seeking an opportunity to bring the British Associations back within FIFA. Friendships were cemented as Heads of Delegations from all the European countries came to the banquet. Pickford presided and as he thanked each delegation I had arranged for their flag to be unfurled from the balcony to complete a colourful scene.

A misunderstanding was all that marred this happy night of European co-operation in sport on the verge of European conflict over politics. As a supreme gesture of French goodwill Jules Rimet announced that he had been authorised by the President of the French Republic to inform Pickford he had been admitted to the Légion d'Honneur in recognition of French respect for his services to football. Rimet's speech was in French and Pickford did not grasp the tribute paid to him, making no mention of it in his final reply. Wives were present at the banquet, and mine was quick to interpret for me and to press me in whispers to get Pickford to cover his gaffe. But though I passed him a note it was too late for him to adjust—or even realise what had happened. And by sad coincidence he was to die before the honour was finally bestowed.

That splendid gathering full of distinguished persons kept the toastmaster busy with his endless string of titles before he called for silence for the next speaker. Listening, I was reminded of a similar occasion on which I had heard Lord Birkett at the Guildhall speak after an equally impressive reference to the assembled dignitaries. He began more simply: 'Ladies and Gentlemen—and that's a compliment to some of you . . .'

War prevented any chance of an immediate follow-up with FIFA. But Britain's part in the war perhaps made Europeans even keener to have us back in their football community and us much readier to rejoin. The sense of comradeship and interdependence was the one happy relic of the conflict. So there was no problem in getting approval for Arthur Drewry, now Chairman of the FA, and myself, to go as delegates to a FIFA Executive meeting in Zurich in November 1945, with the brief to see if re-entry might be negotiable.

There was an interesting team of personalities with whom we held our detailed discussions. Dr Ivo Schricker was the Secretary of FIFA, a German with an international outlook who for years had run FIFA's business from Switzerland. He had no problems of relationships from any residue of bitterness over Germany's wartime role. For we all knew that he had regarded himself for years as more a man of Europe than of Germany and had been antagonistic to Nazi philosophy. Indeed he had been in trouble with Goebbels when he attended an International match in Germany and a photograph showed him with his own right hand dangling limply level with his waist while around him every arm pointed rigidly at the sky in the Nazi salute. His reprimand was countered with a spirited defence that he was there representing the World not Germany and could do as he felt appropriate. Schricker had been an international player himself. In the first ever match between England and Germany at Karlsruhe he was set to mark Billy Bassett of West Bromwich Albion, a winger who was one of the most feared players in the England team. Schricker close-marked him with such dogged determination that when Bassett, for a joke, wandered off the field and walked round behind the goal Schricker was at his elbow all the way. 'Had I gone to the moon, he would have followed me,' was Bassett's comment. Schricker was equally tenacious in furthering FIFA's work and indeed had himself contributed substantially to their funds when the war left them with only debts.

Karel Lotsy, President of the Dutch FA, was another man of unusual talent. He had been the man through whom I arranged the seventy-fifth anniversary match and who raised the European side against us, cannily playing a practice match in Holland first to prepare his team and also raise the money which enabled him to pay off a Dutch debt owed to FIFA. Lotsy appeared cold and unemotional himself and was a clever and calculating administrator. But he had great depth of feeling and the power to arouse it in others. At the war's end his outlook was coloured by the Dutch experience of wartime dread and deprivation. After our first meeting we were sitting in the Hotel St Gotthardt when a cheerful party arrived in the lounge dressed for some function. Intrigued Lotsy went over and discovered this was an annual party for the Swiss Hockey Association. As a member of the International Olympic Committee Lotsy had an interest in their sport and he also found that the President of the Swiss FA was among the guests. Finally Lotsy and I were invited to join them for coffee and Lotsy was asked if he could make a short address. That abruptly ended their merriment. For instead of the pleasant, humorous speech they had anticipated, he coldly contrasted their gaiety with the sufferings of the Dutch and others who had endured wartime tyranny and terror. So moving and vivid was his account that those who had come for a social evening were left in tears.

I was present again years later to hear him achieve exactly the same effect. The Mayor of Lausanne gave a lunch after a meeting of the Olympic Committee and Lotsy was a speaker. Instead of the expected talk on sport or the Olympics he dwelt on a disaster in which thirty children had died in a fire at a children's home at a ski resort. As he expressed his profound sympathy with the parents and recalled the past suffering of Dutch children he again had his audience crying unashamedly and uncontrollably. In day-to-day conversation Lotsy could appear cynical and uninvolved, yet he had this remarkable power to move others. It was a gift I envied him when I had to speak myself at memorial services for my friends such as Dr Schricker himself, Ernst Thommen of the Swiss FA and FIFA, or the closest of them all, that fine tennis player, Nigel Sharpe. The deep emotion I felt myself I found hard to convey to others.

Jules Rimet, whose name is for ever associated with the World Cup, was the FIFA President, but I always couple his name with R. W. Seeldrayers of Belgium. For in this committee, as in all FIFA business, Rimet, who spoke only French, relied heavily on the multilingual Seeldrayers of Belgium. And the fluent Seeldrayers was as likely to express his own views as to give an exact translation of the Chairman's. Seeldrayers was a golfing as well as a football enthusiast. He was a scratch player himself and it was he who brought Henry Cotton, that outstanding performer and teacher of the game, to his club at Waterloo. Seeldrayers was an expert putter. Since he wore enormous bifocal-lensed glasses I used to comment to him that he had an unfair advantage in putting, since ball and hole must have looked so large it was easy as stroking a football into an empty goal.

Rimet himself was small and expressive, a slim grey-haired man quick in speech and lively in gesture. He was conservative by nature wanting to preserve the 'family' of football from worrying change. Of a committee too full of elderly and inert members he commented once to me, 'The "dead" committee man has his use. He prevents unnecessary change.' And when later I was to urge on him the necessity of dividing the rapidly growing FIFA into Confederations, as the only way to avoid a vast central bureaucracy that would soon be out of touch with Asia or America, he would say, 'Some day, Stanley. But you are in advance of the times. Now we must preserve the "family" as a unit as long as we can.'

To complete the negotiating team was Mr Eie of Norway and Professor Pelikan from Czechoslovakia. The professor was an entertaining character who had had to leave Prague without any allownace of foreign money and had bartered his way to the Executive meeting in Zurich by selling the beet sugar with which he had stocked the boot of his car, in order to buy petrol.

FIFA, too, were badly in need of finance, and we were able to help after a basis of re-entry had been agreed. It was broken-time payments which had caused the problem between us, and FIFA agreed to a slight easing of their position. They also agreed that we should always be entitled to nominate one Vice President from the British Associations, a privilege we share only with the USSR. For the Russians were also negotiating entry at that time and made it a condition that any privilege given to us should also apply to them.

Once Drewry and I had agreed the ground rules with Rimet and Schricker, a committee meeting soon followed at the FA offices in London and the British Associations were later re-elected at a Congress in Luxembourg in 1946. After this was fixed I was holidaying in Basle when Ernst Thommen, President of the Swiss FA, invited me to lunch and talked of FIFA's desperate financial problems. It was then that I suggested a celebration match, Great Britain against Europe, with the proceeds going to FIFA as our goodwill gesture on re-entry. I saw it also as a kind of victory salute heralding the return to normal sporting friendships for all, including Germany.

On return I had to sell the idea first to the FA. It was readily agreed there, but unfortunately had been prematurely leaked to the Press from Switzerland. At once I had the Secretary of the Scottish FA on the phone. George Graham rightly complained that the announcement had been made without any consultation with Scotland. He was mollified when I apologised for the embarrassing leak and added, 'Of course we are thinking of playing the match at Hampden Park if that is agreeable to you.' 'In that case I anticipate no difficulty with my executive', said George, rapidly converted to the project.

And what an exhibition match that was, with 135,000 coming to watch and Great Britain winning 6–1. It may be a pleasant reminder for those of us who haven't been so used to British teams winning by that sort of margin to recall the game that marked our re-entry to FIFA. Certainly it was made memorable for me by a marvellous display of attacking skill from a forward line of all the talents—Stanley Matthews, Wilf Mannion, Tommy Lawton, Billy Steel, and Billy Liddell. With such fine players to prompt him Tommy Lawton scored twice, and so did Wilf Mannion. Billy Steel had one and the Italian centre-half, Parola, put one into his own goal as the Rest of Europe's defence became even more confused—despite having Johnny Carey to marshal them. For us it had been a great sporting occasion. For the losers there was the consolation of a cheque for £30,000 which the able Schricker made the basis of FIFA's rapid financial recovery.

8

A Vision Realised

●●

Football was the main strand of my working life, but a remarkable woman was to ensure that I was almost as closely involved in all sport. It was in 1935 that I received an invitation to help form the Central Council of Recreative Physical Training. Under that title, and its subsequent name of the Central Council of Physical Recreation, it became an absorbing interest for me over more than forty years. Yet when Phyllis Colson wrote to me it was no more than an idea in the restless mind of that very determined and shrewd lady.

Phyllis Colson was then in her early thirties. She had trained at Bedford College of Physical Education, and then taught in girls' secondary schools, earning the description 'outstanding student and brilliant teacher'. In 1930 she had become assistant to Phyllis Spafford, organising physical education within the National Council of Girls' Clubs. When, a year later, Miss Spafford became Secretary of the Ling Association of teachers of Swedish gymnastics, Miss Colson stayed on with the Girls' Clubs. In that work she became acquainted with everyone of importance in youth work and physical education, and especially those at the Board of Education. She also maintained her close association with Phyllis Spafford, and was soon acting as Press Officer of the Ling Association, editing their Newsletter and their quarterly Journal. So through the Ling Association she had a further platform for expressing her views, and the chance to establish an ever-widening range of contacts. These were never casual contacts, for those she met were immediately impressed—as I was myself— by her vitality, organising ability, and her lucid thinking.

Her invitation to me stemmed from her knowledge of my physical education methods and demonstrations at Watford Grammar School, which had won wide acclaim, and of my general interest in the training of youth. That was what mattered to her, rather than the bonus of my present position as Secretary of the FA.

Phyllis Colson was a person with a private vision; but she was also one of those very unusual people with the clarity of intellect and the persistence and charm of personality to turn dream to fact. She herself was later to describe the 'vision' which led her to write to me and a score of others:

> Wending my way down Upper Woburn Place, I suddenly pictured a Great Britain in which every youngster had a chance to take part in enjoyable and health-giving physical activity and in which all the people and associations with something to offer to that end— teachers and organisers, sports bodies and youth organisations, educational authorities and industrial firms, and many others— worked *together*, pooling their knowledge, experience, and re- sources, helping each other and tackling their problems by joint effort. Facilities would be first-class; classes of various kinds would be available in every area, rural as well as urban; in the bigger cities, comprehensive centres would provide for youth organisations as well as physical activity bodies; and there would be a plentiful supply of voluntary leaders, men and women who were more than teachers of technique. Yes, it *could* happen if there were a really active 'umbrella' body with provincial branches but no vested interests!
>
> I cannot pretend that the 'flash' was the outcome of reasoning. But perhaps a long period off work had, unbeknown to me, allowed time for two things to become linked in my mind: concern about the bad effects which the unhappy economic position of the country was having on the well-being of young people, and the impressions about the value of physical recreation which I had gained from serving as an Organiser of Physical Education and from watching the quick growth of keep-fit movements.

Phyllis's 'vision' made sense to me too, so I agreed to join the Council of her new organisation.

The Central Council came into being at a meeting on June 8th 1935 and was immediately accorded Royal patronage. The patronage was a measure of the Royal Family's interest in sport and in the social problems of the time, which had already been evidenced in their formation of the Duke of York's camps. The new organisation as yet had no status and no money beyond £400 in donations, yet the King at once appreciated its potential. Once inaugurated, the Central

Council was only able to start work because some of us contributed money to it, and because Phyllis went driving ahead in a whirlwind of effort as honorary Officer without pay. With barely enough to live on herself, she dedicated her whole existence to realising her dream of how the lot of millions might be improved. That spirit is rare indeed in the present day. Fortunately, so are the conditions which inspired it. For the background, so well described in Justin Evans' history of the CCPR, was depressing enough to convince me that there was a need of a new initiative such as Miss Colson proposed.

The nation was passing through a series of financial and industrial crises. The financial position had seemed so grave in 1931 that a National Government was formed, a cut of 10 per cent imposed on the salaries of teachers and other employees in the statutory services and other drastic economies made in public expenditure. The number of registered unemployed varied between two and three million, and unemployment was particularly high among juveniles.

The school-leaving age was fourteen, and less than 10 per cent of the nation's boys and girls went on from elementary to secondary schools. Of that percentage fewer than one-third remained at school after sixteen. For those who got to work at fourteen, wages were low, apprenticeships rare, and 'blind-alley' jobs leading to dismissal at sixteen a common form of employment. Until 1934, those under sixteen were covered by no compulsory insurance scheme against sickness or unemployment, and there was no restriction upon the hours worked by shop boys or factory hands. A large proportion had no holiday whatever except at Bank Holidays, for which they had to work especially hard beforehand.

No dole or unemployment pay was received until after the age of sixteen was reached, and then a condition of receiving it was attendance at what were called Junior Instruction Centres, which met in makeshift premises and offered physical training (often without any changing from ordinary clothing), handicrafts and some games. It was a grim and ghastly time for many young people, which they bore with astonishing fortitude and cheerfulness.

Many of us were deeply concerned that these conditions were sapping the physical and mental health of the country's youth in the years after leaving school. The Education Act of 1921 had given Youth Organisations some statutory recognition but there was little monetary or practical assistance for them, and they were inadequately equipped for a daunting task.

99

In the schools physical education was improving in quality. Colleges for specialist women teachers of PE had grown rapidly in numbers in the early years of the century. And though there was no comparable improvement for a time on the men's side, that was beginning to change, too. In 1933 the Leeds Education Authority opened the Carnegie College of Physical Education, offering a one-year course in PE to trained teachers or university graduates. Two years later Loughborough started a similar course, and these two Colleges made a profound impact on physical education training in the country. But improved standards at school merely underlined the inadequacy of what followed.

Hope for improvement came in the year of the Council's formation. King George V had recently recovered from a serious illness, and when his Jubilee Fund Appeal was launched there was an overwhelming response. The King George Jubilee Trust was to be devoted to 'the physical, mental, and spiritual welfare of the younger generation'. And Lord Portal, Vice Chairman of the Trust, commented that it would aid 'large numbers of boys and girls approaching the age of full citizenship ill equipped for the responsibilities which face them'.

The after-school welfare of young people largely depended upon the work of many voluntary youth organisations such as the Scouts and Guides, Boys' Clubs and Girls' Clubs, the YMCA, the YWCA, and the Welsh League of Youth, all pursuing their own aims and using their own methods. The prospect of aid from the Jubilee Trust fostered a new desire for co-operation.

That desire was the catalyst which allowed our new Council to be ormed. And in time it was to produce a dramatic change from the bleak past and divided present in which we started our work. When I first talked with Phyllis Colson about it in the dingy little office in Doughty Street there was no thought in my mind that this new body, without funds or staff, would grow over forty years to employ a full-time staff of over four hundred and have an income of more than a million pounds a year. Nor did I imagine that for twenty-seven of those years, from 1945 to 1972, I would be Chairman of the Executive Council. The background against which the Council was formed reads strangely today. Consider with how little *real* hardship the nation has passed through even more exacting financial crises in the seventies without any painful echoes of the 'dirty thirties'. Perhaps we are entitled to feel that not a little of that healthier physical and social environment stems from the tireless voluntary effort which made a practical reality of that early vision.

In the year before the Council was formed the Minister of Health, Sir Hilton Young, had asked the medical profession to 'bring home the benefits of physical culture, which is a culture of mind as well as muscle'. The 'healthy mind in a healthy body' concept had always appealed to me, as does the importance of promoting it through voluntary effort. The state certainly has a part to play, but should never be directing sport for its own greater glory, as with Hitler's 'strength through joy' movement, or the modern Russian or East German equivalents, with their robot sportsmen. And the CCPR has always acted in keeping with the British tradition and the ideal of preserving the individual's freedom of action within the general framework of society. Indeed it was characteristic of this country that sport's central organisation should flourish from the inspiration of one person, the voluntary effort of fellow enthusiasts, and later the expert assistance of professionals, who were also dedicated to helping others to fulfil themselves. And if there is now greater assistance and control by the State through the Sports Council, the voices of the ordinary sports enthusiast and the voluntary club administrator continue to be dominant there and in the CCPR. The pattern we set in those early days is continually changing and developing, but cannot be wholly reversed.

Twenty-one years later at the CCPR's coming of age celebrations, Prince Philip, in his first outside TV broadcast, seen by 10 million viewers, was to say:

> The CCPR does two things: it introduces all forms of physical recreation to people and it introduces people to all forms of physical recreation. We believe that a very large proportion of the people in this country like taking some sort of exercise and they feel better and happier for it. I don't think leisure is any problem and if people want to do nothing I have no objection. All I am concerned with is that people should not be forced to do nothing because there is no opportunity for them to do something in their leisure time.

When he could say this about the CCPR our original dream was already established fact. What a simple sounding sentence that is: 'It introduces all forms of physical recreation to people and people to all forms of physical recreation.' But what a wealth of endeavour has gone to achieve today's wide range of sporting facilities and tuition or the great National Recreation Centres at Bisham Abbey, Lilleshall, Plas-y-Brenin, Crystal Palace, Cardiff, Cowes or Inverclyde.

Our inaugural meeting of the Council was held in a Board of

Education conference room in Whitehall, with Viscount Astor in the chair. Lord Halifax, as President of the Board of Education, stressed that they supported us in principle, but that we were no official concern of theirs, and at this stage could only rely on them for sympathy rather than help. The meeting set up our first executive committee of sixteen which included among my fellow members Lord Derby, Chairman of the National Playing Fields Association, and Lord Dawson of Penn, the famous surgeon.

'An organisation of the magnitude of the Central Council, and especially one which aims at co-ordination and elimination of overlapping, must of necessity develop slowly,' we were advised. Our interpretation of that was to 'hasten slowly'. Within a few months a register of Leaders had been compiled, courses started, and contacts made with hundreds of individuals, voluntary organisations, and business companies. Demonstrations too were being given throughout the country and I have a vivid memory of Miss Colson in action at one such demonstration at Plymouth Hoe, with thousands flocking to watch the exhibition she organised. Within eighteen months the Council was firmly enough established to get a grant of £1,000 from the cautious Board of Education, a welcome contribution and an accolade of success.

As the new venture tapped a great reservoir of public interest, it was close to being overwhelmed in the details of day-to-day administration. To keep us moving forward Phyllis Colson invited me to chair a technical sub-committee 'to establish the closest links between the Council and those responsible for physical activities in voluntary organisations, and to investigate the best methods of placing the specialised knowledge of the physical training associations at the service of the population.'

It is often those who deal with the physically handicapped who have the clearest view of physical needs. Miss Bullock at Bushey with her methods of training the deaf and dumb gave me ideas for my own physical education teaching. And now my approach to the technical committee was influenced by the Secretary General of the National Institute for the Blind, W. McG. Eagar. He wrote:

If any agreement between experts is possible the Central Council are most likely to secure it. The physical training world is so riven with sectarian jealousies that the inexpert club leader may safely discount the extremists and devote himself to finding the right teacher rather than the ideal system. Women have gone a long way ahead of us. They did not have to clear the ground of the debris of old Army and German gymnastics systems, intended to make strong men stronger. They have much to teach us in the science of making young bodies fitter.

Our aim in the technical committee was to end sectarian jealousies and give a clear guidance to the inexpert club leader by taking a fresh look at the old and new ideas to select the best.

Throughout this period I worked closely with Arthur Gem, who took over the chairmanship of the committee as I became Deputy Chairman of the Council, which was by now co-ordinating the work of 109 constituent organisations without interfering with the individual character of any of them.

For a time our Council came under the supervision of the new National Fitness Council set up by law in the Physical Training and Recreation Act of 1937. The Fitness Council had a warm welcome from the country and the physical education bodies. It was well funded for its National Fitness campaign, which has given us a useful legacy of halls and playing fields, swimming baths and community centres. But its posters 'Fitness Wins' did not apply to the Fitness Council itself. It lost out within a couple of years as an early casualty of the war, fading away 'unhonoured, and unsung, without an inquest, with scarcely an obituary notice'.

And as it died it tried to destroy our Central Council with it. The day before war broke out an official of the Fitness Council wrote to us instructing the Central Council to terminate the lease of its office and to end the contracts of its staff. It was a silly instruction which we determined to ignore. Together with Miss Colson, Lord Hampden, Sir Percival Sharp and John Catlow I went to see the President and Permanent Secretary of the Board of Education. Our deputation was well received and we had no real difficulty in substantiating the need for the Central Council to continue its work, which was to be of great value for the fitness of the Forces and the morale of the Home Front. We were told to ignore the Fitness Council letter. Our Central Council was already too well established to be killed off so easily.

9

War Games

●●●

English teams touring abroad have always been regarded as ambassadors of their country. Particularly was that so in the thirties when Europeans had much less contact with ordinary English people and many of them had their impressions of us formed by the conduct of such touring parties. Remembering the high standards those teams set it is sad to see the damage now inflicted on our reputation by the behaviour of club supporters, such as those of Leeds, Manchester United, or Glasgow Rangers who have given Britain a hooligan image. It is sadder still to reflect that the image is not too distorted, but a fair reflection of a fundamental change in national character in the past quarter of a century. From being regarded as one of the most phlegmatic, tolerant, and well-behaved of European peoples we are fast deserving our new reputation as one of the most violent and ill-mannered.

The FA were always conscious of the political implications of tours by our national team and we kept in close touch with the Foreign Office over arrangements. For the spring of 1939 we had planned a tour of Jugoslavia, Italy, and Czechoslovakia. Before we left I went to see Sir Robert Vansittart, who was then Permanent Under-Secretary in the Foreign Office, and asked whether it would be wise to undertake this tour in view of Europe's troubled state. He asked when we planned to return and I told him, 'The end of May.' 'In that case it will be all right. It is August which will be the danger month.' How right he proved.

Yet after the match in Italy we were told by the Foreign Office to cancel the Czechoslovakian game because of demonstrations and unrest in Prague and instead we included two matches in Switzerland. One, against a selected Swiss XI, was played on a beautiful ground in

Bellinzona, near Locarno. There were massive snow-capped mountains as the backdrop to the lush green pitch, and the stadium which fitted so neatly into this strikingly impressive setting. Even more striking was a goal Mortensen scored there which is etched still on my memory. From fully 35 yards he hit an angled shot which left the goalkeeper groping as it arrowed into the net.

Our next stop was Schaffhausen. We played there at the request of Max Brunner, an industrialist who was then President of the little local club. Brunner was such an admirer of English football that he often joined our tours, becoming a popular figure with players and officials. We had to play there on a cramped school ground surrounded by temporary scaffolding and improvised seats, which were quite inadequate to cope with the vast crowd which came to see us. The scene indeed resembled a cricket match in the West Indies with spectators hanging out of trees around the ground or framed in the upper windows of the schoolhouse. There was no adequate ground then in the town and the people there had just voted against paying an extra 50 centimes on the rate to provide one. Such was the enthusiasm this match aroused however that a new poll was at once demanded, which proved heavily in favour. It was a pleasure to return after the war to see our youth team play on Schaffhausen's new pitch and find the facilities of the highest standard. We were, however, fortunate that that match could go ahead. While waiting in the porch of our hotel for the bus to take the team to the ground a sudden thunderstorm began to drench us. So I called the players back into the lounge. As we re-entered it a huge chandelier came crashing down from the ceiling, narrowly missing some of our party.

Indeed, there always seemed to be incidents a-plenty in Schaffhausen. On another occasion one of our Council members, Mr Brearley, accompanying the team, dropped off to sleep while smoking. He was fortunate to escape the subsequent flames and the FA was fortunate only to have to pay for a bed and bedclothes destroyed in the fire. It could have been so much more damaging, but for the prompt preventative action. Perhaps it was all just retribution on us for an embarrassing slight on that first friendly visit. Most of us were highly appreciative of Max Brunner's invitation and delighted to help a man who was so well regarded by our team. To add to his kindness Max entertained us to an excellent lunch in the beautiful Casino garden before the game. Unfortunately, it was the FA Honorary Treasurer, Albert Ansell, who was the first to comment. He was apt to be sour in outlook and was noted for his *faux pas*. And now he said aggressively, 'We didn't want to come here. We were dragged here instead of going on to Prague as we should have done.' Perhaps the extra travel expense had niggled him but for the rest of us a visit to Schaffhausen was a real pleasure, though it was not so easy to convince our host after that ungracious comment.

The distant drums of war did not disturb our normal programme of preparation for the football season of 1939. Their insistent beat was in the back of our minds throughout the long hot summer, but we were more preoccupied with the arranging of courses and all the administrative plans for a fresh season. Norman Creek, John Witty, my assistant on many courses, and I were at Loughborough College organising one for coaches and referees when it became clear at last that Europe was again at the brink. With war so obviously imminent we asked the members of the courses if they wanted to take a chance and continue, or hurry home before the storm broke. We were relieved that there were no echoes of Drake as all opted to get on with the war, rather than finish the game.

To hasten them home there was the latent threat of the unknown, with fears of air or gas attack in the opening minutes of any new conflict. And indeed Chamberlain had hardly announced the following day that we were at war than the sirens began their eerie wailing and everyone headed for the shelters. That was a false alarm, and instead of the anticipated blitzkrieg there were long months of 'phoney war' before the storm finally broke and the German whirlwind was upon us in all its power.

We had no expectation that there would be such a leisurely start to hostilities for us, and all was bustle at first as the evacuees were hurried out of London and the volunteers and reservists hastened to join the Forces. As Britain concentrated on war all regular sporting fixtures ended and football seemed momentarily irrelevant.

Twelve months earlier a Consultative Committee of the FA had decided 'That in the event of war, a meeting be convened comprising the officers of the Football Association and the Management Committee of the Football League for the purpose of deciding the course of action to be taken with regard to the game.' I therefore arranged for that meeting to be held at Lancaster Gate on September 8th with fifteen of us present. It was the first meeting of the 'War Emergency Committee' which was in effect to be the executive body for the next five years. It seemed at first there would be little for the Committee to do. For our main decision was that in accordance with Government proclamation and our own Rule 27 all organised football, except for the Forces, would be suspended until official notice to the contrary.

However, I had already been in touch with the GOC Home Forces and discussed with him the desirability of putting at their disposal our panel of qualified coaches, trainers, and masseurs and helping in any other way we could. He was instantly enthused by the offer and I was able to tell the Committee that he was considering how best the scheme might work.

With memories of my army training at Portman Road and how we had had to make our own recreation, I had urged clubs to make their facilities available for the troops' recreation where possible, and was already able to report an excellent response. For the rest it seemed that the blackout on football would be as total as it was on our cities at night.

My mind turned immediately to rejoining the Army and as I went to report I found myself by happy coincidence being interviewed together with Jack Orange, the knowledgeable football correspondent of the *Evening News*, with whom I had established a friendly working association. Both of us received our postings and I prepared to travel to an anti-aircraft battery at Fishguard in South Wales as a Lieutenant in the Royal Artillery.

On the eve of my departure Lord Wigram came to see me. He had just been asked to establish a sports committee of the Duke of Gloucester's Red Cross Organisation and needed guidance on how to do it. When I told him that I was leaving to join the Army, he insisted that it was more necessary I stay to help raise funds and organise the many sporting activities, which would become essential to maintain civilian morale. He at once arranged to see General Auchinleck and have me released to become a member of his committee.

'Spiv' was to become a wartime word of abuse for the small-time profiteer. But it was a nickname I accepted with pride for my fund-raising activity. We set up a 'shop' at Lancaster Gate which acquired the prizes for the multitude of money-raising competitions we organised from which the funds flowed in. Bridge parties, whist drives, and darts competitions were all indoor money-spinners. And as the numbers being organised grew ever greater, so did the requests for prizes. When the Beaverbrook drive for metal for aircraft and tank production led to its use being banned in many ordinary articles I hurried to buy up cheap the stock of a handbag manufacturer whose production of bags with metal frames had to cease. When a bomb damaged a Bond Street store I was round making bulk purchases of the scent and cosmetics being sold off at give-away prices among the debris. The 'shop' at the FA offices soon became the centre of a sizeable organisation far larger than we had needed to run the country's football. With so many small competitions to organise, so many thousand pounds coming in in small amounts each day, so many prizes to buy and distribute, we had at one time thirty-three working at Lancaster Gate. This was the mainspring of the effort which brought in almost £3 million for the Red Cross & St John Fund including a donation to Mrs Churchill's 'Aid to Russia' Fund. That was big money for those days, yet all collected in small sums on the 'little drops of water, little grains of sand' principle.

Lord Iliffe was chairman of the main Red Cross Committee and at one of the early meetings he was looking for ways of raising large amounts. 'If the war goes on as long as we expect you will be glad of the pennies too' had been my comment. It was instantly taken up by another member suggesting a 'penny a week' fund and that too was soon established; these tiny individual contributions netting vast sums over the years of war.

Darts proved one of the most popular and profitable of the small competitions, and as I was not myself very proficient I went to seek advice from the President of the Darts Association. He was the landlord of an Islington pub, a burly, cheerful man and a real enthusiast immersed in the jargon of 'flights' and 'trebles' and 'double tops'; when he took me through the existing rules I was amazed how lengthy and complicated they were and suggested they might be simplified, particularly to help those coming fresh to the myriad local competitions we were organising. It ended with my being asked to rewrite the rules and producing a shorter, more positive version. For competitions we also shifted the emphasis from the 'league'-type matches then popular to the one evening knockout. This was necessary because in so many Service camps turnover was too quick to allow league-style tournaments to be completed before half the players had left.

A less entertaining side of our work was attendance at court cases. Inevitably there were instances when organisers of the sporting events were accused by those present of not forwarding all the money known to have been collected. Such incidents were fortunately rare, but Ernest Miller, who usually attended to give evidence of what we had received, always complained that this was a particularly distasteful chore.

The Red Cross and St John Appeal Sports Committee was officially formed at a meeting at the Mansion House on October 10th 1939. Colonel the Rt Hon Lord Wigram was Chairman from the start and I became the Deputy Chairman and Secretary. By February 1943 we reached our first million pounds when a cheque for £15,000 was handed over by Lord Mottistone, Chairman of Wembley Stadium, to Lord Wigram after an England *v* Wales football match. All sports, big and small, had made some contribution, but the breakdown of that first million may give a pointer to war-time recreational interest. £365,478 came from whist drives, bridge parties, dances and socials. £79,919 from billiards and snooker; £72,186 from darts and bowls; £67,711 from soccer; £67,375 from golf; £27,965 from athletics; £22,996 from cricket; £22,015 from lawn tennis; £25,183 from boxing; £50,561 from greyhound racing; £2,595 from American football; £480 from hockey; £76 from lacrosse; £36 from stoolball; and £8 from fencing; with many other sports helping to the million target. The appeal fund incorporated Mrs Churchill's 'Aid to Russia' fund and a number of other funds registered under the War Charities Act 1940, such as the Agriculture Fund. But the main work was summed up by the President of the Red Cross and St John Fund, HRH the Duke of Gloucester, in his introduction to the illustrated booklet we published *Sport scores a million*.

> With every year the work of the War Organisation of the Red Cross and St John increases. A vast network of services, supplementary to those of the State, brings help to the wounded, to prisoners of war, to civilian air-raid victims, and to others who suffer as a result of war.

Football had from the start a close link with the Committee as I ensured that both the FA and League Chairmen, Mark Frowde and Will Cuff, attended the first meeting. And it was not long before I was again heavily involved with football matters. At the first meeting of the War Emergency Committee we had agreed to donate £1,000 towards equipment for Army teams. That sum was soon doubled. My proposal over the register of coaches and trainers was also quickly followed up by the Army and I was soon being asked to recommend coaches and players for training at Aldershot and Uxbridge prior to being passed out as Sergeant Instructors APTC. Many outstanding footballers such as Joe Mercer and Matt Busby were posted to Aldershot and many of them were able to play matches at Reading where a formidable war-time team was built up. For the total ban on football lasted only a few days as the initial fears subsided and the Government began to appreciate the need for recreation to continue as normally as possible, both as an outlet for maintaining physical fitness and as a stimulus to morale. Within a few days friendly matches were permitted again and I had started discussions with the Home Office. Ernest Bevin represented to me that it was preferable for football, as a national sport, to continue to be organised by an official body. We agreed to give our full support to the organisation of both friendly and competitive matches, but to confine the competitive games to local and regional groups on Saturdays and holidays. We also agreed to limit the number of spectators to avoid large crowds travelling. For the first six months, indeed, the number of spectators at major grounds in evacuation areas was limited to 15,000. Before long we were also organising friendly Internationals as part of the endeavour to shrug off the discomforts of war, the bombing, the rationing, the restrictions on everyday life.

Just because our lives were so cramped, and because the threat of sudden death was with civilians as well as soldiers, there was a heightened enjoyment, an uninhibited relish among players and spectators, which made these matches a special experience. One in particular was as memorable as any I have watched. The International between England and Scotland at Hampden Park was a unique occasion, a unique game. In April 1942 Scotland won an enthralling game 5–4. That was the highest score ever in an International at Hampden and players like Matt Busby have rated it the best match in which they took part. It might be an austerity war-time game not counting in official records. But with Tommy Lawton at his peak for England and Billy Liddell making his debut for Scotland the forward play has rarely been matched. 'Jock' Dodds scored a hat trick, with Billy Liddell and Bill Shankly getting one each to give Scotland victory. But next year it was England's forwards who dominated in an 8–0 win.

Football matches became so important a part of life on the home front that our small war-time organisation had in the end to cope with fixtures different in character but little less complex or numerous than in peace-time. Sunday football for industrial workers had been sanctioned by September 1940; special programmes were arranged for the fourteen to eighteen age group; and there was a growing proliferation of Charity matches, Service matches, Civil Defence matches, Inter-Allied Service games and ordinary Cup matches. The first Wartime Cup Final was held at Wembley on April 10th 1941 with Preston drawing with Arsenal to keep North and South happy. With troops from many countries packed into Britain another major competition was run with our aid—the Inter-Allied Services' Cup. So popular did this become that by 1943 eleven separate teams entered and the final between the British Army and the RAF at Stamford Bridge was watched by 31,000 including King Haakon of Norway, a great enthusiast for sport.

In my dual roles with CCPR and FA I was able to promote another successful scheme started jointly by these two bodies. In the desperate days after Dunkirk recruitment was stepped up and the age of joining the Services lowered from twenty to nineteen as the country cast around for manpower to defend against the expected invasion. The Home Guard was one answer, but that concentrated on training the more elderly. In conjunction with the Service Ministries we prepared a scheme aimed at the young called 'Fitness for Service'. The title aptly expressed the aim of preparing young people for Service life by improving their physical fitness and giving them a basic grounding in elementary drills. The FA donated £1,000 towards the project and soon there were 190 training centres set up with more than 40,000 availing themselves of the opportunity provided to have physical training and games instruction from experts, and a taste of Service drill as well.

There was also a new contact for me with broadcasting as I was invited to talk on the radio to the 'Rock' at Gibraltar giving details of war-time sport for the interest of Servicemen there. And as a result of my suggestion to the BBC a new programme was started introducing home listeners to early morning exercises. May Brown of the Scottish CCPR became responsible for the women's exercise routines but I was much involved in the designing of exercises for both men and women. The meetings were in Glasgow and the frequent trips there by rail were unpredictable and uncomfortable in those days of air raids and dislocation.

Another major interest for me was the Civil Defence Sports Committee formed in the autumn of 1941. Again this was a joint FA/CCPR venture and I found myself elected Chairman of this new Committee. Our task was to ensure that the vast number of Civil Defence Units, often small, often isolated, usually bored, had games enough to keep them fit and amused. The scheme extended also to other small units such as fire stations or barrage balloon crews, who were in need of recreation and entertainment. Inevitably this had to be a scheme to promote self-help. We could give the lead by coaching instruction, by training PE leaders for units, by providing tests and examinations for the more skilful and interested. But above all these small groups had to take their own initiative in organising their sport. All they needed was guidance. The enthusiasm was certain to be there. So I produced myself for circulation to all such sites a booklet on organising games for small units. Some 400,000 copies were distributed and, as with the Fitness for Service scheme, there were hundreds of letters of appreciation of the help given. There was also a Parliamentary complaint that the booklet was not written in proper Civil Service language; but I took that as a compliment.

This was rewarding work, and there was an unexpected but welcome bonus when it led to the award of the CBE. Or so I understood as I was afterwards told that the recommendation was made by Sir Harold Scott, Deputy Commissioner of Police, who had a special interest in the help given to the Fire and Civil Defence Services. I was not as conversant as I should have been with the ranking of such honours. When the letter came by second post—a service which survived the peril of war but appears too difficult for the white-hot technology of the modern age—I was delighted but intrigued by the significance of the 'Commander' in the title. As the letter stressed the confidentiality there was no one I could ask. A few minutes later, however, Phyllis Colson telephoned and it was clear she had also been involved, when she asked if anything special had happened to me. I replied guardedly that I had indeed had a pleasant surprise. 'I must know. Is it M, O or C?' she asked and I was then able to get detailed information from her, as to the difference.

Phyllis Colson, Major Gem and I often constituted a small interviewing panel to appoint instructors to visit these scattered groups and help them organise their games. On one occasion we had a special request to do so from Brigadier Wand-Tetley, with whom I worked closely in operating the scheme. He wanted us to interview a young Norwegian escapee, recently arrived after a daring escape in a small boat. Like many Scandinavians he was blond, handsome, and with a healthy, well-muscled look. He wanted to join the PE instructors as he had himself been a games instructor at an Oslo sports hall. We all took an instant liking to him and to pass the time I asked him about the Norwegian winger at the last Olympic games in Berlin, who would have trained at the same hall. The winger had been engaged at the time to the daughter of the President of the Norwegian FA. They had made an engaging couple so obviously in love that they caught our attention. 'You must know them,' I said. 'Have you seen either lately?' It was an idle question, but for the first time in the interview he hesitated before replying. 'Oh but of course I have,' he then answered, hurrying on to add that they were happily married now and living close to the sports centre. I had asked the question because I knew that they too had escaped from Norway and that he might have visited the family as the wife and children lived close to Lancaster Gate. The answer aroused vague suspicions in my mind and I probed his knowledge of other Norwegian players to get equally wild answers. While he appeared suitably qualified to act as one of the sports instructors, and the others were impressed with him, I now reported my suspicions to the Home Office that he might be a spy. These were dismissed without much investigation as he had been carefully screened on arrival. And he was soon touring widely round the country to a variety of units. But I at least was not surprised when about a year later Lord Haw-Haw's propaganda broadcast started: 'Gairmany calling, Gairmany calling. You sports enthusiasts in Britain may like to know that the nice Norwegian who has toured so many of your military establishments is in fact an agent of ours. Two nights ago he left as he arrived—by boat to a waiting submarine and is on his way now to Berlin.' I got an apology, but the Germans got more information than they should have done.

Council meetings were suspended throughout the war and the emergency committee did not meet very often. Once the raids on London became heavy it used to meet in Nottingham to avoid the disruptions of London travel and living. And indeed Lancaster Gate could be a noisy area, with the FA offices extensively damaged in the bombing. Like most London civilians I had my share of fire-watching and fire-fighting to do, and one of my keenest companions on this duty was Emperor Haile Selassie of Abyssinia. He lived in the Palace Hotel opposite to our offices and I was there with a warden on the night of a heavy incendiary raid. We soon appeared to be at the centre of a ring of flame, spectators of some mad bonfire night. 'Your place is on fire, too', said the Emperor. He was right, and we hurried back to the FA offices to find carpets and furniture alight in many of the rooms which kept us busy with sandbags and stirrup-pumps. We had followed the recommended drill of the time by keeping the baths full of water so that a supply was instantly available. It was doubly effective in this case because by happy coincidence two of the incendiaries dropped straight into a bath of water and were rendered harmless. That was fortunate as it would not have taken much more to have the fire totally out of control.

The offices had also been damaged, but less severely, by another incendiary raid and by blast when a couple of heavy bombs fell on a nearby street demolishing most of the houses and a large garage. My most fortunate escape came after I accepted an invitation to a service at the Guards Chapel having been asked to attend by General Serjeantson-Brook and Captain Ivan Cobbold, father of the present Chairman of Ipswich. Just before I was due to leave my local Padre called in to remind me that I had undertaken to read the lesson at a service specially for Rotary members. As President of the Paddington & Marylebone Rotary Club it would have been taken amiss had I forgotten this engagement. So I had to phone my apologies to Serjeantson-Brook, who was not pleased and said that in the circumstances he would not go either. We were both lucky. That evening I heard on the news that a flying bomb had hit the Chapel squarely in the midst of the service. Captain Cobbold, like so many other officers, was killed as we would have been.

Another of the FA's special war-time efforts was of particular interest to me. With the co-operation of the Prisoners of War Department of the Red Cross and St John Organisation we organised a stream of sports equipment for POW camps. There were many thousands of Allied prisoners by now, and this gave them some outlet from the degrading boredom of captivity. The supplies were supervised by the International Red Cross and I made special arrangements to see they had the names and addresses of all connected with football who were among the prisoners, and tried to ensure that they had their share of footballs.

The Sports Committee and my CCPR work kept me in touch with many different sporting bodies outside football. Tennis was one such interest as I had a special friendship with the Davis Cup player, Nigel Sharpe, who took a leading part in organising exhibition matches and competitions for the benefit of the Fund. Cricket was also helpful with Lord Hawke responding quickly when we pointed out that Lord's was not being used. Many matches were subsequently arranged there. On one occasion near the end of the war a game was in progress when a VI flying bomb came heading over Lord's. To the consternation of the players and the watchers, including the Duke of Gloucester, 'Plum' Warner, and many servicemen, the motor cut out to signal that the bomb was now gliding down to explode in the area. The fieldsmen all fell prone on the grass as a block of flats just beyond the ground was demolished. Unshaken was that elegant Middlesex and England batsman, Jack Robertson. He hit the next ball for a soaring six. And soon Hitler too—in Field Marshal Montgomery's favourite phrase—had been hit for six.

10

Festivals of Sport

●●

The first years after the war were some of the happiest of my life. My wife and I enjoyed the flat at Lancaster Gate which allowed us both to pursue our own divergent interests and yet to share a common pattern of life. I was totally immersed in sport, while her interests were mainly musical. London gave her every opportunity to follow her bent. And, though I was usually kept working late, home was also where my work was with no wasted travelling time. Adrienne was not very attracted by football, though she came to a number of Cup Finals and Internationals. What she greatly enjoyed was meeting the wide range of overseas visitors to Lancaster Gate, and, as an able linguist who could speak three languages, she was of great help to me in entertaining them.

Many came to stay or dine at Lancaster Gate and we also had the sons and daughters of FIFA, UEFA, and other football friends over for visits. Frequent and very welcome visitors were the children of Wiederkehr, Andrejevic, Brunner, and Schwartz. That idyllic phase was not to last for long, for within a few years my wife contracted a long wasting illness, which confined her to hospital in Frinton. It was a dispiriting period for me, since I could not devote as much time to her as I would have wished without abandoning my work. There was no way of forecasting when the final crisis would come; and when it did I was away in France for an International, only able to reach the hospital just before she died.

That early period after the war saw me with an experienced and competent staff who worked so smoothly that I was never cluttered up with detailed administrative matters which could be safely left to them. At the turn of the century there had been just two clerks, Charles Earle and George Neal in the office at 104 High Street,

Holborn. But my staff soon numbered twenty-five, indicating not only the wider range of work covered but also its greater complexity. The framework had now taken the shape I wanted. There was Walter Winterbottom as Director of Coaching and England team manager, both new concepts. His department also controlled publications. There was Ernest Miller in charge of the General Office. There was John Witty looking after the library and publication department; there was Norman Creek helping with coaching and looking after the amateurs' interests, a brilliant player turned capable administrator. There was a department for overseas matches and Internationals, there was a section covering tax and accountancy; there was a highly efficient department filing and indexing the registration forms of all professional and amateur players, each with his own record card recording his clubs, his playing experience, his disciplinary sentences.

As we expanded the staff I was fortunate in my selections for the new posts. Without exception those appointed proved excellent at their job and good colleagues with whom it was a pleasure to work. Not surprisingly there was virtually no turnover. Almost the only person who left went at my own instigation. John Battersby joined us as a junior and during the war he served with distinction in the RAF, becoming a Squadron Leader. Naturally he was ambitious to improve himself on return and indicated to me he might look for another post. I discussed with him the potential in a growing organisation like ours, but he finally commented, 'There's only one job here which would satisfy me. Yours.'

By coincidence the following day Chelsea's manager, Billy Birrell, came to see me to ask if I could suggest a suitable Secretary for the club. So I proposed John, and he served them splendidly for many years. He later became Secretary of Aldershot, and recently of Sunningdale Golf Club. Among the others who made an exceptionally efficient office team was Doug Hawes, whose knowledge and expertise have made him an ever more vital part in the smooth working of the FA. There was another ex-Air Force man in Nigel Bird, who so ably looked after all refereeing affairs. The late John Carvosso, 'Carr' to everyone, was the most friendly and helpful of people, as well as having detailed knowledge of his main field of publications. In charge of the youth teams John Baylis proved just the father figure required, transmitting to them the enthusiasm to develop and ensuring there was both encouragement and discipline. Between them all they made my work easy and enjoyable.

In another sphere, too, a happy relationship developed. We established a Press Room and an effective communication system with the Press, aimed to ensure there was equal and rapid access to all relevant information. The Press in their turn treated us courteously and it pleased me to read a kindly account of my work so far in an *Observer* sporting print:

> Unlike a man who resides in a valley, influenced and governed by the shadows of the valley, Sir Stanley lives at the mountain-top. His views are wide, his horizons limitless. Football is his game and the world his playing pitch. In the short span of sixteen years since he succeeded Sir Frederick Wall as FA Secretary there have been revolutionary changes within the framework of football legislation and policy.
>
> The rigid conventions of seventy years have been quietly disturbed. We now see a Provident Fund for professional players; the British Associations back in FIFA; international youth tournaments; the FA coaching scheme; propaganda linked with films, radio and television; the interchange of British and foreign referees; FA teams and British clubs hopping from cloud to cloud as they span the earth by air.

There are few of us immune from the hurt of public criticism or the pleasure of reading complimentary comment. I am certainly no exception. But pleased as I was to read that account, it worried me to be credited with these changes. In an organisation like the FA one can influence others, but not force new ideas against the general will. Change is a slow and diplomatic process with many contributing to it. Even some Chairmen have had to learn the hard way that the Council can be swayed, but not driven. That did not apply to the man with whom I was then working, Amos Brook Hirst, a quiet-spoken solicitor from Huddersfield who was later knighted for his services. He was more effective than many more forceful personalities, winning people round in his self-effacing way.

Had I been offered the chance of adding anything to the *Observer* encomium, there was one other development in which I took special pride. With the war over and Germany prostrate, it seemed to me that reconciliation could come through sport. We had to forget the past and build a new and friendlier relationship in the present. It was difficult to make the rapprochement through FIFA or national Associations. The FIFA view, as expressed at Zurich in 1945, was:

> As the object of the Federation is to promote the amateur football sport, to control in general the game of Association Football and to

frame friendly relations between the national Associations, it is not possible at present to entertain such relations with subjects of Germany and Japan. Furthermore, the 'Nationalsozialistischer Reichsbund für Leibesübungen Fachamt Fussball' has ceased to exist, and consequently its affiliation with FIFA is terminated.

In soundings with government I was advised that the best way to bring Germany back into the sporting community of Europe was through youth fixtures. That seemed entirely appropriate with a new start for a new generation uninvolved in the causes of war. So I arranged for matches between UAU teams and German university students and then for exchanges of youth sides in 1949. It was a first small step, but I have since taken pleasure in watching the contribution made to world football by West Germany.

It is not without regret, however, that I have seen them far outstrip us in performance in the post-war World Cups. Theirs is indeed a remarkable record, winning the Cup in 1954 and 1974, being runners-up in 1966 and reaching the last four more often than not. German play has been a fine blend of skill and strength, of flair and discipline, but above all they have always been consistent in style and simple in approach. They have recognised and played on their basic strengths while others, ourselves sometimes included, have followed someone else's cast-off fashions.

The first pre-war visit of the German Universities side had been indirectly responsible for a change in our domestic football arrangements. Numbering of players had been tried out in the thirties. For the 1933 Cup Final between Everton and Manchester City the teams were numbered 1 to 22 and there is a well-known picture of 'Dixie' Dean heading home at close range past a goalkeeper numbered 22. The experiment had not been approved, however. The members of the International Committee were always against it, claiming that it reduced football players to the level of jockeys or greyhounds. As a supporter of numbering myself I had made no impression before the Germans' visit in 1936. The letter about the proposed team arrangements was written in German and after I had passed it for translation one passage was found to read 'Our team will be numbered to thirteen.'

It seemed to me that they wished to number their two reserves as well, even though no substitutes were then allowed. We were providing all the equipment for the game and so I arranged for the housekeeper at Lancaster Gate, the very helpful Mrs Rowlands, to

sew numbers on their purple-coloured jerseys. To avoid any discrimination I asked her to number the England team shirts as well.

When the German team arrived I found too late that there had been
a mistranslation. They had merely written that their party *numbered*
thirteen. It was too late to change back, and by coincidence the International Committee, for seniors as well as youth, met in London in
the morning and decided to come to the match at Wembley in the
afternoon. None of them knew the players on either side, so they
found for themselves the value of numbering in enabling them to
identify players from the programme. Thereafter the likes of Sutcliffe,
Cuff, Wreford-Brown and Huband were more easily convinced that it
should be tried in Internationals. Soon numbering was standard
practice.

Another team to show us something new after the war was Russia's
Moscow Dynamos. There was tremendous admiration in Britain for
the supreme courage and tenacity of the Russians during the war, and
there was an especially warm welcome for their footballers. But it was
not anticipated that they would have so many novel and effective
ideas to impart.

The Dynamos lived up to their name with a driving energy which
allowed their players to cover the whole field. This was the first
demonstration of the work-rate and utility principles. They seemed to
have now ten attackers, now ten defenders while our team relied on
more rigid positioning and more specialist performers. The pace was
certainly too fast for Cardiff, who lost 1–10.

Another sensible innovation was not to select their team until they
had had a lengthy warm-up session before the kick-off and satisfied
themselves that all players were fully fit. Again for this session each
player had his own ball while we were used to sides taking out just one
or two for kicking into a goal. Walter Winterbottom was always quick
to look for the benefit in such new ideas, and the visit taught him some
lessons and reinforced my own belief that we had much to gain from
the close study of European football.

The Dynamos gave our players some headaches on the field, and
there was a problem or two off it for me. We could get no advance
information of the time and place of arrival, which made planning
difficult. There were abortive visits to Northolt before we were finally
informed while waiting there that the plane bringing them was about
to land at Croydon. So we were just too late for the planned welcome.
Everything including hotel space was still rationed, and as no hotel
would accept vague bookings we had finally arranged for them to stay

the first night at the Wellington Barracks, where a room was kept for them. As our buses drove in through the gate a Guards Sergeant Major was putting a squad of defaulters through their punishment paces. The Russians watched wide-eyed as they were doubled round the square reacting to the stentorian commands which echoed round St James's Park. They refused at first to get out of their coach as they clearly thought we had brought them to a penal settlement.

To add to my worries the barrack room assigned them did indeed look like one, so bare and uncomfortable was it. So I phoned Sir Guy Bracewell Smith, the Arsenal Chairman, and asked if he could save us further embarrassment by putting beds for them in the ballroom of his Park Lane Hotel. And he saved the day by arranging it without fuss.

The Russian officials were always polite and punctual, but produced some new problem every day. And each one usually took four meetings to resolve, since the first request was never the last, and all answers led to a withdrawal for study and to get instructions. When due to play Chelsea at Stamford Bridge they came to object that the game was not at Wembley, which was to them the national stadium. 'It could not be played there because there is a bus strike and spectators could not get there even if we had planned to hold it there,' I told them. Two hours of consideration later they were back to say, 'Surely the game is important enough to stage at Wembley. So you must order the strikers back to work.'

Our lengthiest discussion was over a banquet planned in their honour at the Mansion House. First they were doubtful if they wished to attend and I had to explain the unusual privilege being accorded them. Then they were back to say the ambassador wished to bring his wife, so ladies must come to the dinner, too. Only the last of their many requests proved impossible to meet: 'We want no extravagance, no ostentation at the dinner.' I relayed this message to the Lord Mayor, who commented, 'We have arranged to get out the gold plate in their honour and they will have the choice of eating off that or the floor.'

During the war I took the opportunity to consider the future pattern of soccer over the next quarter of a century, and plan the steps we should take. My report became known as the 'Post-War Memorandum' and charted the course of the FA's future development. The report was divided into sections dealing with development in England and in international football. Some of the proposals were thought revolutionary but all were in time implemented. Among the more important were that we should start a county youth championship, and a Football Association competition for youngsters under eighteen, both amateur and professional. I also proposed an 'under-23' international competition and the widening of the scope of full International matches. The design I had in mind was to produce a 'ladder' which any youngster with the ability could climb. He could progress through competition of widening scope with the best reaching the international team already fully trained and experienced in international competition. As that plan slowly took shape it became copied in many other countries and sports.

In the memorandum I also urged that the four British Associations rejoin FIFA as soon as possible, and the early realisation of this was a matter of great satisfaction to me. So, too, was the progress made on other proposals recommending the establishment or improvement of specialist courses for football's various groups—referees, players, coaches, managers, trainers and administrators. There were many difficulties in getting some of these organised, but over the years all interests were fully covered. In particular, the FA coaching scheme was developed through Walter Winterbottom's work to a point where it became forerunner and model for most other sports.

There are always some who question the value of coaching and point to the 'natural' geniuses like Greaves or Matthews. But for the development and maintenance of the game at all levels a national coaching scheme is a must. We have never suffered here from being 'overcoached'. More often we have suffered in recent years because other countries have worked even harder at mastering the skills. At least the FA coaching scheme ensured that we have only ourselves to blame when ability does not match expectation. The opportunity is there for those who take it.

As a change from looking ahead for soccer I was soon immersed in one of Britain's great sporting occasions.

As Chairman of the CCPR I was involved in the planning and staging of the 1948 Olympics in London, the 'austerity' Olympics. There was still rationing of food, an absence of luxuries, and a shortage of accommodation. Viscount Portal of Laverstoke was President of the Games and from the twelve of us on the Organising Committee of which Lord Burghley was the energetic Chairman, he co-opted Eaton Griffiths and me to be his special aides.

As Chairman of the Great Western Railway, Lord Portal stayed in the Great Western Hotel, where Eaton and I met him daily in the final stages of planning, and while the Games were running. Eaton was a civil servant with vast experience of government offices and all the contacts to get matters arranged swiftly. And through the Central Council I was in close touch with all sports and able rapidly to get their views or co-operation.

Housing the competitors was in itself a major problem, with London still not fully recovered from the war-time bombing and with too little money available to contemplate building a separate village just for the Olympics. Fortunately the Olympics then were still seen as primarily for the competitors and had not yet escalated to the present point where the staging is all important. The presentation becomes a matter of national pride with each determined to outdo the previous presenters until the Games have become an almost unbearable financial worry to a host country. The 1976 Games in Montreal came close to bankrupting the city, and in preparation were a constant source of anxiety. And yet our utility Games, dictated by the necessity of the times and making no undue demands on resources, seemed to generate a rare spirit of enthusiasm and comradeship among the participants. They were billeted in Nissen huts in Richmond Park, or in Service accommodation as in the RAF stations at Uxbridge and West Drayton. But the somewhat dismal surroundings seemed only to stimulate the sense of fun and friendship among the competitors.

While I was concerned with all sports I naturally took a special interest in the football. British teams had a fine record in the Games so long as the amateur definition was clear and limiting. We won the first football competition in the Olympics in 1900 and took the gold again in 1908 and 1912. Then came the disputes after the First World War and our withdrawal from FIFA. In a conference at Brussels in 1919 Belgium, Luxembourg and the four home countries threatened to withdraw rather than play matches against Germany, Austria and Hungary, so bitter were the feelings after that war. And when those who had been neutral like Sweden and Norway, and some of our fellow combatants, such as Italy, opted to play these Central Powers, we carried out our threat. When peace was made with FIFA again in 1924 and the home countries rejoined, one controversial issue was left on one side: the definition of an amateur. British Associations had always opted for a simple, clear-cut definition, since to make exceptions was to encourage an endless slide. So our definition of an amateur footballer read:

Players are either amateur or professional. Any player registered with his national Association as a professional or receiving re-muneration or consideration of any sort above his hotel and travelling expenses actually paid, shall be a professional. Training expenses of amateurs, other than the wages paid to trainer or coach, must be paid by the players themselves. A player competing for any money prize in a football contest shall be a professional.

When FIFA and the Olympic Games Committee reversed an earlier ruling and allowed 'broken time' payments to compensate amateurs for lost wages in the 1928 Olympics in Amsterdam, the British Associations withdrew once more from FIFA on this issue. And even when we re-entered a football team in the Games, our more purist view of amateurism handicapped performance by giving us a more limited selection than some countries with more elastic concepts. For these 1948 Games a special compromise had to be achieved with FIFA, the FA somewhat reluctantly accepting a declaration which read:

An amateur is one whose connection with a sport is solely for pleasure and for the physical and moral benefits he derives therefrom without material gain of any kind, direct or indirect. This definition is liberal in so far as it admits the reimbursement of actually lost salary and of real expenses of the athlete. In fact if the amount paid to the athlete covers his actual expenses or the loss of salary such reimbursement does not represent any material profit, direct or indirect, for the athlete.

Though this was a mere verbal gloss on the contentious issue of broken time I urged our acceptance to avoid any controversy souring the London Games.

In retrospect we may look a bit stuffy with our opposition to such payments, but the fear that one concession might start many more has been only too correct. The problems have remained with the Olympic movement ever since, with the insidious progress to 'State Scholarships' and 'State Athletes' until some countries just enter the best eleven players they have, while others struggle to retain some amateur concept. With our own game we have now at least accepted this *reductio ad absurdum* and started classing all footballers as 'players'. No doubt the Olympic movement will soon have to be equally honest in admitting it has lost all power to make any genuine distinction.

Even by 1952 the Olympic final in Helsinki was between perhaps the two best professional teams of the day, Puskas's Hungarians and the Jugoslav national side. But in 1948 the standard was still genuinely amateur and there were some challenging games to watch. Outstanding for the British team was a stirring match with a fine Dutch side which we won at the last 4–3. We then beat France 1–0, and after losing to Jugoslavia 1–3 were only beaten 3–5 by Denmark in the play-off for third place.

On Finals Day I was asked to act as usher in the Royal Box. Unfortunately, at the moment I was meant to leave to line-up for presentation with other officials, King Haakon of Norway and King Gustav of Sweden arrived at the Box and had to be shown to their seats. So one of the fastest sprints on Finals Day was by a tall figure in top hat and morning coat. With tails flying I was barely in time to make it breathless to the line for my handshake with King George, who appeared amused by my predicament.

Certainly that earned me no black marks with him, for shortly afterwards he was to bestow a knighthood on me in the New Year Honours in 1949. And I was given to understand that the recommendation came from Lord Portal and was related to the successful organisation of the Games. It was a particular pleasure to me that the honour should come in time for my wife to share. She was delighted by it, though concealing her excitement: 'The only difference I notice in becoming a Lady is that the tradesmen charge double.'

The Festival of Britain in 1951 gave us a splendid opportunity to cement international relationships. The Football Association encouraged clubs to invite their overseas counterparts, which often led to the two becoming 'sister' clubs and maintaining close links. In all more than twenty of our clubs invited sides from abroad or played those who came at the FA's special invitation. Permission was given for the matches to be arranged out of season in May and June, so that there was no fixture problem. There was already a fund of goodwill for British soccer throughout Europe, and indeed throughout the world. And the Festival matches further enhanced that happy relationship. It is galling now for those of us who worked so hard for the good name of English soccer, players and administrators alike, to see the damage being done to our reputation by the thoughtless and violent 'hangers-on'. The 'wild' men who wrecked Luxembourg's stadium in October 1977 are typical of a new breed who harm our name abroad. It is sad to see so much dedicated effort of the past being so quickly and so mindlessly destroyed.

The receipts of the Festival Games were all donated to King George's Jubilee Trust, which has continued as a permanent organisation supporting youth clubs and youth organisations in the British Isles. I was pleased to be a member of the Trust almost from its start, as its aims and action were admirably in tune with the needs of the time. Only when I reached sixty-five years of age did I retire from it. The Officers are appointed by the Queen, and it is a rule that retirement at that age is automatic to ensure that there are new faces and new ideas. The late Duke of Gloucester was President then and, as a retiring present, I was delighted to receive his signed photograph while the Queen sent me also a signed photograph of herself and Prince Philip, both of which have pride of place in my study.

Meetings of the Jubilee Trust were rarely dull. The Secretary for many years was Commander J. B. Adams, known to everyone as Bill. With his breezy nautical bonhomie he was apt to address everyone as 'mate', no matter what their rank. On one occasion at the start of a meeting the Duke of Gloucester asked for the minutes to be read. There were pages of them, all in Bill's own hand. He sat there silently turning them over one by one with great deliberation, then looked up and said, 'Do you want the bloody lot, mate?' At which Sir Ivison Macadam hastily intervened with, 'I think, sir, that we might take them as read.' And so we did—then and in the future.

Once when I was senior member present I had to receive His Royal Highness, who was looking very businesslike as he shook hands with us all without speaking. Then as everyone waited expectantly for some important announcement he fixed his eye on me and said, 'Prince William wants to know why Stanley Matthews isn't playing for England on Wednesday.' So did I, but I did my best to explain the selectors' reasons as the non-footballing members of the Trust became ever more bewildered by the discussion.

Another youth project with which I was concerned from the start was the Duke of Edinburgh's Award Scheme. The basic idea of awards to encourage initiative in the young, and set standards of achievement, was a wartime development with a short-lived county badge scheme started at Kurt Hahn's prompting. There was another abortive attempt in 1948 when Michael Wardell produced a memorandum advocating a 'British Fitness Badge' and the CCPR tried to get sports organisations to participate. But the scheme was felt to be impractical so soon after the war with some feeling that it had unfortunate echoes of the Nazi 'Strength through Joy' movement. A few years later Prince Philip, influenced no doubt by the educational ideas of Kurt Hahn whose outdoor activities at his Gordonstoun School were run on similar lines, decided the time was now ripe for such a scheme. With the help of Lt-General Sir Frederick 'Boy' Browning a committee was formed on which I served with such as

Jack Crump, Dr Kurt Hahn, Sir John Hunt, Sir Arthur Porritt, the
Bishop of Portsmouth, General Sir Gerald Templar, Lt Cdr Michael
Parker and Dr Roger Bannister. Starting in late 1954 we had monthly
meetings at Buckingham Palace, presided over by Prince Philip, to
establish the standards anyone participating in the scheme had to
reach to obtain a gold, silver, or bronze award. We hoped this scheme
would be made available to *any* youth organisation, without trespass-
ing on its autonomy or character, and that it would strengthen the
appeal of these organisations. In football too development of youth
continued to be a main concern. Back in 1922 when I first became
Secretary of the West Herts FA a study of the FA regulations made
me aware we could claim £100 towards the administrative costs of
youth football and immediately I formed an 'under-16' league in the
county. Later, when I was at the FA, the Council approved rules for
a national FA Youth Cup and a national county FA youth amateur
competition, both of which are still operating.

My next step was to propose an international youth competition
with eight countries sending teams to Biggin Hill Air Force camp in
1948 for the first tournament. Next year FIFA invited the Netherlands to organise the tournament and it continues to move from
country to country annually. The organising responsibility was passed
to UEFA when it was established in 1957 and it was a pleasure to be
made first President of the youth committee formed to look after it.
So many European National Associations now enter a team that the
final round has to be limited to sixteen. With UEFA regarding me as
the 'father of the tournament' it is a pleasure still to be invited each
year to this final round wherever it is held.

Other Confederations soon followed the UEFA example. Indeed
such is the popularity of the South American youth championship that
at one final in Bogota I saw the gates closed on a full stadium and
eager youths sticking twenty foot poles into the ground which they
climbed to peer over the crowd on the terraces. In Asia too there has
been overflowing grounds for the successful tournaments promoted
by the Confederation Secretary, Koe Ewe Teik, which I have watched
in Kuala Lumpur, Bangkok, and Tokyo. It was one of my principal
aims at FIFA to help promote and finance such projects. Encouragement and training of youth is for me the most essential part of
sporting organisation and such schemes have always had my immediate support.

11

President of FIFA

●●

FIFA became an ever growing interest and influence on my life from
the moment that England rejoined. At once I was heavily involved in
its work. There was a constant need to prepare detailed briefs for
Arthur Drewry, who was appointed Vice President in 1946 to represent the British Associations. He rightly realised that it was essential
for us to make the proper impact at the start and that we could only
win acceptance of our views if they were convincingly argued.

In addition I was immediately made a member of World Cup
Organising and Olympic Games Committees and of FIFA's Referees'
Committee. The Referees' Committee was naturally a special interest
of mine and one where I could make an immediate contribution.
From pre-war days I was familiar with its work, for even though we
were not in FIFA I had been co-opted as one of its four members. It
had then been called the Rules and Regulations Committee and most
of its meetings had been held in Italy under the chairmanship of Dr
Mauro, with Henri Delaunay of France as Secretary. Dr Peco
Bauwens of Germany and myself completed the quartet.

Our main task was to answer queries from national Associations
and take decisions on the problems they posed us concerning refereeing method or interpretation of the laws. But it was interpretation of
language which was our main difficulty as we tried to ensure that
nuances and meanings were identical in French, German, Italian, and
English. Without any expert linguists among us, that was a laborious
task which stretched the meetings out for two days or more.

Dr Mauro spoke little English, but had enough pidgin French to
explain his view to Delaunay, who was more fluent. The usual drill
was for these two to converse with each other for a time after which
Mauro would say: 'Monsieur Delaunay, ayez l'amabilité d'expliquer

à M Rous et au Dr Bauwens mon point de vue.' In time we came to understand each other well enough, but despite Delaunay's fluent English, discussions were often tedious and involved, with much checking needed to ensure that the final version was right in all languages.

By 1946 the Committee had been renamed and Dr Bauwens was no longer a part of it. He had been a member of the FIFA Executive Committee from 1932 until Germany was expelled in 1945. The happy personal relationships we had previously established on our Committee, now enabled me to play a part in healing the divisions of war. Unlike Dr Schricker, Bauwens had been no obvious opponent of the Nazi regime. And there was some resentment in countries such as Belgium, Switzerland, and Holland that he had tried to arrange for German teams to play against nationals of those countries. FIFA, however, was primarily concerned with the re-establishment of good relations throughout Europe and, like the other members of the Rules Committee, I had retained a personal liking for him.

We all still respected Bauwens as an expert referee in his day and as a knowledgeable and friendly past member of the Committee. The nightmare years of war found no echo in our personal feelings. We had all been caught in the gale of the world, and were now glad to treat each other as individuals again. When Dr Bauwens was appointed President of the German Football Association in 1949, I was glad to work closely with him to try and get the German FA accepted back into FIFA. This was successfully achieved in 1950, and what a major contribution Germany has since made to international football.

More FIFA work came my way in 1950, when Dr Schricker resigned as Secretary. He had been a remarkable unifying influence and had done much to regenerate FIFA after the war. His resignation came during the World Cup finals in Brazil and I was immediately approached to take over as FIFA Secretary. As my Chairman, Arthur Drewry, was with me in Brazil we had immediate discussions on the offer and its possible effect on the FA. Both of us were keen to help FIFA, if we could, and the passionate enthusiasm for the game of South American players and crowds had reaffirmed for me that football was indeed a world game. In the heady atmosphere of Brazil it was natural to wish to play a central part in a sport in which so many of the exciting innovations were occurring outside the narrow confines of the British game. Yet the more we talked it over, the clearer the reality became. It was only feasible for me to combine the two jobs if the FIFA Secretaryship could be established in London. That set Rimet

1. The Mutford village team in 1912. The author kneels (second from left) beside
schoolmaster Cobb, who guards the loaned ball

2. The St Luke's College team with goalkeeper Rous in the back row

3. Serving in Egypt
   in 1916

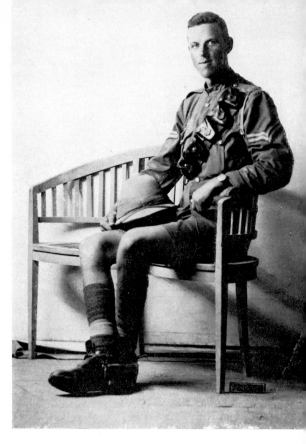

4. Giving swimming
   instruction at Watford
   Grammar School

5. About to start the Hungary *v* Italy match, October 1933. Rous stands between Hungarian captain Koranji (left) and Italian captain Cesarini. Far right is the Hungarian linesman, Fryges Kann

6. Refereeing the 1934 Cup Final as nineteen-year-old Frank Swift gropes for a Portsmouth centre. Manchester City won 2–1 with two goals from centre-forward Tilson in the last fifteen minutes

7. Taking leave of Sir Frederick Wall as the FA secretaryship is handed over

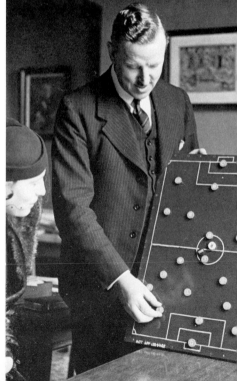

8. A lesson in tactics for a sports journalist from Austria visiting the FA

9. Escorting the King to meet the players in a war-time International at Wembley. On the right is Eddie Hapgood (No. 3) with Stan Cullis (No. 5) next to him. Beyond Hapgood is Sergeant-Major Voysey, the Millwall trainer

10. Mrs Churchill at Lancaster Gate checks progress of her 'Aid to Russia' Fund. Watching from the left are Charles Wreford-Brown (FA Committee member), Lord Iliffe (Chairman Red Cross Committee), Lord Wigram (Chairman Red Cross Sports Committee), the author, Miss Holden (Secretary for Indoor Sports), and Ernest Miller (Secretary for Outdoor Sports)

11. Winston Churchill is introduced to the Newcastle team by Joe Harvey before they beat Arsenal 1–0 in the 1952 Cup Final. Bob Stokoe is on Harvey's left as Churchill shakes hands with Bobby Mitchell

12. The author with his wife after receiving his knighthood in 1949

13. FIFA's goalkeeper, Zenian of Austria, punches clear from Nat Lofthouse with Stan Mortensen lurking near as England draw 4–4 in the match at Wembley to celebrate the FA's ninetieth anniversary in 1953

14. Watching as Billy Wright and Joe Mears carry a wreath at a service for Eva Perón, who died as the England team was visiting Argentina in 1953

15. Leaving for Moscow with the Arsenal team in 1954. To the author's right are the manager, Tom Whittaker, Jimmy Joyce, Alec Forbes, and Chairman, Guy Bracewell Smith. On the steps are Tommy Lawton (top right), trainer Milne, and Don Roper; Peter Goring (right) and Jack Kelsey; Derek Tapscott (right) and Walley Barnes

16. All smiles as England beat Scotland 9–3 at Wembley in 1961 and the Queen presents the International trophy to Johnny Haynes, the England captain

17. Watching as Jimmy Adamson presents the Burnley team to the Duke of Edinburgh before the 1962 Cup Final, which Tottenham won for the second year running

18. Meeting the Pope as His Holiness gives audience to members of a UEFA Congress in Rome. Behind the Pope are Michel Daphinoff, Asst. Sec. UEFA (left); Gustav Wiederkehr, UEFA President (facing, between the Pope and Sir Stanley); Jose Crahay, Sec. Belgian FA; Sandor Barcs, Hungary; Herbert Powell, Wales; and Hans Bangerter, Gen. Sec. UEFA (on the right of picture

19. Field Marshal Lord Montgomery of Alamein at the FA offices with Walter Winterbottom (left), Graham Doggart, and the author

20. In 1966 the Jules Rimet Cup is handed to Sir Stanley by Dr Luiz Murgel of Brazil, the holders. World Cup Organising Committee members in the background are from the left Gustav Wiederkehr (Switzerland), Lim Zee Sion (Malaysia), Harry Cavan (Northern Ireland), and Dr Ottorini Barassi (Italy)

21. The height of enthusiasm as some ticketless spectators are up the pole in their determination to see the 1964 final of the South American Youth Tournament in Bogota, Colombia

22. With Gillian Gilks and John Conteh receiving the first Manning awards in 1975. The author was the sports writers' first choice for outstanding services to sport

23. Receiving a decoration from the Senegalese Government on his eightieth birthday in April 1975

24. Watching the final of the first Gulf Cup staged in Kuwait

25. Watching football in Burma in the Asian zone pre-Olympic tournament (*Photo: Maung Maung Tin*)

26. Organising the charity cricket match at Eastcote in 1955

27. Being entertained in Japan. Dr Käser, General Secretary of FIFA, is on the left; holding the chopsticks is Rosemarie Breitenstein, the author's secretary

28. Taking part in the activities at Plas-y-Brenin National Recreation Centre with Sir John Hunt (at back), and Prince Philip (centre), who talks to one of a group setting out on an exercise

and his Committee a problem for the offices were based in Zurich on the understanding that this would be a permanent headquarters. No long-term compromise proved possible, and the best I could do was to agree to act as honorary Secretary jointly with Dr Barassi until Kurt Gassmann, a Swiss, was appointed a few months later.

The Rio Congress was the prelude to the World Cup matches which ended with a memorable final—so long as one was not Brazilian. For the host nation lost unexpectedly to Uruguay despite the thousands willing them to win. Sitting in the special box with the President and his family, I noticed that many were in tears in those last minutes as the game slipped irretrievably away from Brazil.

It was a custom in that country for white handkerchiefs to be waved round a stadium to signal that a team was beaten beyond hope of recovery. As Brazil fought desperately for the elusive equaliser a stewardess among a BOAC crew, for whom I had acquired tickets, fainted in the heat and noise of a stadium crowded with 200,000 fanatical enthusiasts. Her companions tried to attract a first-aider's attention by waving a white handkerchief. They were nearly lynched by those around, who misinterpreted it as a derisory gesture.

After the opening match the President had asked to see me because he had been offended by referee George Reader's action in starting the game punctually, although the President was a few minutes late and had not reached his box. I explained that referees had instructions to start punctually as so many others depended on it, the public, the transport services, the journalists with deadlines, the broadcasters with fixed programmes. The President smiled and said, 'You can be sure I will be punctual at the final.' Indeed he and his family were twenty minutes early, and I felt for them that they should be so disappointed in the result. And George Reader, far from being rebuked, was refereeing that final and handled an emotional occasion with such a firm, sure touch that over the years many expert referees have told me it was the best refereeing exhibition of any final. Certainly I have never seen a better in the World Cup.

While I was in South America there was an opportunity for me to further an innovation which seemed particularly desirable if FIFA were to maintain both its growth and its cohesion. The growth had been steady rather than startling: six member countries in 1904, forty-four by the twenty-fifth anniversary in 1929, seventy-three as we met for the Rio Congress in 1950. As with everything else in the modern world, the pace was likely to quicken, however. And indeed in the next quarter of a century the number of members has more than doubled. With that as the prospect, it was essential in my view that FIFA decentralise rather than become a vast bureaucracy based on Europe and out of touch—or thought to be out of touch—and unsympathetic to the needs of other continents.

Drewry and myself had drafted proposals for confederations involving a change in FIFA's statutes and we duly got these accepted for the agenda. By coincidence Argentina and Chile were thinking on somewhat similar lines, and also submitted proposals for a modification of the statutes. We were invited by Argentina to discuss our proposal in advance to see if differences could be ironed out and a united front presented to the Congress. So we arrived in Buenos Aires a week before the Congress in Rio and had fruitful discussions, only slightly disturbed by an agitated telegram from Brazil indicating that our presence in Argentina was not welcome to them. Brazil was the first nation to stage a FIFA Congress in South America and were understandably nervous about any breach of protocol. There was, however, no reason why we should not talk to the Argentinians and we established that their proposals were much less far-reaching. Their main concern was over confederations controlling competitions, whereas we envisaged them dealing with the whole range of football development, including youth tournaments and standards of refereeing. There was amicable agreement that our wider concept embraced theirs.

Jules Rimet introduced the discussion of the proposals with a heavy emphasis on his 'family' concept and his view that change should be gradual and minimal. As he put it, 'FIFA had existed for almost fifty years and it is the only organisation which has succeeded in rallying all the world's Associations. It is true everything is in a state of continuous evolution which the International Federation cannot escape, but it is only with great prudence that its statutory rules, which have proved their value in the course of long years, should be touched.'

Arthur Drewry then spoke on behalf of not only the FA but of Argentina and Chile as well. He finally proposed a Commission to report to the next Congress on what action should be taken and that members of the three countries who made the proposals should be on this small Commission. That proposal was accepted and I was appointed adviser to the working party then set up.

The Rio Congress marked Jules Rimet's thirtieth year as President. He spoke little during meetings, but he was a fine orator when the spirit moved him. At Congresses his main effort was reserved for an opening address which was both a masterly summary of FIFA's progress and emotive statement of his view of football. Extracts from this address to this conference give an indication of the passionate commitment to the game which allowed him to head FIFA for so long, and of those beliefs which motivated him:

This is the first time that the conclave of world football has been held on South American soil, where it gives me great satisfaction to see the representatives of the affiliated Associations foregathered in a manifestation which would demonstrate, were such a demonstration necessary, the perfect unity that holds us together, the spiritual community to which we all adhere with one heart and one will. This [twenty-seventh] Congress is a milestone in the history of FIFA.

Since the London Congress in 1948 world unity of football, the essential goal of FIFA, has been an accomplished fact: unity both moral and material.

The laws of the game are respected throughout the world; the rules laid down by the FIFA are unanimously recognised and applied; its advice and opinion are sought, its arbitration is called for to settle the rare disputes that arise between the Associations. Football is in favour with the crowds, and the number of those who take an active part increases from year to year. The World Cup has become the most important international competition.

These results are not a matter of chance; they are the fruit of voluntary action resolutely pursued, the consequence of the magnificent enthusiasm displayed by an elite of directing minds in all the national Associations, of the work, often obscure but always persistent, of the devoted moving spirits of large and small clubs, of the referees who put up with abuse because they have faith, and finally of the patient plodding of all, apostles and disciples, towards a common ideal that fully deserves to be held aloft. It is by putting forward every effort to attain it that we remain on the right track. It can be expressed in four words: football is a game. It is a game under whatever label it may be played. The professionalism which might seem to deflect football from its true function is a necessity imposed by the very success of the game. . . .

But even though professionalism, or its masked brother 're-muneralism' . . . may make football a 'job', whether full-time or part-time, our sport remains a game. It must remain so for all those who engage in it, and must continue subject to the laws which are its strength and give it its value, as a channel for imparting the finest human qualities.

Discipline freely consented to—team discipline—discipline required by the rules, by the decisions of the referee, by the captain, leads the young man to recognise the benefits of such discipline in the course of the match, and to accept discipline without constraint in the other circumstances of his life. . . .

Loyalty to the spirit of the game, fairness to the adversary, is perhaps the most remarkable quality of football; without it a match would be devoid of all meaning and would return to the condition of the barbarous games of antiquity.

Moderation, too, that major quality; moderation in victory, moderation in defeat, is constantly displayed in a conspicuous degree in football.

And finally, solidarity is not with us a word that has no meaning; imperative in the life of the clubs and in the conduct of matches, it imbues the spirit of the players and brings within their reach the practice of one of the finest of virtues.

Need I remind my hearers of the splendid spirit of solidarity that illuminated the entire world of football on the occasion of the Superga catastrophe, when the Turin club lost its entire team and Italy a large proportion of its best players?

Our aim must be to transfer these idealistic qualities of the game to our everyday life.

There was much in that address to reflect the spirit of the time, and much that the modern footballer could ponder with advantage.

While Rimet had been cautious in his approach to confederation and change in statutes, it was France who gave the vital push to implementation. At Rio there was no more done than set up the working party and provide a few extra seats on the Executive, mainly for Africa, Asia and South America. Delaunay, however, soon called a meeting of the European national Associations in Paris followed by one in Basle, at which the first true Continental Confederation was provisionally formed. There were already existing Confederations in South, North and Central America, but these were concerned almost entirely with competitions and championships and not with the whole range of administrative work.

The European Confederation, UEFA, took shape at the Basle meeting in 1954. The earlier one in Paris had been largely abortive because it seemed a spur-of-the-moment decision by Henri Delaunay to hold it. There was no agenda for the meeting, nor any prior consultation. Dr Barassi, who spoke fluent French, was elected to the chair but difficulties of interpretation made for a lengthy and inconclusive meeting. England, Scotland, and Wales were all represented and we all approved in principle.

When Thommen called the Basle meeting a few months later most of the European nations attended, with a few exceptions such as Wales, Czechoslovakia, and Albania. Barassi was again Chairman with Delaunay of France and Crahay from Belgium acting as Secretaries. At first we seemed likely to lose our way in a procedural wrangle as Poland sought permission to vote for absent Czechoslovakia. To end the argument I proposed that Poland vote for Czechoslovakia while one of our representatives, Joe Mears, should vote on behalf of Wales, who had asked us to represent them. This was passed. After a couple of hours' more talk I asked the Chairman to put a motion to the meeting 'That a European Union should be formed' and this too was passed unanimously.

I then proposed that a 'steering committee' be formed for a year to prepare statutes and regulations for approval and to draft any necessary regulations for a European Cup. Furthermore, I proposed that no member of the FIFA Executive Committee be appointed to avoid overlapping. Among the names I put forward for the steering committee were Dr Josef Gerö of Austria, Dr Munoz Calero of Spain, Sir George Graham of Scotland, Ebbe Schwartz representing the Scandinavian countries, and José Crahay of Belgium. The proposal was approved and a number of meetings followed during the year. I was asked to draft the statutes, regulations and rules for the first Cup competition and these were passed with only minor amendments when we met again in Vienna in March 1955. Sadly Dr Gerö had died a month before, and Henri Delaunay was absent with a fatal illness when we met under the chairmanship of Ebbe Schwartz. The Executive Committee which was then formed included Alfred Frei of Austria, José Crahay, Dr Peco Bauwens, Gustav Sebes of Hungary, and Constantin Constantaras of Greece with Pierre Delaunay, Henri's son, becoming Secretary. So UEFA became reality as the first genuine Confederation. I became a member of the Executive Committee in 1958, and Vice President two years later, though I had to give up this position as soon as I was elected FIFA President—a casualty of my own rule!

Pierre Delaunay was soon to be in the kind of dilemma which often faced me. As Secretary of UEFA and the General Secretary of the French Football Federation—FFF—he was finding the workload too heavy. I was asked to arrange a meeting in Paris in March 1959 between Schwartz, Bauwens, and myself and the then President of the FFF, Pochonet, and three officials of his Federation. There it was put to Pierre that he had to choose between being full-time UEFA Secretary or Secretary of the French Federation as he clearly could not cope with both jobs. To help him we undertook that UEFA Headquarters would move to Paris if he became Secretary. After a night of agonising Pierre finally decided to stay with the FFF. We then had to find new accommodation for UEFA headquarters and Thommen most helpfully provided us with offices at the new 'house of sport' in Berne.

My next proposal was that FIFA's Assistant Secretary, Hans Bangerter, be appointed UEFA Secretary. While I believed him to be highly competent, I knew he was unhappy in his present job and upset to have been told that he would never become FIFA Secretary when Kurt Gassmann, the holder, retired. I had myself seen the excellent work Bangerter had done as publicity manager at the impressive Swiss Physical Recreation Centre at Macolin and had full confidence in him. Hans had already been to a language college here to improve his English and he was to prove a most efficient Secretary and a pleasant working partner.

Although the problem was happily resolved in the end after further difficulties in Hans' appointment I seemed unable to avoid involvement in UEFA's more awkward situations. As the senior Vice President in 1961, the Executive Committee requested me, together with Lo Brunt, Secretary of the Dutch FA, to tell Ebbe Schwartz that the European associations were no longer happy with him as President. My brief was to ask him to give up the office; in return UEFA would propose him for a vacancy as Vice President of FIFA. That was hardly an attractive swap for him or a pleasant assignment for me, particularly as I was a very good friend of Ebbe and his family. However we persuaded him, and Gustav Wiederkehr of Switzerland was elected President with outstanding success at the 1962 UEFA Congress.

Once the European Confederation had been approved FIFA's statutes had to be redrafted and I was asked to make the amendments. Rimet's objection to the formation of the Confederation had been expressed to me as 'decentralisation will destroy FIFA, only direct membership will retain FIFA as one family'. But I was confident that dual membership, properly organised, would add strength.

I submitted the new statutes to the London Congress in 1961, and though they were not universally welcomed, they were adopted as the new basis for FIFA's operations. Eleven years after we had launched the idea Confederations had become fact. And if that seems a long time, it was relatively fast progress for a radical change affecting the whole future of a world game. It is right that such alterations should be considered at length, or you get the kind of upset which has afflicted cricket when Packer and his players tried to force overnight change on the established structure of the game.

Once established, the Confederation had a major role to play, but I had to keep pressing that they did in fact fill their full function as outlined in the paper drafted by me for FIFA in the 1960s as the confederation idea spread to embrace football world-wide:

The growth of international football at all the many levels—schoolboy, youth, 'under-23', 'B', as well as 'A' teams, and so on—needs the guiding hand of bodies responsible to FIFA. Members of the Executive Committees of Confederations are certainly in a position to have a profound effect on the development of football, and the more encouragement they can give to teams and individual players the better. Soccer is still the most popular game in many countries, but it will only keep this pride of place if it is remembered that social habits are changing, and that young people are being offered a wider range of leisure-time pursuits than ever before, many of them much less exacting than soccer. . . .

Because their role is such a vital one, it is important that Confederations should elect officials to FIFA who can spare time to play a fully active part. Ideally, each Confederation should be represented by its President on the FIFA Executive Committee. They, together with a permanent Chairman of Finance, should form a Consultative Committee or General Purposes Committee of FIFA. In this way, continuity—very necessary in such an organisation as FIFA—could be ensured. Too frequent changes of the officials of any body are bound to retard its development.

Consultations have already taken place between the members of the Emergency Committee of FIFA and representatives of the Confederations during which many problems have been solved and ideas exchanged, with the result that projects which have proved successful in one continent are being tried out in others. In my view, Confederations should aim to have full-time Secretaries; only then will they be able to deal adequately with all the current work and, at the same time, to initiate and develop new projects. . . .

To enable Confederations to fulfil their role in world football, (it is necessary that):

1. The statutes of FIFA should be altered so as to allow the constitution of the Executive Committee to include the Presidents of Confederations as Vice Presidents and that they, together with the President and President of the Finance Committee, should then form a General Purposes Committee, thus ensuring continuity and development.

2. Secretaries of Confederations should be full-time paid workers.

3. An educational programme should be introduced in conjunction with FIFA, so that the technical resources of the world can be used to full advantage.

4. The financial resources of FIFA and of Confederations should be utilised for practical purposes connected with the development of the game, as little as possible being spent on Committees and other meetings. Small 'sub-committees' and working parties could undertake more of the routine work at much less cost.

Co-operation and progress will only be achieved if Confederations regard it as their responsibility to provide for all who wish to play football in all countries in their areas and to ensure that the game is never used for any but sporting purposes.

Arthur Drewry's appointment as FIFA President, succeeding Seeldrayers in 1956, gave a fair wind to the Confederation proposals, which he strongly supported. But when the 1961 London Congress passed the new statutes I was myself in the chair as President.

Drewry's death earlier that year was a special sadness for me, as we had travelled and worked together for so long. There had been quite a resemblance between us, and we were often confused. In the Austrian Embassy at a reception the Ambassador's wife came up to me and said, 'Sir Stanley says you will provide us with twenty tickets for tomorrow's match.' 'But I *am* Sir Stanley' was not a response to deter her. 'You cannot play that trick on me,' she answered, 'Sir Stanley himself pointed you out, Mr Drewry.'

Considering his world-wide services to football Drewry was unfortunate not to be knighted, which was an ambition of his. I was told that this was proposed to Mr Churchill when he was considering a sportsman to honour. But following his own sporting interest, he awarded the knighthood to Gordon Richards instead. Certainly Churchill rarely came to watch football and did not appear greatly interested. He did come to Wembley for a war-time match in aid of Lady Churchill's Aid to Russia Fund. He was just back from a wearing trip to meet Roosevelt and spoke little during the game. At the end he started leaving the Royal Box down the narrow side of the staircase and I put out my arm to steady him warning that it was easy to fall. He shrugged it aside: 'Leave me be. I am perfectly capable of falling downstairs myself, thank you.'

Drewry, appropriately enough for a Grimsby FC Director, had prospered in the fish business which allowed him to devote much time to football, and he had been the League's choice as FA Chairman. Drewry gave himself wholeheartedly to his job and this made him a man with whom it was easy to work.

It had never occurred to me that I might be considered as his successor at FIFA, and I played no part in the nomination. I was just past normal retirement age, but still immersed in the FA's work. From my contacts in FIFA I knew that Ernst Thommen of Switzerland was the favoured candidate of the many nominated. The Swiss Secretary, Dr Käser, naturally preferred a close working association with Thommen, who had been President of the Swiss FA and was managing director of the Swiss football pools. In the early stages there was no British nomination at all. Then at a meeting of the International Board in Porthcawl Harry Cavan, President of the Irish FA, proposed that all British Associations nominate me. He had just been with his national team to Czechoslovakia, and the officials there had asked hopefully whether Britain would nominate a successor.

The British members of the Board agreed that if I was proposed they would support me themselves and approach other national Associations to join with them.

Graham Doggart, the new Chairman of the FA, had detailed discussions with me, encouraging me to accept. He was keen to cement our relationship with FIFA and it was apparent that he had someone in mind as a replacement for me. Still, it was not an easy decision. Since paid officials were not eligible it meant I had to give up my salary of £3,000 a year and the flat which went with the FA job. There had been little opportunity for me to save money paid me as a schoolmaster, or as FA Secretary. It meant taking on a new and challenging position just as most men are thinking of retirement. It meant the risk of giving up the FA post and then not being re-elected by FIFA nine months later, though Graham Doggart assured me that I would anyway be kept on as a consultant. And in fact when I finally agreed to let my name go forward, it was in the belief that there was little hope of being elected.

Ernst Thommen seemed to me certain to be elected. He was a Vice President of FIFA and was already acting as President since Drewry's death, a position which gave him every opportunity to canvass for votes. While I was a member of the FIFA Referees' World Cup and Olympic Committees I was in no position to make appeals for support. Dr Käser, the newly appointed FIFA Secretary, and a keen supporter of Thommen, had also prejudiced my possible election by circulating a memo to members stating that as paid officials were not eligible to be members of the Executive Committee, this probably ruled me out. He was informed that from the date of my nomination I had ceased to be paid and was acting only in an honorary capacity, as the FA again made clear.

Thommen, however, made the mistake of putting the election of the President on the agenda for the extraordinary Congress in London, which was arranged to decide the alterations to the Statutes, as he thought more delegates would be present there than at the Congress scheduled for Chile in 1962 at the time of the World Cup.

There were other strong candidates apart from myself and Thommen, such as Professor Andrejevic of Jugoslavia and Dr Barassi of Italy, though the latter finally withdrew just before the election. There were long arguments going on at the Executive Committee meetings prior to the Congress about my eligibility as an ex-paid official, and whether the election should take place at an extraordinary Congress. There was also some misinterpretation in the French version of the statutes. These arguments continued during the first part of the Congress until it was resolved that I was eligible and that the election should take place. I was not present when the first ballot was held as I had to leave early with Ernest Miller, my senior staff member, in order to arrange the seating at the Mansion House for the lunch the Lord Mayor was giving to the delegates.

When they arrived I learnt the result of the ballot which was 35 votes for me, 18 for Thommen, and 14 for Andrejevic. The necessary two-thirds majority was not obtained and a second ballot was necessary after lunch. For the first time I began to realise that I might indeed become President, and reflected a little anxiously on how it would affect my life. The outside chance looked like coming off, and I was not mentally prepared for it. So it was in a mood of doubt and self-searching rather than elation that I finally heard the announcement that I was to be President. Thommen had withdrawn before the second ballot in which I received 51 votes to Andrejevic's 14.

It had been a difficult decision for me to choose between continuing as FA Secretary or accepting the Presidency of FIFA, particularly as there was so much in hand at the FA. Already with

Walter Winterbottom I had made the preparations for the FA Centenary celebrations in 1963 and would naturally have liked to have seen them through. In addition, although the World Cup to be held in England was five years distant Walter and I had already completed the detailed plans. That too I would have liked to organise and had been much encouraged by one Council member writing to me in June 1961 to welcome the forty-page memorandum drawn up by Walter and myself so enthusiastically:

> The index alone proves what a comprehensive, precise, and forward looking document this is, and in point of fact it would really enable the Football Association to go into action and stage the World Cup almost any time. I was particularly impressed with the four pages 'Statistics and Analysis' under Finance, which is a matter of such great importance. Everything seems to have been clearly set out including the committees required, schedule of dates, grounds and their requirements, travel and accommodation. The detail is remarkable even down to the six suggestions of the form souvenir gifts might take and the note about the possible clash of dates with the Wimbledon tennis.

Though all the preliminary work for the World Cup was done, that was too far ahead for any realistic expectation on my part of being the man to implement the plan. But I still hoped to be actively involved with the Centenary celebrations. Indeed I was not convinced myself that it was impossible to continue as honorary Secretary of the FA as well as FIFA President. I had after all acted as honorary Secretary of FIFA as well as Secretary of the FA without finding any intolerable strain of loyalties or too great a workload. The reverse situation should not have been too difficult. However, my Chairman, Graham Doggart, had determined early on that this was not possible because the two jobs might involve a clash of interests. I received assurances however that I would continue for a period as honorary Secretary, and thereafter in a consultative capacity.

Now, however, the words 'urgency' and 'emergency' began to be bandied about in relation to appointing a successor after my appointment as FIFA President on September 28th. The Chairman and Officers asked the Council to approve a recommendation that I be appointed honorary Secretary 'until the date, not later than June 1st 1962, fixed for the new Secretary to take office'. The Council approved this, but there were immediate anxieties. My own worry was that my appointment as FIFA President had to be confirmed in the next FIFA Congress in Chile at almost the same time as was now being set as the last date for a new Secretary to take office. It was a natural worry that I might find myself out of *both* jobs if the FA did not wait to see what happened.

Others were concerned for different reasons. I had a letter from Major Michael Hawkins, private secretary to the Duke of Gloucester, the then President of the Football Association:

> I am directed by the Duke of Gloucester to say that he was very relieved to hear from you today that you are willing and able to continue to watch over the interests of the Football Association and to continue carrying out the duties of Secretary in an honorary capacity whilst you hold the World football office to which you have recently been elected. His Royal Highness is particularly anxious that this arrangement should, in fact, be continued, and indeed when he said that he would remain as President until after the Centenary Year, had assumed you would still be acting as Secretary during that important year.

The League appeared equally anxious, because I had always gone out of my way to cultivate an easy relationship with them. I had a private letter from one Council member saying that he had seen the League President, Joe Richards, because he wished to make three points to him. First that the new Secretary should not be appointed until after the 100th birthday of the FA, and possibly not until after the World Cup; second that there was no valid reason why I could not combine my new obligation to FIFA with my responsibilities to the FA; and third that the FA would lose prestige by severing ties with me just when my world position might enhance this. He went on, 'With all these points I found Joe Richards in complete agreement. Len Shipman assured me that all the members of the Management Committee of the Football League are appalled at the situation that has arisen and they are unanimous in their desire to retain your *active* association with us as *long as possible*.' The upshot was that Lt Col Linnitt of Dorset County proposed at the December meeting that the words 'not later than 1st June' be deleted.

It was soon clear that the motion if put would be carried by a large majority. It was also clear that if it was, and my honorary secretaryship was extended, a difficult working relationship was inevitable with my Chairman and some Officers. To save embarrassment for them at the time, and for me later, I accepted a compromise. Linnitt withdrew his motion on the understanding that, as the minutes later recorded, 'The Chairman further reminded the Council that Sir Stanley had been assured that the Association would be glad, after his ceasing to hold secretarial office, to use his services in an advisory capacity, especially in connection with the Centenary celebrations in 1963.' In fact, except in so far as use was made of the detailed plans I had left, I was not consulted again. More important to me however was the evidence of support and trust for me from almost the whole Council. In writing to thank Linnitt I expressed these feelings:

> Thank you for your sympathetic speech to the Council on Monday. There was no doubt that if your proposal had gone to the vote it would have been carried almost unanimously.
>
> That being the case, the Council will have to watch most carefully the type of man appointed to succeed me. The double first and triple blue may be all right for the rugby world but not for soccer. If people like you and I have met with any success in our football relations it is because we have been able to appreciate the feelings of the man on the terraces as well as the 'Gent' in the Royal Box.

In any organisation like the FA or FIFA there is always a difficult relationship between a working Chairman or President, and the full-time paid Secretary. The Chairman's is the senior appointment, but the day-to-day matters go through the Secretary and inevitably he is the man with the most contacts and the ability to get things done. In my case this tendency was intensified by the length of time I had been in the job, which meant that so many people came to me for advice. I appreciated that this could be difficult for Graham Doggart, who was newly appointed while I had been so long in the job. Fortunately, I had worked harmoniously before with Graham, who had been an outstanding footballer in his day. At a time when the Selection Committee members often lacked practical experience I had pressed his appointment as selector, although it was unusual for a University representative to be on the International Selection Committee. And while the situation caused us some problems, our established friendship enabled these to be overcome.

It was all the easier for me to understand Graham's position, as the reverse applied at FIFA. Dr Käser had only recently taken over as Secretary from Kurt Gassmann and was taking efficient control of the job. My predecessor, Arthur Drewry, had left most of the detail work to the Secretariat. But I had been so long and so deeply involved with FIFA's work that I aimed to master all aspects of it rather than be in any sense a figurehead President. So it may well have appeared to Dr Käser that I was undertaking work he would have expected to do himself. To avoid confusion, and relieve him of the burden of keeping me informed of all that was going on, I set up frequent discussion periods with him and René Courte, the able Assistant Secretary. As a rountine I arranged that I came with a list of matters on which I wanted information and they came with a list of what they thought I needed to know. If Käser omitted anything, then Courte usually had it on his list. So not only was I fully informed but the follow-up discussion instantly settled outstanding points.

I missed the same full exchange of views at the FA when there was no attempt by the Appointments Committee to sound out my view of the qualities required of an FA Secretary, or of the best of the seventy or so applicants. Perhaps it was known I would favour Walter Winterbottom as a successor. He had an international reputation, was acceptable at all levels of the game, was brilliant administratively and was a forward thinker of sound, but original judgement.

No doubt for those who felt too much had devolved onto me for too long our close association may have proved a handicap to their acceptance of Walter. But what really defeated him was a Press campaign on his behalf. It was bad enough that the papers should trumpet that Winterbottom was the obvious choice. It was worse that they should in some cases make bitter, unjustified and derogatory attacks on his main rival, Denis Follows. Some who had told me they were certain to vote for Walter, now came to say that they were not going to be dictated to by the Press and would change to Follows to show their independence. Many were particularly incensed when, just before the meeting, a Sunday paper listed details of the three men thought to be short-listed. The article spoke in glowing terms of Walter's record and was generous to George Clark, an ex-Lieutenant Commander, RN, who refereed the Chelsea *v* Dynamo game in 1945; but Follows was headlined as 'cool, pedantic, plain, prim' and referred to as 'plump, red of face, a nailbiter, horn-rimmed spectacled and nobody's fool'. That offensive comment may well have been a vital factor in giving Denis an overwhelming majority over Walter by 50 votes to 20.

There was nothing wrong in the choice in itself, but they seemed to me to have plumped for the good at the expense of the excellent. In a roundabout way I had myself been responsible for Denis becoming FA Honorary Treasurer and being in a position to challenge for the job. For years I pressed for the Universities Athletic Union to have a representative on the FA as had Oxford and Cambridge. This was opposed by many county Associations who did not feel they contributed enough to the running of the game to justify it. Eventually, however, they accepted the logic of my argument that soccer can only be healthy if it is properly supported in the schools, and since so many teachers come via universities, it was desirable for them to be fully represented. As Chairman of the UAU Denis became their member and had much of the negotiating skill one would expect of the Secretary of the British Airline Pilots' Association. He has a tidy mind, is a master of detail, and has always been able to present his views concisely and forcefully. Appreciating his efficiency, I soon involved him in the Treasurer's work. His BALPA office was in the same building as that of the British Olympic Association, with which he is also involved, and Lancaster Gate was on his route to work. As I was keen to have all the cheques and payments disposed of on a regular weekly basis, he was in all ways the right man to take over the Honorary Treasurer's work, and was soon making significant contribution to the running of the FA. So there was no question of his being an unsuitable choice. And indeed sport as a whole was to benefit, for Walter naturally would not stay after being passed over. Fortunately there was a demanding position waiting for him due to the retirement of Phyllis Colson as General Secretary of the CCPR. He filled that void and has since done outstanding work at the CCPR and later as Director of the Sports Council which earned him a well-deserved knighthood. At the FA it needed two men of stature, Alf Ramsey and Allen Wade, to fill the gap he left. That was the measure of his value to English football.

Denis and I were occasionally to find ourselves representing different points of view, as it was inevitable that FIFA and the FA were not always in accord. He had his way over the future of the Fairs Cup in conflict with me, and I had mine when he tried to prevent me from replying on behalf of FIFA at the FA Centenary banquet. But in general we had a satisfactory relationship, neither expecting to interfere with the other's field except where FIFA and the FA had a conflict of opinion. It was no surprise to me that the Football Association never implemented its undertaking to call on me for advice. The same was to happen to Denis in turn: inevitably the new men want to be seen to do things their way. If you are not there you're done without.

Leaving the FA meant reorganising my life and facing difficult financial problems. The flat at Lancaster Gate had insulated me from many of these. Now I had to move to a small flat in Ladbroke Road, not too far from the centre of London, and also set up a *pied-à-terre* in Zurich so that rooms were permanently available to me there on a bed-and-breakfast basis. I had travelled a lot in the past. Now I was living in London, commuting to Switzerland, and making flying business trips world-wide. At sixty-six I had the most exciting and the most exacting thirteen years of my life still in prospect.

12

The Inter-Cities Fairs Cup

●●●

In the 'Post-War Memorandum' which aimed to chart the FA's course in the years of reconstruction, I had stressed the need for international exchange and competition at club as well as national level. The World Cup had existed since 1930 and clubs did occasionally indulge in friendly matches or tours. But there was then no European club competition, no European Cup, or Cup Winners' Cup. This was one of the developments much on my mind in the fifties. In the wake of war there was a new spirit of co-operation within Europe and football was proving an ideal medium for healing old animosities and establishing new friendships. But in the aftermath of fighting and destruction, immense problems of organisation and rebuilding had made an extensive interchange of footballing teams hard to organise. My chance to assist in the development of European club competition came when I and Dr Ottorino Barassi of Italy were approached by Ernst Thommen of Basle, the most influential man in Swiss football. He, too, had been interested for years in the idea of promoting international football at a level below competition between national teams. And he had taken the opportunity of the celebrations of the Swedish FA's fifty years to sound out others. Many of those he met and talked with in Stockholm were favourably disposed to the idea. So he approached Barassi and me to see if FIFA could help. He had come to the right people. For Dr Barassi was also of a like mind on the role of football in developing international co-operation. He had been one of the keenest supporters of the World Cup competition, and indeed had kept the golden Jules Rimet Trophy hidden under his bed during the war. He could not bear the thought that Italy, the holders, should lose the trophy and but for his care and ingenuity it might well have been looted, or scrounged, or 'won' by any of a variety of armies.

We immediately welcomed the proposal and formed ourselves into a small 'initiative' committee, not as the 'three wise men', but as the three who were fired with enthusiasm for the project. Barassi and I were well placed to ensure that FIFA accepted the new competition and that the competition was framed in a way acceptable to FIFA. My main concern was that this should be a competition run for the clubs and by the clubs, organised in accordance with *their* wishes. My English experience had shown me this was both desirable and possible. That was how we had let the League develop, running its own affairs largely independent of the FA, but in close co-operation with it and conforming to its rules.

This principle was accepted by the others, and was to be one of the distinctive features of the competition. It was indeed to be a chief reason for its outstanding success, and also of its destruction, when it was finally done to death by, of all people, the British Football Associations.

We had other difficult decisions to take at the foundation meeting of the three of us in April. Our aim was simple: 'To further international sporting relations and to contribute to the friendship amongst nations.' And we aimed to do so by matches on an inter-city basis providing a new level of international competition and so bringing more people together by means of the games.

Whom to invite into such a competition was our first concern. But consideration of our aim brought us an obvious and satisfactory solution. Before the war representative teams drawn from various cities had played each other on a friendly basis. We saw this as the established base on which to build. And when we came to consider choice of cities we opted for a competition between those cities which had staged international trade fairs and exhibitions. This had three advantages. Such cities were all large and were widely spread, East as well as West. They already had an organisation of a sort based on Paris. And such a competition might increase international co-operation on a much wider base than football, bringing a new form of contact for administrators and businessmen as well.

So the Inter-Cities Fairs Cup was born in 1955. Since we had designed it to be run by the clubs themselves, with those in the competition taking the future decisions, we expected that it would keep changing in shape and size to meet changing needs. And so it proved. The idea of one composite team representative of a whole city soon proved difficult to arrange. As commitments grew so cities began to nominate just one club to represent them, until it was clubs, not cities, which entered. The leisurely pace of the first competition was speeded for similar reasons, so that the final competition was five times as large, yet finished three times as quickly, as the first. The limitation to cities with fairs was soon ended as the competition's popularity brought a flood of new applicants to join, and as existing members decided to widen the scope. All this was as the three of us had wanted. We put a premium on the clubs themselves deciding what they required, and on the organisation being flexible enough to adapt rapidly.

We foresaw also that our relations with national Associations would have to develop naturally, but carefully, with the onus on us to see we did not clash with them or with UEFA, if this could be avoided. UEFA and the national Associations, through FIFA, had agreed the competition's start and its organisation, for which I drafted the regulations.

During its sixteen years of competition there were only two serious complaints against the Fairs Cup. The first involved the English FA's concern that national Associations and UEFA did not control disciplinary measures. The complaint arose after a fight on the field between Chelsea and Roma players. The Fairs Cup Committee responded rapidly by amending the disciplinary regulations of the Fairs Cup so that they could conform to those of UEFA. The other main complaint was by the Scottish FA that each competing city could only be represented by one club. This regulation too was promptly amended to meet their requirement, though in fact exceptions had already been allowed. Yet these two points, so quickly and reasonably resolved by the Fairs Cup Committee, were dredged up again by England and Scotland as their only reasons for leading a move which killed off the Fairs Cup. It died finally after Leeds had won the trophy in 1970/71, then lost a play-off match in Barcelona against the first holders for the right to keep the Cup in perpetuity.

What the Fairs Cup had achieved was summed up in a foreword I wrote for its official history:

The competition was a pioneering effort; it began life as a tournament between representative sides drawn from cities where international trade fairs were held. In the post-war years such cities were Birmingham, Copenhagen, Frankfurt, Lausanne, Leipzig, London, Milan, Stockholm, Vienna and Zagreb.

In the first competition over half a million spectators in ten European countries attended the games. By 1970/71 over eighteen million people had paid to watch games in the competition. The clubs taking part during those sixteen years had benefited financially by about £283,000, a considerable contribution to European football.

More important was the contribution to the cause of international football in Europe; the opportunities in international competition were extended to a much wider range of clubs and players.

The competition, after an uncertain beginning, became one of the most successful club competitions ever created; there had been nothing like it before, and none of the other European competitions had been mounted. It grew to take in sixty-four clubs from twenty-nine European countries.

It was unique in another particular: the competition was organised and administered directly by an executive committee elected by the participating clubs; it was directly responsible to them, and was organised in their interest and for their immediate benefit.

The Fairs Cup competition became too successful. This success, coupled with its democratic organisation, caused various agencies to seek to take control of it.

The competition goes on after 1970/71 under new auspices. I hope, in its new form, it will be allowed to continue to make the valuable contribution to international football that it did during the first sixteen years of its existence.

The beginning was indeed uncertain. The first match was launched only six weeks after our 'initiative' committee held an inaugural meeting open to all interested parties. On June 4th 1955 London beat Basle 5–0 in the St Jacob Stadium to start the 'Inter-Cities Fairs Cup', as it was called before later becoming the 'European Fairs Cup'. But it was almost three years before that first competition was completed when on May 1st 1958 Barcelona beat London 6–0 in Barcelona to win the final 8–2 on aggregate. The twelve participants from nine different countries had started in four groups. But the home and away matches took time to fit into existing programmes and representative teams, perhaps involving players from five or more clubs in a city like London, were difficult to organise when so many clubs had conflicting commitments. Like all the problems that arose, these early difficulties were smoothed over in time and in accordance with the wishes of the clubs involved, and the competition was soon running so well that it kept expanding under the weight of demand.

At first the competition was dominated by Spanish clubs, with

Barcelona, Valencia, and Real Zaragoza winning six of the first eight competitions. Not until the tenth did an English Club win when Leeds beat Ferencvaros of Hungary by the only goal of the two-leg final. England indeed established late dominance in this Cup, winning all the last four competitions through Arsenal, Newcastle, and Leeds again. So it seemed odd that the British Associations should kill it off —or at least kill off its independence. From time to time UEFA had considered doing so, but it was at the Annual Meeting in 1966 that they decided to act. It was Tom Reid of the Scottish FA who made the proposal. He was supported by the FA Secretary, Denis Follows. Follows pointed out that though the competition was the most popular in Europe from the point of view of the Clubs participating it was not either directly or indirectly subject to control by the national Associations. This view prevailed on some others, and the take-over was voted by 11 votes to 10 with 11 abstentions. The British Associations all voted together and their four votes were clearly decisive in the single-vote win.

The odd part of their thinking was that not only was this an un-necessary and regressive act, but it was quite contrary to the wishes of the Leagues. In view of the indecisive nature of the voting the President of UEFA delayed implementing the decision, but it was con-firmed at the 1968 Congress by the same narrow margin, and with Scotland and England again taking the lead. In April 1968 the Foot-ball League members of the joint liaison committee recorded in the minutes that they opposed the take-over. They also recorded later: 'This matter had been discussed in the Professional Committee of UEFA, which is composed of representatives of professional Leagues, and in every case it has been stated categorically that neither the Leagues nor their member clubs wished to see any interference with the present organisation of the Inter-Cities Fairs Cup competition, which was run by professionals for the benefit of professional clubs and was, in fact, a successful, well run competition.' That record was part of a paper accompanying the agenda for an extraordinary meeting of the English Football League on November 7th 1969 which not surprisingly included the motion 'That the Football League clubs deprecate the action of the FA in supporting the take-over of the European Fairs Cup competition by UEFA without prior consulta-tion with member Clubs.'

Naturally, I have a biased view of the take-over of a competition with whose growth I was so closely connected. But the take-over achieved just what we had tried to avoid. A competition which had been flexible in development and involved an even wider variety of clubs settled into a narrower, more rigid mould—or rut—without the clubs themselves having a say in its future.

More important, it seemed to illustrate an attitude which has led to some unnecessary confrontation in recent years between the FA and the League. My own outlook had always been that the FA must stand up for any vital part of principle and not let the League dictate on such matters. Yet equally it should avoid conflict where possible, and particularly where the prime interest involved was the League's. The FA had given the League a great deal of independence to develop as it wished and in my view should always respect that independence, just as the League must respect the FA's overall supervision. Finally, it had always been of vital concern to me that where conflict was likely we should head it off, if practical, by prior consultation. To that end I arranged early in my FA career for discussions with League officials in advance of all FA general meetings so that any conflicts of interest were foreseen and removed or recognised. But here the FA seemed to be gratuitously flouting the League and without consultation. And the ill-feeling that generated no doubt played a part in other unfortunate conflicts, such as the League's growing reluctance to release players for training for England teams, and the relegation of the once popular Home Internationals to the fag-end of the season when interest is drained.

I had tried to avert the final adverse vote in 1968 by a memorandum stressing the merits of the Fairs Cup as it stood. The three main points on which I harped were:

1. Match attendances showed that the competition was popular in all countries concerned.
2. The equal division of nett profits among all participating clubs was universally welcomed (and in the final competition that amounted to £1,000 profit to each of sixty-four clubs).
3. No member Association appeared opposed to the competition in principle. In fact most valued it as giving more clubs the opportunity to compete at international level.

So it was a considerable disappointment to me that the feelings of the clubs should be ignored. The disappointment was the more acute that the FA should take such a leading role in what I regarded as a niggling and retrograde act. The illogicality of their position is perhaps clearer today. Then they stressed the need to control a competition which was already well under control, risking a clash with the League to achieve this. Yet a few years later the FA has allowed teams of professional players, members of a number of clubs, to undertake foreign tours unrelated to, and unsupervised by, any national Association. That is a much more difficult development over which to exercise control, and one which really has latent dangers.

There is never any point continuing to fight lost battles; and once this was clearly lost my concern was to salvage the best possible solution from the wreck of a competition. That made me unpopular with the more wrathful members of the organising committee, who wanted to wind it up and terminate it, rather than hand over their success to UEFA. I had to remind them that our aim had been to improve international co-operation and there was no reason why part of what we had tried to do could not still be accomplished by UEFA, as indeed it has been. The last Congress of the European Fairs Cup competition was held at Sitges in September 1971. I asked, as Chairman, that those who attended take pride in what they had achieved in that its very excellence had led to the take-over. Further, I asked that all should support the new competition and wish it well. To my old friend, Hans Bangerter, UEFA's General Secretary, who was present at the meeting, I wished equal success in handling the future of the UEFA Cup as it was now to be. Though I knew he was in no way to blame for the demise of the Fairs Cup, I could not resist an unusual moment of sarcasm as I remarked that it was nice to be praised for our success by 'the powerful organisation which has crushed us out of existence'. Hans was well aware that this was intended not for him, but for the eleven responsible, including all the British representatives, whose judgement I felt had so sadly erred.

Much of what Thommen, Barassi and I had hoped for in starting this competition had indeed been realised. So this was not for me the death of a dream. It was a moment to look back in thankfulness on achievement and on the personal friendships along the way.

The misgivings I had about the future of the Fairs Cup were largely dispelled when Hans Bangerter became responsible for it. The competition may have become more limited and rigid than we envisaged, but UEFA has ensured that it is exceptionally well run. Under Hans' direction it remains a worthwhile competition, and our efforts in starting it have not been wasted. UEFA took over from us a highly competent Secretary, Pierre Joris. Joris was a modest, meticulously thorough man who was a director of the Swiss pools and though he had the offer of continuing in the job as a full-time member of the UEFA staff he declined it as he felt he had better prospects in Switzerland's 'Sport Toto'.

Though I had made some contribution to the Fairs Cup it was truly Thommen's brainchild. Later he was to be tragically killed when, as he was returning from the Swiss Cup final of 1967 his car ran off the road and hit a concrete pill-box. His son Harry specially asked me to speak at my old friend's memorial service, and I was struck then by the range and the depth of feeling of the tributes to him. He had well deserved such high regard and the world of football had cause to be grateful to him.

The Fairs Cup was the first of the major European club competitions, but I was less directly involved with the most prestigious of them all, the European Cup. This was the brainchild of the French journalist, Gabriel Hanot, editor of the sports paper *L'Equipe*. He was rightly critical of exuberant claims in English newspapers that Wolves were club champions of the world because in 1954 they beat at Molineux the Russian team Spartak, and then they narrowly defeated the Hungarian Honved side, which was almost the national XI with Puskas, Kocsis and all. Hanot was sceptical of English euphoria: 'We must wait for Wolves to visit Moscow or Budapest before we proclaim their invincibility. There are other clubs of international prowess, notably Milan and Real Madrid . . .' Hanot's paper then outlined plans for a European tournament to give a practical test to the jingoistic boasts made whenever one important match was won.

Hanot had just asked me to place his daughter with an English family, and I had arranged this for him. He now discussed with me how he could promote the competition. I advised him that this was not possible for a paper, but since he had aroused wide interest in his idea, he should call a meeting of leading club officials who could help him launch the competition through the European Football Association. There had been limited competition in regions of Euope before—the Mitropa Cup before the war, the Latiflu Cup after it. But Hanot's idea embraced the whole of Europe and his enthusiasm soon had it launched to spectacular success. The French had a talent for instigating great competitions, but it was Spain who dominated the early years of the European Cup with the remarkable Real Madrid side winning for the first five years. Perhaps the best game I have ever seen was that fifth successive victory in the European Cup final, when with 127,620 other spectators at Hampden Park I watched Real beat Eintracht Frankfurt 7–3 with Puskas and Di Stefano sharing the goals in an exhilarating display of the attacking skills which made them the two greatest players of their era.

The League at first refused to allow English clubs to enter, barring

Chelsea when the competition started in 1955. The stated reason for this new dose of isolationism was a fear of fixture congestion. The following year Manchester United were also told not to enter, but Matt Busby was eager to try out his fine young side against the best of Europe. He and his Chairman, Harold Hardman, came to see me for advice. I suggested they read the League rules carefully, but added: 'It's your ground, and your players. As long as you meet your contractual requirements to fulfil League fixtures with your best team there is nothing to prevent you from entering. The FA certainly has no objection.'

Manchester United did indeed lead us into the European Cup, despite the Football League; and it was appropriate that they should be the first English club side to win the trophy in 1968. That was a night to remember as Wembley became a 'Son et lumière' soccer pageant with the great stadium ablaze with light and noise. An unusual headed goal by Bobby Charlton, an equaliser by the busy Graca, and a magical save by Stepney from Eusebio, prolonged the suspense into extra time. Then Benfica were swept away by the stamina and attacking skills of Best, Charlton, Kidd, and Aston. For two men particularly that was triumph from the ashes of disaster. For how could Matt Busby and Bobby Charlton not think back to that other European Cup day of agony in 1958 when so many United players perished on the way home from a 3–3 draw with Red Star of Belgrade which had put them through to the semi-final? The crash on Munich's snow-covered airport shocked the country as if it were some national tragedy embracing us all. When the news came I was in Edinburgh arranging an annual charity match there. At once I returned to Lancaster Gate, although there was nothing to do but grieve the death of so many fine players. From my own sense of shock and loss I could appreciate the wave of emotion which swept the country, as if this was a truly national disaster.

Attending the memorial service for Duncan Edwards was the moment which touched me most deeply. He had fought so hard for his life, and he had been such a young giant of a player. This was the man round whom England could have built a team for a decade. Quiet and modest off the field, he was an irresistible force in play, a wing-half who snuffed out attacks or scored goals with the same ferocious power. Some of his goals remain vivid in the memory. The most vital was a surging run and a blistering shot which sent England on the way to a 3–1 win in Berlin over World Champions West Germany in 1956. But even more remarkable were two goals in a 'B' International in Bratislava against Czechoslovakia. Our forwards could find no way past a stout defence, but once in each half Duncan arrowed in a shot from twenty-five yards or more to leave the goalkeeper helpless. 'That's how you should do it,' he called to Johnny Haynes and his fellow forwards. But Duncan's talent was unique.

It was not only a great Manchester United side destroyed at Munich airport. A fine England team disintegrated as well. We had just beaten Brazil for the only time in our history, winning 4–2 at Wembley despite missing two penalties. France we had defeated even more easily. Brazil was shortly to win the World Cup in Sweden, and France to finish third. Had Roger Byrne, a left-back with the speed and skill of a winger, Tommy Taylor, a centre-forward with the all-round ability reminiscent of Lawton, and the incomparable Duncan Edwards still been playing, England might well have won in 1958 instead of waiting another eight years. The sadness was heightened for me by the death of Frank Swift, one of the writers with the party. 'Big Swifty' had been one of the game's characters. As a nineteen-year-old Swift kept goal for Manchester City in that Cup Final I refereed in 1934. As he heard my final whistle, with Manchester ahead 2–1 after being down at half-time, Frank fainted on his goal-line from the excitement. That was the only time I have known him quiet. On so many England tours he was the lively humourist who kept the party amused without ever overdoing it. Out of all that black misery, this was the most personal loss of an old friend. In a lifetime of football there has been nothing to stir me as deeply as the Munich disaster.

13

Final Achievement

●●●

The years past the normal age of retirement have been some of the most fruitful of my working life. I was sixty-six when I was first elected President of FIFA, but I certainly did not see this as being pensioned off with honour. Rather it was the climax of a career for which I had served a long, but wholly enjoyable apprenticeship. Here was the chance to use all my experience and to indulge my lifelong interest in international co-operation. FIFA's Referees' Committee once marked me highly for refereeing 'in a large manner'. And I hoped the same might be said of my presidency, in that I was determined FIFA should take the broadest view looking at problems from a world viewpoint, not from Europe's or South America's. I was determined too that FIFA should keep the game moving smoothly on without undue checks in the pattern of development.

My close connection with FIFA had given me an insight into possible areas of improvement, and I started from the simple philosophy that innovations which had worked when introduced in England might well be valuable in a wider context. And my own enthusiasms would be kept in control by the need to get wide acceptance of any change. For another simple feature of my philosophy was that if your idea was not good enough to persuade others of its value, then it was in any case not good enough to implement. For me, consultation and obtaining a reasonable consensus was the best way of working, rather than trying to force one's own views regardless of others' opinions.

Considering the funds and influence it had, FIFA had seemed to me to be unnecessarily limited in scope, keeping to traditionally narrow functions. These were impressively performed, but there was clearly much more it could do and I had to lead it to a more adventurous frame of mind. To achieve that, a drastic change of structure was necessary to enable FIFA to cope with its expanding membership and opportunities. But this had to be seen as a gradual evolutionary process rather than as a revolutionary new concept, which might have aroused opposition from existing members. Having pinned my faith on the importance of Confederations in keeping FIFA both unified and flexible, my first aim was to strengthen these, pressing for each to have a full-time Secretary and pressing FIFA to give financial support where needed.

The next important step was the setting up of the specialist committees to support a more extensive service. Five new ones were formed and named: Technical, Consultative, Medical, Press and Publications, and Disciplinary. The Technical Development Committee, approved by the Executive Committee in 1963, was of prime importance starting under the chairmanship of Valentin Granatkin until Harry Cavan took over in 1969. Under its direction a panel of lecturers and instructors was established, speaking a wide range of languages, so that we were able to organise courses for coaches and referees worldwide. At first we also used several itinerant lecturers to give talks in countries or continents requesting them. But in 1967 Dettmar Cramer, the excellent West German coach, was appointed FIFA's main instructor, and during the seven years of his contract visited almost every affiliated country. Dettmar also directed for the Asian Confederation FIFA coaching schools lasting up to three months. Forty-two applicants from 12 different countries attended the first in Tokyo in 1969, and numbers increased for the subsequent schools in Kuala Lumpur and Tehran.

Walter Winterbottom was a most valuable member of the Technical Committee and in 1966 headed a group formed to study technical aspects of the play, refereeing, and organisation, of the final round of the World Cup. Their report was included in FIFA's general World Cup report and became a standard feature of it. As an aid to referees the Technical Committee also had films made such as *Referee and Linesmen—a Team*, and made tapes of any important talks given by members of the Referees' Committee or panel lecturers. At their request I also produced a handbook for use by referee-instructors and a history of the Laws.

A main feature of the Committee's work was to be a grant-aid scheme to help develop the game in the newly emerging football nations. To assess needs and possibilities at first hand I travelled widely and made copious reports on the need for grants. My emphasis on the educational aspect brought the occasional exasperated comment: 'He's playing the schoolmaster again.' But Valentin Granatkin and Harry Cavan gave staunch support in converting the Executive to these ideas, and in 1964 I was able to put the wide-ranging plan before them knowing it would be acceptable. A united decision was essential for this had to be something in which FIFA believed and not just a hobby horse of my own. With vital support from Dr Barassi, as Chairman of the Finance Committee, I was able to get the grant-aid scheme, to cost some 500,000 Swiss francs, launched in these positive terms: 'The Executive Committee having decided to formulate grant-aided policy and having approved, in principle, the recommendations made by the Finance and Technical Committees and the proposals made by the President following his visits to many countries, particularly the emerging countries, and also the suggestions by Presidents of the Confederations, the following scheme is outlined. . . .'

The scheme was designed to aid a wider use of coaching courses and trainers' courses; to give financial support to enable all Confederations to implement my recommendation that they had a full-time paid Secretary; to encourage conferences on coaching; to produce technical films and make them available to members; to build a library of text-books available in several languages; to help Confederations with the administrative and equipment expenses involved in improving their own courses; to encourage tournaments, particularly at youth and amateur level; and to assist emerging nations to invite leading teams from other parts of the world.

Valentin Granatkin of Russia was an ideal choice to chair the Technical Committee in its early days. He was a most helpful member of the Executive Committee of which he was both senior Vice President and Deputy President. He was always very thorough in his preparation, having read translations and memorised all the various committee reports and minutes, and his comments were shrewd, concise, and constructive.

The Medical Committee started as an *ad hoc* arrangement in 1966 to supervise anti-doping tests during the World Cup, but it soon became a standing committee with a wider brief. It acted as an advisory board for the Executive Committee on all medical problems, gave advice to national associations, carried out any special projects required and undertook scientific research into football's medical problems.

The Press and Publications Committee was formed to establish the close relationship with press, radio, and television which I felt to be so desirable for an international body. It was also intended to improve communications with national associations, and as a contribution to this I had the six-monthly FIFA Bulletin changed to a monthly magazine, *FIFA News*.

The Disciplinary Committee was required mainly for tournaments organised by FIFA and was intended to ensure that there was reasonable uniformity in the penalties awarded. To assist its early work I wrote a memorandum on disciplinary measures which was adopted by the 1964 Congress as the basis for punishments which the national associations should apply.

To emphasise my own interest in all these new committees, I attended every meeting of each one of them throughout my thirteen years as President.

Apart from making such assistance available through FIFA, it was also part of my job to advise countries on how to organise their football to ensure success. That was the question so many asked me when I visited them. A lot of them wanted some magical short-cut formula for producing World Cup-winning teams. Always I had to warn them that there was no way of buying instant success. Building it was a long, slow process which I would outline for them. First, it has to start in the schools, with proper coaching and with enthusiasm for the game encouraged. Then a sound base is needed of Clubs and facilities covering the whole country. To that must be added a nation-wide coaching scheme. There need to be youth and intermediate teams as feeders for a national side. Top-level teams from other countries have to be played and studied as part of the long and humbling learning process. Where others have a century of development and experience behind them, there is no hope of emulating or outstripping them in a decade. Buying in a Puskas or a Revie cannot suddenly give you a national team to compete with the best in Europe or South America. The top will never be right until the foundations are solid, and that demands perseverance, patience and commonsense endeavour over many years.

This was not always a popular message for football is the glory game where victory *now* is so important. As one of my FIFA colleagues used to comment, 'The only way to satisfy the craving for immediate achievement is to change the laws so that both sides win.' All I could do was to help them face reality, to persuade FIFA to give every aid to shorten the educational and development period, and to give them the vision of what could be done if they had the will to persevere.

Africa was typical of a Confederation with the will and zest to overcome massive problems of development. Visits to the African Games impressed me with the improving standard of play and with the organisational arrangements. These were held at Brazzaville and in Nigeria, while 'Jeux d'Amitiés' in Abidjan and Dakar were staged in the 1960s. But in many African countries there were massive problems to be overcome if they were to develop to a high standard. There were few grounds or stadia of the proper quality. The make-shift pitches on which youngsters learnt the game were often little better than dust-bowls. Travel and ground difficulties hampered the development of any nation-wide League capable of sustaining top-class football. The young were often poorly equipped and might well learn to play barefoot. And even in the best teams there seemed to be a lack of stamina, perhaps due to a diet which put more emphasis on cereals than meat. Too many who looked to have the needed ball skills and the acceleration over short distances lacked the staying power to challenge the leading European or South American teams.

There were other problems for any smooth development of football on the African continent, not least the rivalries and bad relations be-tween the former French and former British colonies. The very popularity of football as the leading game in the continent meant that it was soon subject to Government interference and dictation to national associations. As a result, many were more concerned with politics than the administration of the game, and there was a tendency to act against FIFA rules, as for instance when a Government ordered matches to be played against unaffiliated teams. As officials were often Government appointees there also tended to be constant change making it difficult to establish a basis of continuity and effective planning.

The Supreme Council of African Sport was founded in 1966 and un-fortunately accentuated the political bias. Its Secretary, Claude Ganga is an energetic traveller and speaker at any sports congress or con-ference in the world on its behalf. However, the African Football Confederation—CAF—with headquarters in Cairo is making signifi-cant progress in the organisation of tournaments and championships and raising standards of refereeing, so that General Mostafa was able to report steady improvement at our FIFA Executive meetings. The President of CAF, Mr. Tessema, has been working hard to develop football in the Continent. He had been a FIFA member and with his forceful personality he ensured quick progress. Though I had many differences of opinion with him we maintained a friendly relationship and I appreciated his driving determination to raise the standard of African football.

There was indeed much for him to build on. The enthusiasm was there and the desire to learn. Any idea that the heat in these countries made for a lethargic population not suited to energetic sports was far from the mark. There was an eagerness and joy in their play which reminded me of the earlier days of English football, when for so many the game was a release from boredom or toil. Here was an area ripe for FIFA to help with visiting teams and players giving them a vision of what they might one day achieve themselves. No one player could make the impact on their football that Pele was later to achieve in America. Yet I was pleased to find that the magic name for many countries was Stanley Matthews, who travelled widely in the twilight of his great career. He was the man so many wished to copy and he took a leading part in coaching, particularly in South Africa.

Addis Ababa was one of the African centres it was a pleasure for me to visit, when we staged Conferences in the magnificent 'Africa Hall', or watched matches in the fine stadium. Emperor Haile Selassie, with whom I had shared fire-watching duties, made me welcome. He was a football fanatic, and apart from ensuring splendid facilities for the game in his capital saw to it that major football matches were presented with style. For the Emperor's entrance the richest carpets were laid down leading up to a massive chair carved like a throne. Before one match I was being escorted to meet him there when I tripped on a fold in the carpet. At once a small chihuahua poked its head out of a pocket in his robe and barked at me. Apparently it was a tradition that the dog warned him thus of the approach of enemies. It proved much easier to maintain friendly relations with the Emperor than ever to establish them with his dog.

African spectators, though excitable, were usually kept in order by strict security measures. Yet occasionally they could not control their feelings as at an excellent final at Dakar, which ended level after extra time. With the teams lined up in the centre I was asked to go and draw lots to decide the winner. As I was entering the field an enormous, muscular man ran up to the Sudanese team and felled their goalkeeper with one blow, as other players scattered for safety. Later I went to hear the culprit tried. From the salutary sentence he received there was clearly no toleration of hooliganism. But his heartfelt plea in mitigation: 'That goalkeeper was too much to bear. He alone prevented my country winning', indicated how passionately the people felt about the game.

There were exciting developments also in Asia where I travelled extensively. Grounds there are generally of high standard with especially impressive stadia in Bangkok, Djakarta, Kuala Lumpur, and

Tehran. Having seen the equally high standards of skill in the whole area, it was not so much of a surprise to me when the North Koreans startled European football in the 1966 World Cup. With their elimination of Italy and their 3–0 lead in the quarter-final against Portugal, before Eusebio's brilliance wrested the game from them, North Korea gave an indication of Asia's potential in world football.

In Asia, too, politics were apt to intrude as in the Djakarta games of 1962 which I attended with Dr Barassi. Israel and Taiwan had been given guarantees that they could compete, but at the last minute their players and officials were refused visas. Even Lee Wai Tong, then secretary of the Asian Confederation, was turned away because he had connections with Taiwan. Mr Maladi, the Indonesian Minister for Sport, had invited all delegations to a concert where he himself conducted the orchestra. When I was asked to speak to him afterwards about the ban I took the universality of music as my theme and reminded Maladi that music knew no political or national boundaries. A composer's race was no bar to his music being played worldwide and leading musicians were welcomed everywhere. My impassioned plea that the Games should similarly be free of politics appeared to move Maladi, but the ban stayed.

Meanwhile, Mr Sondi, a member of the Indian delegation, tried to persuade Barassi, myself, and other sports representatives, to leave the Games in protest. Barassi and I felt that with spectators and competitors looking forward to the contest it was too late for such action without causing even more trouble for the many prepared for the Games and uninvolved in the politics. However, Sondi's action was soon known to the Press who started a campaign against him. One evening when we returned to our hotel, 'Indonesia', we found thousands of demonstrators protesting outside. It certainly scared us. But it didn't worry Sondi. He had already been smuggled out and flown home. What a pity it was that politics should have marred these Games for the football itself was enjoyable as were the exhibition shows every night both by the countries taking part and by hundreds of Balinese dancers.

Despite the occasional political set-back it was my aim to maintain the sporting unity of football and on my travels I was able to encourage the formation of the youngest Confederation, Oceania. This centred round Australia, New Zealand, Fiji, and Papua and New Guinea. Its Secretary, Charles Dempsey, has battled bravely with the immense problems it faces. Distances make communication and competition difficult. Rugby is a more popular game in New Zealand and

Australia, whose support is so essential to it. And though Taiwan joined, and Tahiti, New Caledonia and the Solomon Islands all showed interest, the Confederation has too few members to be represented yet on the Executive of FIFA. Yet Australia's performance in the final round of the World Cup showed in 1974 that football standards were improving fast in Oceania. Their problems are not dissimilar from another Confederation whose development we encouraged, Conacaf, the North, Central, and Caribbean Confederation. In some cases Conacaf members cannot travel direct from country to country without a detour via Miami or New York. Yet with strong administration from their office in Guatemala and with Mexico making an important contribution Conacaf has knit into an effective Confederation.

The USA could hardly be classed as an emergent nation. In the first World Cup in 1930 the Americans headed their group, beating Paraguay and Belgium each by 3–0. Though there were six former British professionals in their team, five Scots and an Englishman, the team reflected a reasonable standard in the country as a whole. Trained by Jack Coll of Brooklyn Wanderers, they were fast and fit, packing their defence and relying on three forwards to launch sudden raids. My friend John Langenus of Belgium was the outstanding referee of the competition and was entrusted with the final won by Uruguay. He told me the Americans gave an impression of crude vigour, many of them formidably strong athletes with thighs like tree-trunks. At least they were good enough to reach the semi-final for which they were billed as favourites. In fact Argentina beat them 6–1, but it was to be another thirty-six years before a British team reached the semi-finals.

Langenus also refereed that match against Argentina and had an altercation with the American medical attendant, who ran on the field and roundly criticised his handling of the game. To emphasise a point he hurled down his box of medicaments, smashing the bottles inside. One of these contained chloroform and to Langenus' relief the official had to be helped from the field as the fumes enveloped him. Their performance in that World Cup seemed to indicate that American football had come of age, at least on the field, and had made great strides since they first entered a team for the Olympic Games in 1920. And how could I regard the Americans as 'emerging' when they had inflicted that humiliating defeat on us in our first World Cup attempt in 1950? I was, however, keen to hasten the development of the game in a country where it was still a peripheral sport, but which had, and still has, the capacity to become a world leader in the game.

In this great sporting country, with its British connections, soccer seemed doomed to remain a marginal activity, almost as far as cricket from the mainstream of American sport. The American representatives on FIFA had given little evidence of vision, or of that flamboyant determination to improve, which is so characteristic of their country. Old Dr Manning, with his English background, had been a charming man, but no ball of fire. Then my friend Jimmy McGuire proved little more effective despite a life dedicated to soccer. He was an Irishman, who had learned his football in Scotland and played in England for Northampton. With the overlay of an American accent, his linguistic pedigree sometimes made him incomprehensible to me, particularly as he was usually smoking a large pipe and talking through clenched teeth. Jimmy was a lovable character and had been one of the candidates for the presidency of FIFA, but withdrew early as it was apparent he had little support. He was, however, a delightful travelling companion. On several occasions he came with me as FIFA representative to some conference or function, together with 'Mordy' Maduro of Curacao. Mordy was an impressive character, with a large share in many business projects in his home island. He bulked large in our council, too, for he weighed over twenty-two stone. At the dinner in 1963 to mark fifty years of American soccer Mordy and Jimmy were both present with me, so I was able to relate a story from a recent joint visit of ours to a meeting in Cairo.

Mordy wanted the traditional picture of himself on a camel beside the Pyramids. Jimmy and I arranged it for him, but I forgot to warn him of the one danger. You mount the camel in the 'Barak' position, where it is crouched and couchant. Then you must grasp the front of the saddle with one hand and the rear with the other, or you may nearly dislocate your neck as you are hurled forward then back as the camel rises convulsively to its feet. The camel-driver had too many problems getting Mordy on at all to tell him what to do. So it was a very white and shaken Maduro who was returned to us, 'And what he does not know,' I added, 'is that the drover later claimed compensation, because when he removed the saddle the hump had gone.' And if that jocular reference to Mordy's weight was not strictly accurate, this is an exact record of my conversation with the drover when he tried to get me to take Mordy's place. 'Too late,' I told him. 'I had my picture taken like that forty-five years ago when I was here with the Army, and by the looks of it probably on the same camel.' 'But of course, Your Excellency, I remember you well!'

I was convinced that soccer could take off in America, as in all other major countries if only it was given a proper chance. And the post-war period seemed to offer special opportunities. Many American servicemen in Britain and Germany had been involved in playing or watching soccer, and so had their children. With my belief in the essential importance of arousing interest young, I had involved an American team in the first youth tournament after the war, and I found there were enough soccer-trained sons of servicemen to give them a respectable side. The teams were also given coaching and taken to see top-class League soccer. This the Americans thoroughly enjoyed, and if their performances on the field were not remarkable, they were the liveliest in those do-it-yourself utility days in providing the entertainment at the Biggin Hill Air Force camp, where teams from a dozen countries were housed.

We were quite happy for soccer to stand comparison with American football. And while encouraging them to try our game, I was also instrumental in getting an American football match staged at Wembley between Forces teams. That brought me several abusive letters, particularly from one man who said, as if it was the ultimate deterrent, that he had sent a copy of his letter to the *Daily Mirror*. After complaining that 'Wembley had been desecrated by these antics' and objecting to the cheerleaders, and the players 'padded, cotton-woolled, and helmeted', he ended: 'You know it was stupid to allow this. I certainly do because after the game one of the players ran off with my wife.'

More seriously, I took every opportunity to visit the States and help develop the game there. Walter Winterbottom and I attended a conference in New York for some four hundred coaches. And since standards of play so often depend on standards of refereeing, Dr Andrejevic and I toured the States for FIFA talking at a series of referees' courses and trying to recruit more to be interested enough to take it up. Since many attended the meetings out of condition and smoking cigars, the need for referees to be as fit as players was one of our themes.

In Chicago I found Andrejevic unusually anxious about its reputation as a gangster city. We were in penthouse rooms at the top of a hotel with a connecting balcony running past outside. When I knocked on his door in the morning it was bolted and, when at last he had satisfied himself of my identity, I heard him removing piled furniture in order to let me in. The balcony also acted as the platform for diners to walk round, viewing the city lights, but the sound of their talk outside his window had convinced Andrejevic he was about to be assaulted.

We found some strong clubs playing good football, particularly in the New York area. But only after the success of the 1966 World Cup had acted as a stimulus was there a real effort to promote the game. Within a year six rich Americans called on me together, a couple of them having to sit on the floor as they crowded uncomfortably into my small office. Among these millionaires was Lamar Hunt, Jack Kent Cooke, owner of the Forum in Los Angeles, and Judge Roy Hofheinz, director of the Houston Astrodome, as well as the management of baseball clubs like the Atlanta Braves and Chicago White Sox. They and the CBS television company pumped millions into promoting soccer and at first disastrously. Three thousand was a large gate. Several clubs lost more than a million dollars in their first season. Five went bankrupt. Their questions to me were based on the thought that they had the stadia and the TV coverage, but what they needed was good teams. How could they buy them? One had the fancy, and thought he had cash, to buy up Wolves, another Derby County. I had to explain that this was not the way. They must work through the United States Soccer Football Association and if they wanted the game to last they must give it a firm base in the country rather than just import some good teams. In effect I suggested a threefold programme to them.

Some individuals they imported should not be the usual elderly Fourth-Division-type players on the way out, but high-quality performers capable of selling the skills of the game. From the more elderly professionals they should look for good coaches to give proper instruction to youth. And while they could add frills to the presentation and packaging of the game for the American public, they needed to keep to the basic rules within the guidance of FIFA, since otherwise they would be no part of world soccer.

My advice was sought again when the North American Soccer League appointed a Commissioner. Out of the hundreds of applications Phil Woosnam was a happy choice. There had been a faintly American look about him, with his crew-cut hair, as he played so intelligently at inside for Wales. He was a science graduate of high intelligence and, like most articulate Welshmen, had an enthusiasm and a smooth flow of words which appealed to Americans. His appointment was one breakthrough in popularising soccer there. But first FIFA and myself were involved in a Packer-type conflict, with a 'pirate' circus suing the USSFA and FIFA for breach of the anti-trust laws in denying them a franchise to form a new professional League.

Football organisation in America had been weak and unambitious, with no attempt to form a truly professional League until a lawyer and commercial dealer, William Cox, organised summer tournaments with League clubs taking part. At first the USSFA accepted these when they started in 1958, to be run for five years. As FA Secretary at the time I was more chary of involvement, but our League ignored FA advice and allowed their clubs to participate. Soon arguments flared between Cox and USSFA and the existing American League as USSFA asked for a higher percentage of the 'take'. When I attended the USSFA Congress in 1963 I told them, 'If the grass is not good, weeds grow', indicating to them my belief that if they did not see the opportunities and adapt some of Cox's ideas for a professional League, they would find themselves in trouble. The trouble duly came in 1965 and when Jack Flamhaft, Counsellor at Law and guiding hand of the American League, wrote for my support I had to remind him, 'Cox is still trying in an irregular way to do what your Association should have taken the lead in doing. I said so at your Congress and still believe the USSFA could and should organise such a League.' By waiting they had been pre-empted by the energetic William Cox, who was proposing the formation of a National Soccer League which the USSFA was proposing to 'outlaw'. Flamhaft wrote agitatedly to me,

The problems concern themselves with a Cox-dominated national professional soccer league; the relegation of the USSFA to a secondary role in the government of the game; and the possible destruction of the game as it exists here today. If Cox were allowed to organise this venture under his terms it would mean the extinction of most of the Leagues in the United States, who depend on gate receipts and foreign tour income to support themselves. A Cox League could not exist without television subsidy. Television, without appropriate protection, would ruin the other organisations.

Since I believe that a national professional soccer league cannot exist without television it follows that it must, as baseball has done, destroy the minor league organisations. The difference is that when baseball went into television and acquired new territories, for instance California, it at least had the decency to compensate the minor baseball leagues it was about to destroy.

Those who favor the Cox league contend that the American League has not served its function of creating professional football. The history of the American Soccer League from its inception in 1923 has been marked by ups and downs. Concededly, it is not in one of its prosperous cycles at present. In fairness, one must remember that the only era of soccer prosperity and great development in this country, circa 1925 to 1932, is entirely attributable to the American Soccer League.

The choice lies between a private promoter and speculator and the organisations which are integral parts of the soccer life of this country.

Reference to good times thirty years ago seemed illustrative of the ossified state of American football, and I was relieved when the quarrel was temporarily patched up. It flared again a few years later in another argument over franchises, and in 1970 I found FIFA being sued for $1½ million as co-defendants with USSFA and the American League. The Cox complaint was that FIFA control of the game amounted to a breach of the American anti-trust laws. The lawyers' wrangling continued in Switzerland, but I finally told the USSFA that a sensible settlement must be reached. Flamhaft was a difficult man to persuade to compromise, obsessed as he was by dislike of Cox. But after an all-night session in the Dolder Hotel we finally resolved the problem. Cox was allowed to operate profitably, but agreed to stay within USSFA.

I had a lot of sympathy with Cox for jolting reality into the game and applying a needed stimulus. Equally, it was essential that soccer stayed within FIFA's rules if America was to develop as part of the world game and not as an entirely different one.

Inevitably there were difficult problems of recognition for FIFA, some related solely to a country's football, some to international tensions. In the first category came those countries where rival national Associations competed to be the one body to be represented on FIFA, which by its rules could not recognise more than one association per country. Usually this stemmed from a national Association being too weak and unrepresentative at the start, or from the national League making a take-over bid. Colombia, Venezuela, and Cyprus all gave us this kind of problem.

With China it was simply a question of international politics. In Sweden in 1958 they left FIFA because it continued to recognise the Association from Taiwan. The dispute was further aggravated by Taiwan calling itself National China and the name-calling spilled over from the United Nations to FIFA. The split had occurred before my presidency and I made attempts at reconciliation in meetings with their ambassador in London, and with their Sports Minister and delegates attending conferences in Nigeria and elsewhere. Always the response was, 'put Taiwan out before we join'. I stressed that it was not *governments*, but national Associations who were in membership of FIFA. So long as a country was internationally recognised to exist and had a reputable national Association representing and properly organising the majority of clubs in the country, FIFA's rules required us to give recognition. Not even the argument that in FIFA there were two Germanys, two Vietnams, and two Koreas had any effect. Nor did the offer that the name problem be erased by FIFA recognising Chiang Kai-shek's country only as Taiwan. In 1978 the problem still existed in more acute form, since the Asian Confederation took China into membership against FIFA rules and expelled Taiwan. FIFA has also eased its rules to allow China to make exchange visits of teams with Cosmos and British clubs, such as West Bromwich Albion, being permitted to play there, while West Germany and other European countries arrange matches on a home and away basis. This is a dangerous course for FIFA, if it wishes to keep football under one umbrella organisation for the world. It should rather maintain its position that no member association can play against an unaffiliated association or its clubs. Once this position is abandoned the slide into politics, with all the divisions that brings, can only be accelerated. The most complex and perplexing of these problems with which I was involved was the tangled web of football and political confusion posed by Rhodesia and South Africa. I was caught up in it almost from my appointment as President, and a thankless task it was to make judgements on those unhappy disputes. The good administrator's job is to find the facts, give the parties the chance to state their case, and then decide according to the organisation's rules, not any personal opinion of his own. I was soon to find how hard this is in the South African situation, which is bedevilled by emotion. But in any assignment I have been given on South Africa I have always been prepared to see at first hand and to let everyone put their point of view before a decision is made. I have little respect for those who will not even try to find the facts, let alone face them, in case it interferes with their second-hand prejudices.

In Santiago in 1962 FIFA decided to investigate the position in South Africa, whose membership was already suspended, not over apartheid policies as such, but because there were doubts whether the mainly white Football Association of South Africa was genuinely the national Association rather than the South African Soccer Federation. In particular, FIFA were concerned to discover whether by rules relating to colour, or for any other reason FASA was preventing clubs from joining its Association. Naturally, I thought it my duty to see at first hand, and aimed to take a small but representative delegation with me, so that the facts would not be in dispute. We wanted two representatives from North African countries so that there should be no suggestion of bias in our party, but those invited found various excuses to avoid coming on what should have been a priority mission. So America's Jimmy McGuire became the only man to face the problems with me. The Executive Committee had asked us to visit South Africa to try to find a solution to the obstacles preventing all associations and clubs from becoming members of a United South African Football Association. The suspension was to be lifted if we reported that the FA of South Africa was not responsible for clubs remaining outside their Association. This had already been reported to them and our job was to confirm or contradict this. Our terms of reference were simple: 'To ascertain whether FASA was in any way responsible for Associations and Clubs not becoming members of that Association.'

In January 1963 we went to South Africa interviewing organisations and representatives of the then National Associations of Northern and Southern Rhodesia, Basutoland, Nyasaland, and the Sudan. Among the representatives from whom we took evidence were those from FASA from the South African Soccer Federation, from the South African Indian FA, from the South African Bantu FA, from the South African Olympic Council and the South African Foundation, from the Non-European Affairs department of Johannesburg and the Coloured community who were trying to form an FA with the object of affiliating to FASA.

On the detailed evidence we received we had to conclude that FASA was not acting then contrary to FIFA's rules and was not responsible by its actions for any Associations or clubs not becoming members of FASA. From a complex survey the main reasons for this decision were that, notwithstanding the Government's policy of separate development, FASA was not itself practising racial discrimination. It was ready to accept as affiliate any other association, had already accepted the South African Bantu FA, and the Indian Association of the Republic of South Africa, and was about to accept the South African Coloured Association. We also noted that the National Professional League, formed in 1960, was affiliated to FASA and had representation on its Executive, that the Bantu and Indian Associations were also represented there and expressed themselves as happy to be affiliated, that the Constitution of FASA was open to all and that some of the stadiums provided for Non-Whites were as good as any for whites. We were also greatly impressed by the manner and enthusiasm of the FASA officials we met, and it was clear that there was a general advance in popularity and performance of the game under their control. FIFA was not—or by its rules should not have been—concerned with the *government*'s policies and attitudes. Our brief was not to find if the government was discriminatory in outlook, only if FASA was. And FASA at the time was one of many groups of sportsmen in the country working towards close integration *despite* the government.

At that stage the situation in football was quite different to that in some other sports. In cricket, for instance, the South African Government had intervened to force discrimination by banning an MCC side, with D'Oliveira in it, from visiting South Africa. FASA, however, was planning to enter in the World Cup a side which could include black South Africans, and as a FIFA member might have had to accept and play in South Africa coloured teams from other countries in the World Cup. To remove FASA from FIFA then would therefore have been a blow against the integration in sport which was being demanded. And though South Africa was later to be suspended again from FIFA it was right that this should not happen until Government policy forced FASA itself to be discriminatory.

South Africa is such an emotive issue that anyone involved with it is likely to be misunderstood or misrepresented. And because of that report I was sometimes accused in FIFA meetings of being too sympathetic to white South Africans. Certainly I have been sad to see a country with so much potential put itself outside the pale of world opinion. Certainly I have acknowledged the debt that English football owes to many fine South African players like 'Nivvy' Nieuwenhuys, who captained Liverpool in the 1940s, or Perry, who scored the winner for Blackpool in the 'Stanley Matthews' Cup Final in 1953. Among so many others were the Charlton connection with manager Jimmy Seed bringing over players like the long-legged John Hewie, and those two talented cricketing footballers, Leary and O'Linn. And the one who made the greatest impression on me was Eddie Firmani, fine inside-forward and principled manager, who has since made a significant contribution to American football as well.

But such reflections never affected any judgements I made in trying fairly to relate facts to FIFA's rules. And it is equally true that I have always disliked apartheid, or indeed any form of discrimination. For my aim for soccer has been total integration, world-wide with no barriers between sportsmen because of race, colour, religion, or politics. But as an administrator I have always held as a first principle that all sports bodies should be fairly treated by the same rules. To make special rules for one country which is specially unpopular can only lead to long-term trouble. As McGuire and I ended our report: 'FIFA cannot be used as a weapon to force a government to change its internal sports policy. To do so would wreck FIFA's true purpose.'

Historically, it still seems sensible that FIFA acted with restraint over South Africa. For one special exception soon leads to another, as the Olympic movement found when the Montreal Games degenerated into a political wrangle which even sickened a hardened diplomat like Lord Killanin. The tangles of world politics are best left to the United Nations, while FIFA concerns itself with world football and jealously guards its own constitution. Sports administrators are poorly qualified to weigh the righteousness of one country against another, when today's rebel is so often tomorrow's hero; or yesterday's father-figure today's discredited despot.

From South Africa I went on to Salisbury to see representatives of the Southern Rhodesian Football Association, and also those from provincial Associations, soccer enthusiasts such as Mhlanga from Mashonaland, Musararwa from Matabeleland, and Zimuto from the Midlands. My purpose was to try and help them fuse the three organisations administering football in the country and to ensure that any national Association so formed be non-discriminatory. Despite the many problems, we found satisfactory solutions with the meeting ending in a firm agreement. This included the resolve to form one national Association merging the Southern Rhodesian FA, the Southern Rhodesian African FA, and the Southern Rhodesian Football Board. It was further agreed that it should include all clubs affiliated to these three organisations, directly or through provincial Associations.

Oddly, most argument centred on the close season. With football a main sport for so many, and weather conditions so favourable, it seemed desirable that there should be as much opportunity as possible for people to play. But a Scotsman in the Southern Rhodesian FA was very insistent that it should be as long a shut-down as in Britain. Finally, I got him to admit he was an international bowls player, who followed this sport in the close season, and to agree it would be selfish to deny playing opportunity for so long to those who had no second sport to amuse them. So a more liberal clause was inserted that: 'A "close" season shall be determined, but provision for the granting of an extension in special circumstances shall be made.' In Rhodesia there was no difficulty in also ensuring the inclusion of a clause: 'Where matches are staged on grounds under the direct control of the national Association no discrimination shall be permitted.' The meeting indeed ended on a cheerful note when I was asked to recommend whether the new Association's colours should embody colours of existing Associations. 'The best colours for you,' I told them, 'are black and white stripes.'

During the Rhodesian visit I received much help from the British High Commissioner and Brigadier Prentice, a twin brother of Tom Prentice who joined the FA staff in my time there, and whose father was the Secretary of the Rugby Union.

At the Cairo meeting immediately after our trip the vote had been 11–6 in favour of South Africa's suspension being lifted. However, the suspension was reapplied at the Tokyo Congress the next year and maintained until at the Montreal Congress in 1976 South Africa was finally expelled from FIFA by 78 votes to 9 with 13 abstentions.

Rhodesia was still in membership with FIFA when they entered for the World Cup qualifying matches in 1969. With visas being refused to Rhodesian players by many countries they finally had to play Australia in Mozambique. And in 1970 a sub-committee was set up to study the case of Rhodesia and especially its affiliation to the English FA as an associate member. The 1970 Congress in Mexico suspended Rhodesia because of the uncertain political situation and problems relating to the 'nationality' of players following UDI. That should be open to review when the country's future is settled.

My involvement with African and American problems has to be multiplied many times to indicate how much of my time was devoted to individual countries as well as dealing with the ordinary business of FIFA. If any country wanted to make use of my experience I was always glad to help. With so many nations keen to develop the game the requests were frequent. It was the same with my grant-aid scheme which expanded so rapidly that soon half a million Swiss francs were being allocated in one year rather than four.

Appointment as FIFA President inevitably meant a complete change of life-style. Living 'rent-free' at Lancaster Gate had meant that I had no financial worries, even though my salary left little scope for saving. But now I had to depend on my FA pension, and on such money as I had been able to save or had been left, though FIFA refunded all expenses incurred in my work for them. And while I had travelled widely for the FA, I now had to adjust to being almost continuously on the move and become an expert in living out of a suitcase.

My trips to the various continents had to be fitted in with the regular routine of FIFA work. Once or twice a month I would commute to Zurich for three or four days to clear all outstanding business. In my rooms there I kept a complete wardrobe so that I could fly out at a moment's notice and still be self-sufficient on arrival. In London, too, I had my instant travelling-kit always available for quick departure, with one of the two suitcases filled with lightweight clothes for the hotter climates.

Correspondence became a problem since so many people wrote to me individually. More than half the letters came to my London flat, and every week there were a hundred or so to be answered. It was entertaining to have worldwide contact with correspondents, and had I been a stamp collector I would soon have had an impressive collection. But replies on this scale were more than I could cope with unless I had secretarial assistance such as was available to me in Zurich. And in due course I persuaded one of the secretaries who helped me there, and had previously worked for me for a year at the FA, to come to London. Rosemarie Breitenstein, who speaks five languages, soon became indispensable not only in dealing with correspondence, but in organising my somewhat hectic life. She has acted since as interpreter, friend, fellow traveller, and companion in years which might otherwise have been considerably less happy and inspiring.

14

Faces and Places

●●●

Travel world-wide has been a bonus from my work for football. There is no country in Europe, except Albania, which I have not visited on football business. And it is much the same with other continents. Of the 150 countries in FIFA membership I have been to more than a hundred. Friends from many of them still invite me to attend conferences, from Kuwait to Buenos Aires, even though I am semi-retired. Indeed, one of the happiest surprises of my life came on my eighty-second birthday. I had assumed few would still keep in touch. Instead hundreds of letters, cards and telegrams came from all over the world. That made me think back on the places and faces which have contributed to such a full and satisfying life. From so many memories there is only space for a small selection.

There have been many pleasanter trips, but none more intriguing than my first visit to Russia in the days of austerity a few years after the war. We had admired Russia's wonderful struggle as our partner in the fight against the Nazis. There had been an almost mystical quality in their total recovery after being on the brink of total disaster. The passionate love of their homeland expressed in that courageous battle against odds inevitably made it a country one wished to see at first hand. And there was an inscrutable quality about the Russians which made them something of an enigma to us. They had just surprised us with the vitality of their Moscow Dynamo team on its successful tour of Britain. They had amused us, too, by their ostentatious national pride and their determination to make political capital out of sport. When Arsenal paid them the compliment of including some guest players in their side they issued a communiqué claiming victory over England when they won the friendly 4–3 in a fog that made a farce of the game.

That game led to an invitation to Arsenal to go to Moscow for a return match, and I was invited to accompany the team. We left Northolt in two Dakotas, flying first to Prague. There I was immediately struck by the strict formality so characteristic of Russia and the countries she dominates. Some friends came to meet me at the airport as we waited there, but were kept penned so far away we could only shout greetings. Our plane was then diverted to Warsaw to pick up two of their government officials, before we met up with the rest of the party again in Minsk. Bad weather forced us to stop the night there, to the dismay of the locals who were unprepared to put up so large a party in a town badly damaged in the war and still only partly rebuilt. The group of players in the first plane, together with Bernard Joy, Roy Peskett, Clifford Webb and the other accompanying journalists, were the fortunate ones who were finally taken to a hotel. For the remainder of the team, the directors, Jimmy Joyce and Guy Bracewell-Smith, together with Raymond Glendenning and myself, there was an eerie night in a hostel.

As we were taken there at midnight, the building was in pitch darkness. A lady with a candle met us at the door and took us upstairs and down a long corridor. We had expected a drab house, but by the flickering light we could see it lined with exquisite paintings. Finally, we came to a silent dormitory with only a candle left to light us to the four unoccupied beds, one in each corner. All the other beds were filled with shadowy forms so still that it seemed like a mortuary and Jimmy Joyce asked in a whisper, 'Are they all dead?' The players were in the next dormitory, experiencing the same uncanny stillness from the normal occupants who had presumably been instructed to make no sound to disturb us. Tommy Lawton was so unnerved by the motionless bodies that when he folded his trousers and the money clattered out to roll around the floor he was too unnerved to pick it up, since even that made no impression on his motionless room-mates.

In the morning the same lady woke us at six, pointed to a washroom, and made signs to hurry. No one in the other beds stirred as we dressed and tiptoed away still wondering if our fellow guests were human. We learnt afterwards that they were in fact a group of engineers brought into aid the rebuilding of Minsk, who had been ordered under no circumstances to disturb us. The triumph of their military discipline over their curiosity made it a bizarre experience for us.

Our welcome in Moscow was remarkably effusive for just a Club side, although Arsenal's past reputation still meant that they were regarded abroad as the leading English team. We stayed in the Metropole

Hotel in Red Square, an oasis of luxury in that post-war period of shortages and austerity so apparent elsewhere in Moscow. Nikita Kruschev himself presided at a dinner in Arsenal's honour. We also had the privilage of seeing all Moscow's most spectacular entertainment, including a magical performance of *Swan Lake* at the Bolshoi. There was a visit to the Moscow State Circus, which was the highlight for most of us. We also had the unusual honour of being shown round the Kremlin and seeing the extraordinary wealth of *objets d'art* and jewels housed there. Equally impressive was the display of Czarist uniforms and the outstanding collection of furniture and pictures. A more typically Russian display was the exhibition 'village' to which we were taken. On permanent show there were traditional houses from every area in Russia, each with some distinctive feature of the region. The Georgian house, for instance, had trays of apples built up to form imitation pillars. But the Russians were even more proud of their 'sports house' in the main Moscow stadium, where every trophy won by Russia, or its replica, was on display.

To us the facilities in the multi-sports centre were more remarkable. In particular we were fascinated by the water section. This included a rowing area in which an artificial current could be created of the exact strength to simulate Henley or wherever their next race might be. And for those who trained there, every subsidiary service was provided from dental and medical treatment to haircuts. The State decided who was more equal than the others, but the privileged were still well looked after.

And so were we with the red-carpet treatment culminating in the floodlit match with the usual exchange of flowers. Catching the mood, I tossed mine to the crowd in an expansive gesture of goodwill. Some months later I was presiding at a CCPR meeting when Baroness Burton thanked me for the bouquet I had given her. When I denied any knowledge of sending her flowers, she told me she had been at the match that night with a visiting parliamentary delegation, and I had unknowingly thrown my bouquet straight into her lap.

Arsenal was certainly a magic word then in Moscow. While photographing the Kremlin Guy Bracewell Smith was arrested and hustled into a guardroom. I followed after him, apprehensive of the difficulty of explanation with neither of us able to speak Russian. However, when an officer came on the scene the repetition of 'Arsenal' was good enough to bring immediate release and profuse apologies. We then completed the visit by viewing what the Americans crudely termed 'the cold cuts'—the embalmed bodies of Lenin and other cult-figures.

Only one request of mine was evaded. As a magistrate myself, I asked to see something of the Soviet system and to visit one of their detention centres. This was never refused, but always there was some difficulty. 'You will have to start at six in the morning and perhaps that will be inconvenient?' I replied that it would suit me very well as I usually woke up at five. But then it appeared that the road was blocked by snow, and there was always some reason why I could not go.

On a later visit to Russia with the FIFA Referees' Committee, I went on the long night-train journey to Leningrad. We had a young interpreter with us, who carefully checked the carriage for any bugging device then began to talk of his disenchantment with the authorities. But this was no political diatribe. All that had upset him was that he and his fellow interpreters were not allowed to accept the normal FIFA fee for his work as this was a special assignment.

On the return journey my companion, Andrejevic, was unlucky enough to fall from his bunk, fracturing ribs and lying in pain for some hours. His wife finally succeeded in notifying the guard who arranged for an ambulance to be waiting for him on our arrival in Moscow. Before he left we commiserated with him on the accident and praised his fortitude. 'You won't believe it,' he said, 'but I lay there laughing because the incident reminded me of one of your funny stories, Stanley.' This was a shaggy cat story I had just told him the punchline of which involved a fall from a roof. I was surprised he still found in humorous. In the story the victim died.

Travel to Eastern European countries has many happy memories for me. In Hungary, Bulgaria, Czechoslovakia, the DDR, and Roumania there was always a warm welcome and no attempt to introduce politics. My hosts were particularly kind and attentive, and my visits there always enjoyable.

Africa was another area where there was always something unusual or exciting on my many trips. When I visited Kenya in 1968 I was asked to attend a match in my honour on the eve of departure. As we reached the stadium all was turmoil with the game cancelled because the Abaluhya club had failed to turn up. Apparently their witch doctor had predicted many injuries if they played and they were not prepared to risk it. His advice may have saved their limbs but the fine harmed the club's pocket.

It seemed there was more witchcraft afoot when I was staying in the government guest house in Basutoland, now Lesotho, on a visit to their Association who were keen to join FIFA. In the next room I suddenly heard Prince Philip's unmistakable voice apparently being answered by my own! On investigating I found that it was only a group of Basutos using a British Council tape-recorder. The tape was of an address by Prince Philip to the Sheffield amateur club on their hundredth anniversary with a reply by myself.

There was another strange experience after I had attended the first African Games in Brazzaville in the Congo. I was presented with an intricately carved ivory walking stick, a much prized emblem of one of the tribes. I took a special fancy to this gift which was too long to pack, so that I used it on my way home. As I tried to fight my way through Brazzaville airport packed to overflowing with returning competitors and officials, the stick seemed to develop magic properties. Suddenly the mass of people began to divide before me leaving a clear path. A little man took my arm and the hall began to echo with his cry in French of 'attention'. As everyone gave way deferentially to me I suddenly realised that this was no miracle. With my white stick, and wearing dark-tinted glasses against the glare I had been mistaken for a blind man!

Perhaps that was not inappropriate. For while soccer has its violent side it is also a great fund-raiser for charitable causes, not least for the National Institute for the Blind. The Sunshine Homes for blind children were a special interest of mine, and as a patron I used to help with their sportsmen's night.

One of the memorable occasions during my presidency was to go to Mexico City for a week-end visit in May 1966 to open the monumental Aztec Stadium in company with the then President of the Republic, Gustavo Diaz Ordaz. I was asked to visit him at the Government Palace, together with my friend Guillermo Canedo, the President of the Mexican Football Federation. We were then invited to travel the twenty-five miles to the new stadium with the President in his car. The police had been trying from early morning to keep the motorway free of traffic, but it was jammed nonetheless and scores of broken-down or abandoned vehicles had to be pushed on to the side of the road to let us through. As a result we were one and a half hours late for the opening of as magnificent a stadium as I have seen in the world.

A humorist after my own heart is Teofilo 'Lito' Salinas, who has acted as President of the South American Confederation. That is not always an easy task, but he performed it with real efficiency and a sense of fun. At a final of the South American championship 'Copa de los Libertadores', which I attended in Buenos Aires, a cardinal asked me who was about to sit next to him. I introduced Salinas from Peru and added straight-faced that he was the biggest sinner in South America.

The match went into extra time and afterwards I asked the cardinal if Salinas had confessed all his sins to him. He replied that if it had not been for the extra time he wouldn't have been able to complete his confessions! Salinas wasn't at his best in the early morning and he had trouble getting ready in time to address a referees' course in Buenos Aires with his talk scheduled for 8.30. We had to call his room before he came dashing down wearing one black and one brown shoe. When I pointed this out to him he said, 'How odd. I have another pair like that in my room.'

The Middle East is an area where I have watched the swift growth of soccer to become the leading sport in oil-rich nations. Their rulers have no difficulty in providing bread and circuses for their people out of the oil money, and soccer has been a chosen form of entertainment. And it is to Englishmen that they so often turn for advice or assistance. The ruler of Bahrein has been a very generous host to me from the time I first visited his country to talk to the Bahrein Football Association and to their referees. At the time there was still a large British Army camp in the desert outside the capital. The troops had excellent sports facilities and had been instrumental in arousing interest in soccer. But though they had many able referees in the camp they were not allowed to officiate at civilian matches, since there was a policy of non-involvement in the country's affairs. Before leaving, however, I managed to persuade all concerned that a little sporting integration would be for the good of all, and that as both civilian and Army referees had come to my lectures together, they might continue to work together. And it was soon reported to me that they had amalgamated into one society.

The ruler himself had riding and racing as a main hobby. He supplied me with a car and chauffeur and arranged for me to stay in the Government's hospitality villa in the Anglo-Bahrein Oil Company compound, where there was also an impressive sports and social centre, shops and an English church. The first time I met the ruler he asked me to go riding with him, but I had to decline for lack of practice or suitable clothes. Instead he took me to see his eight stables with some hundreds of magnificent horses. Only in Teheran had I seen any other collection to match these beautiful animals. There the President of the Iranian FA, Kambiz Atabai, was also Master of the Horse and took delight in showing me the Shah's special breed.

After the stables the ruler took me to see a Bahrein race meeting. The track for the camel and horse racing was made from some oily, rubbery substance laid in the sand. Within the track was a golf course.

They were similar to the Ludlow race-track and golf club, but both were made out of this substance, bunkers and all. And though it looked primitive the going was excellent, the meeting well organised. The banquet in the royal palace which he organised for me was attended by ambassadors and by uniformed army and naval officers. We walked in silence down a long room with the guests seated on either side as the ruler led me to a settee at the top. He was not the largest of men, and as I tried to adjust my pace to his, he put his hand on my arm and, looking up at me, said, 'You will be careful not to tread on me, won't you?'

Saudi Arabia I still visit at intervals to watch the progress of Jimmy Hill's effort to organise football properly throughout the country. Perhaps because his method is so much in line with my own teaching —that the game must be organised throughout the country, starting in schools and clubs, and not just in a national team or league— Jimmy invited me to be President of his World Sports Academy. Spending a fortnight in Saudi Arabia in 1977 I was able to see its progress, with league matches played on artificial turf and attracting crowds of 30,000. As most of these raced down the single-track road to the stadium in large, fast cars driven at alarming speeds, getting there was a perilous sport in itself. On one occasion I noticed no less than seven accidents in the last two and a half miles. John Harding, a former Oxford blue, has done a thorough job out there as controller of the match programme throughout the country and in organising a network of instructors and referees. Jimmy's son, Duncan, a former Millfield schoolboy, was the resident director. With a good standard national league, and with Bill McGarry, now the Newcastle manager, then running the national side, Saudi Arabia had become well organised on European lines. Only one problem seemed to remain. Good football has often been the offspring of poverty, which gave players like Pele the driving ambition to escape from drab surroundings. But when a small population has money to burn the commitment seems less intense, the enthusiasm not so spontaneous.

In the Concacaf Confederation Mexico was the country I visited most often making many friends and enjoying the exuberance and generous hospitality of the country. But Bermuda, Trinidad, Guatemala, and Netherlands Antilles also attracted me while I had a memorable stay in Haiti in 1973. I was in that beautiful island for the preliminary World Cup round in which Haiti qualified to go to the finals in West Germany. The hospitality was overwhelming, but so was the security. Instead of the occasional outrider to clear a way through traffic here my car was preceded by three 'Tontons Macoutes' on powerful motorcycles. The chauffeur and officer in my car both had machine guns and we were followed by another car with four armed police. When we drove each day from the mountain hotel in Petionville to Port au Prince the sirens and the cavalcade attracted hundreds into the streets. I doubt if they knew who was in the black government limousine but they cheered wildly all the same—an embarrassing experience for me. To make it worse some of our football delegates were among those whose cars were precipitately cleared from the street. Once they had discovered who was in the car they took to shaking their fists at me in mock anger.

There were fourteen Asian countries which particularly attracted me with their extraordinary range of scenery and cultures. The President of the Asian Confederation, and then the Prime Minister of Malaysia, was Tunku Abdul Rahman Putra whom I met on my visits to Kuala Lumpur. He proved a keen golfer and race-horse owner, but a man with a love of football from the days he played soccer for his Cambridge college.

Having helped to form the Oceania Confederation it has been of special interest to see in recent years how they are developing. In 1969 Papua and New Guinea invited me to attend the South Pacific Games at Port Moresby. Though preoccupied with many meetings to advise on their administration of the game and on joining Oceania, I saw some of this land which at the time was still being administered by Australia. As the roads did not lead inside the country most of my trips were made in small planes. There was more enthusiasm than skill about the play and in up country games the locals seemed to have trouble with football boots which never seemed large enough for their outsize feet. Indeed I had to confirm that the rules allowed them to play barefoot as teams and this appeared to increase their enjoyment.

In August 1977 I made a three-week visit to Oceania on behalf of the British Council. Fiji is not likely to be a power in the game, but football was flourishing there stimulated by the colourful and dynamic figure of the country's Ombudsman, Justice Moti Tikeram. The Fiji FA had also worked hard to develop the game, played there in beautiful settings on Suva Island. The grass pitches are mostly open with wonderful views to the sea. But there is one ground, in common use by soccer and rugby, which has stand accommodation and can stage Oceania Cup matches.

New Zealand has greater potential to develop, and the country's intent to become a force in soccer as well as rugby was apparent in my welcome, when I was accorded a parliamentary reception arranged by Mr Highet, the Minister of Sport. An inhibiting factor in the development of the game there is the time and expense of travel involved in any truly national competition. But in recent years the country has tried to build a proper base for success by strengthening the grass roots of the game and instituting national youth competitions and a national League. With the energetic Secretary of the Confederation, Charles Dempsey, living in Auckland I was delighted to find how popular the game had become there with over 150 youth teams in the area.

New Zealand has plenty of good soccer stadia and its playing standards seemed not far short of Australia's. But it is there that progress has been fastest in the last decade. It was no fluke that Australia qualified for the 1974 World Cup final round and played with distinction in West Germany. In England we were better able to judge their rising standards when Alston from their World Cup team found no difficulty settling into League football with Luton and then Cardiff.

To me it seemed that the 1956 Olympics in Melbourne were crucial for the development of the game in Australia. Before that Australian football had been regarded with amusement in Britain as a filler for the summer pools coupons, with the play itself not to be taken too seriously. Certainly Australia had made none of the impact at soccer that the country makes in so many other sports.

Australia already had good stadia and some good players. What the country lacked was nationwide interest in the game, grass-roots teaching, national youth competitions, and a national league—all the essentials in fact for sustained improvement. With some of the best of European football on display in that Olympic tournament, a new zest for the game was born. The final was between Russia and Jugoslavia, with their full national teams playing. That was the only match staged in the vast Melbourne cricket ground and it attracted great interest. I watched with Prince Philip, and two incidents especially intrigued us. As at all their matches at their other stadiums, at half-time and at the close, mounted policemen came from the four corner-flags riding their horses towards the centre of the stand to make a protective lane screening the referee and linesmen as they walked off. And during the game there was a clash between a back and his winger behind the referee's back. Unnoticed by him it ended with a headlong chase outside the touchline with the winger just swift enough to escape being caught by his infuriated pursuer.

Whether it was the skills or the red-blooded challenge in those Olympics which caught the Australian imagination, there was an instant surge of interest in football. When Walter Winterbottom and I gave talks there to coaches and referees on our way to the 1964 Tokyo Games we were impressed with the progress made. And that has been sustained until Australia has the basic structure and the ability to develop to European or South American standards.

Much of the push has come from Sir Arthur George, a forceful spokesman for Australia over the years in both Oceania and FIFA. Sir Arthur comes of emigrant Greek stock and is an influential man whose energetic support of soccer has been a boon to the game. On the recent visit I lunched with Sir Arthur at the exclusive Tattersall's club in Sydney's Castlereagh Street. The discussions with him confirmed that the country's soccer should develop vigorously after tasting World Cup success. And that is the aim of the efficient Secretary of the Australian Football Federation, Brian LeFevre, who has suffered on my account. For it was after he had arranged a press conference for me that he lost an eye in an accident on his way home.

Another remarkable Australian who has given soccer, and sport in general, his strong backing, is Vivian Chalwin, whose Chalwin Castle is a centre of cultural life in New South Wales. The castle is a kind of Australian Glyndebourne. Open-air concerts and operas are performed in the Italian garden of this white castellated building as well as in its indoor theatre. The castle and gardens are laid out in the eighteenth-century picturesque style, with the interior lavishly decorated in the Georgian neo-classical manner. It is indeed an enchanted setting for the music which floats over the blue waters of Sydney's middle bay.

Australia seems now to have taken the last step in its ordered development. Max Garrett, a journalist I met on the trip, wrote later to me: 'At last we have seen formed a national league which should break down the isolationism of States and ethnic groups which has so inhibited us.' The youth competitions which I had pressed them to organise had started earlier and in Sydney I was able to present the 'Sir Stanley Rous' Trophy to the winners of the national youth championship.

There is another national youth championship trophy which bears my name. At least I hope it does. For when I was invited to give my name to the Japanese youth competition trophy my delight was tinged with amusement when the dictated letter included the sentence, 'We would like to inscribe the trophy "Sir Stanley Lous".' During the Olympic Games in Tokyo I had got used to seeing my name spelt with an L since there is no distinction between L and R in the language. This had obviously defeated the typist, but not, I hope, the engraver.

I have always fought hard to retain soccer in the Olympic programme despite the inescapable problems of amateurism. For Olympic soccer has so often stirred interest in countries where the game was dormant. This was the case in Japan. One of the Olympic matches in Yokohama was so sparsely attended that naval cadets were 'invited' in to give atmosphere. But with a Japanese centre-forward, Kamomoto, catching the home spectators' fancy, and with fine matches to see, interest built up until there was a 50,000 crowd for the final. For the Japanese, too, football was about to take off. No one has done more to help them sustain that interest than Leslie Taylor, Hon. Secretary of the Middlesex Wanderers, who acts as the Asian Confederation representative, and has arranged for teams such as Manchester City and Coventry to play in Japan as well as Arsenal, who attracted a 70,000 crowd.

My interest in the Olympic Games was broader than in its football, having been deeply involved with the Olympic movement and having attended every Games from the Berlin Olympics in 1936. When the International Olympic Committee held an Olympic Congress in Varna in 1973 and set up a 'Tripartite Commission for the Organisation of the Olympic Congress' it was a privilege to be elected to this Commission. The Commission consisted of members from the International Federations, the National Olympic Committees and the International Olympic Committees. At the Congress I read a paper pointing out that it was the International Federations who produce the performers, and the National Olympic Committees who financed their delegations, yet it was the IOC which often imposed decisions on them. As a result the Tripartite Commission has become a permanent committee of the IOC ensuring greater co-operation.

The Montreal Olympics three years later also gave a boost to Canadian soccer, and it would be appropriate if this can keep in step with the development in the USA. For back in November 1885, Canada's first international was a 1-0 win over America.

Canada has yet to make any real impact on world football, but her recent performances have shown a steady improvement. In August 1975 Canada lost only 2-3 to a strong Hungarian team. A few months after the Olympics Canada beat Mexico 1-0, and the United States 3-0 in Haiti. For the first time Canadians could cherish genuine hopes that they might qualify for a World Cup final. And though their con-

fident expectations of a trip to Argentina were later dashed by
Mexico, it should not be many years before they reach a final.

Many Canadian players are recruited into America's National
Soccer League, and a few have experience of the English League as
well. Of the Canadian World Cup squad, several were with American
teams such as Minnesota Kicks, Seattle Sounders, or Tampa Bay
Rowdies. One of their best defenders was Bruce Twamley, only the
second Canadian-born footballer to play in our First Division, when
he was selected for Ipswich against Wolves in 1975. 'Buzz' Parsons,
the first man to score ten goals in an International for Canada, was
also briefly with Ipswich six years earlier. Wes McLeod, Canada's
youngest international, was recruited by Tampa Bay Rowdies after
fine performances in the winning matches against Mexico and the
United States. Wes scored his first League goal against New York
Cosmos in June 1977 before a crowd of 62,000, who also saw a hat
trick that day by Pele. Canadian and American soccer is indeed so
closely interwoven that progress in one will be reflected in the other.

The driving force in Canadian football of recent years has been
Eric King, the Executive Director of the Canadian Soccer Association.
He is a valued friend and was an entertaining companion during the
1976 Olympics. When I was appointed FIFA inspector for Canada's
match against North Korea in the soccer tournament I was glad to
accept a lift with Eric from Montreal to the ground in Toronto. Six
hours of driving in his company passed more quickly than would have
the ninety minutes of boredom on the booked plane flight. Eric
appeared to enjoy it too judging by his account in *Canadian Soccer
News*:

En route we stopped at a restaurant in Kingston for lunch. Returning to the car Sir Stanley slipped on an oily patch and struck his
head on a concrete support, bloodying the side of his face and fore-
head. Showing determination worthy of a man half his age, he continued to Toronto, scarred and bruised, and was at Varsity Stadium
to complete his assignment.

The following morning we were heading back for Montreal. The
six-hour journey passed quickly for me as my passenger told me one
soccer story after another. We were back in Montreal in time for
Sir Stanley to accept an invitation to lunch with the President of the
Iranian Olympic Committee. There he was greeted by many
friends made during his thirteen years as FIFA President. After
lunch it was back to the hotel to change and then down to the

Stadium again. Sir Stanley is still drinking deep from the cup of life and having spent two days in his company I know the contents of the cup will be 'good to the last drop'.

Indeed they will, and it is friends like Eric King who will keep it tasting sweet.

Through FIFA I have also established close ties with football in Thailand, a happy reminder of those early days at St Luke's when two Thai students played in the College team. The President of the Thailand FA, Lt General Torsakdi Yomnak, has always kept a firm friendship for this country and a keen eye on its football. The General still sends Thai internationals to visit me and to be passed on to clubs like Arsenal to study our training methods.

As a Police-General, and ADC to the Royal Family, General Yomnak has had the responsibility for the security of their King and Queen. A man of wide interests and unfailing courtesy, he has improved football in Thailand by organising youth tournaments and by arranging for the expert West German coach, Dettmar Cramer, to raise the standards of coaching in Thailand and Malaysia. As Vice President of the Asian Football Confederation, and as its representative on FIFA, General Yomnak, together with Koe Ewe Teik, Secretary of the Confederation, has done much to advance Asian football. Their close links with this country are maintained by Leslie Taylor, the Asian Confederation representative in London. Leslie's cheerful devotion to helping footballers has ensured that many Asians continue to study the game here. And though our national performance may not at present excite others or ourselves, the general standards and methods of our League football rightly attract admiring imitators.

Our Royal Family's close links with sport inevitably have given me the privilege of personal contact with them. But it was at a remote and respectful distance that I first admired their demeanour at the great sporting occasions. For the first Wembley Cup Final in 1923 I was a steward on the ground as that tidal wave of people surged in, breaking down the barriers, scaling the fences, flooding the pitch. County Associations all appointed stewards, and as the representative for Hertfordshire I was asked to help direct guests to the Royal Box. Not many of them fought their way through the crush of people as quarter of a million came flooding in to Wembley as remorselessly as a spring tide.

The situation was already totally out of hand as King George V took his place in the near-empty Box. As fresh thousands came seeping in at the back, those in front were being pressed remorselessly on to the pitch, until the whole playing area was packed with people. No one seemed capable of ordering that vast crowd, good humoured as always in those days, but pressing in towards disaster under its own relentless momentum. The King was quite unmoved and his presence had a magical effect. As he came to the edge of the Box there was a stillness at last in that eddying, swaying mass. An elemental force moving mindlessly forward was suddenly transformed to an ordered human response as the crowd gave three cheers so thunderously loud that they must have echoed to Westminster. The King quietly acknowledged them, taking off his bowler hat in response to this spontaneous welcome. His presence was a stillness at the eye of the storm, which gave Constable Scorey and his white horse, Billie, the chance to pass into legend, as they slowly restored order on the pitch.

As there was so little to do in the Royal Box, Sir Frederick Wall asked me to try and help control the crowd. Control the crowd! I was soon a piece of flotsam carried along in its current. Before I was swept away from the entrance steps I was amused to notice that there were still some disciplined enough to hand in their 5s entrance money, as they were pressed past the pay booths, which looked like sentry boxes. But the official receivers had long since left in despair. Every few minutes one of the opportunists in the crowd would go into the booth and shout for payment. Having collected a few five shillings for himself he would melt away to be succeeded by another smart scrounger.

I was soon being carried along at the whim of the crowd. Big and strong as I was, there was no possibility of independent movement and a frightening sense of utter helplessness. I was still wearing my steward's badge and I could appreciate the feeling of a man who called to me, 'I've paid a guinea for my ticket, but I will give you two to get me out.' I was powerless to help, pressed so hard against a man with a whisky bottle in his capacious pocket that I was bruised down the whole of one side and had to cancel my next refereeing appointment because I was too sore to run. And I never could get back to the Box to see Bolton Wanderers beat West Ham.

In later years as FA Secretary I was beside King George when he presented the Cup at the Wembley Finals. He had done it many times before, but the lid of the Cup was awkwardly balanced and he told me he was always nervous it would fall off as he was presenting it. The following year I arranged to decorate the Cup with the ribbons in the winning team's colours tied to the handles. The King mistook the purpose: 'Well done, Rous. I see you have had the damned lid tied on at last.'

Queen Mary also took a close interest in the Finals. And it was she who first introduced the singing of 'Abide with me' in 1927. The *Daily Express* had organised community singing before the game with Radcliffe, a personality of his day, conducting the crowd in songs of his choice. The song sheet had to be approved, however, and Queen Mary asked for the inclusion of her favourite hymn, 'Abide with me'. That became so much a feature of the match that for some it was the highlight of the afternoon. Indeed there was one distraught lady who asked me to get her a Cup Final ticket as she had failed for the first time in years to buy one. So I asked how she came to be so keen on football. 'It isn't the football I go for. It's the singing of "Abide with me".'

In the post-war Cup Finals in particular there was a fervour in the rendering of the hymn which made it an occasion in itself. But custom stales everything and it seemed to me by 1959 that we should drop it quietly from the programme before it lost its power to move. That may well have been a sensible decision, because supporters were beginning to chant their own songs, drowning whatever might be on the song sheet. But the horrified response when the change was announced made it clear that I had been premature and I rapidly agreed to its reinstatement. However, I did have support in one letter to *The Times*:

> Sir—I am the vicar of the parish in which the Empire Stadium is situated and have been an appreciative guest at Cup Finals for many years. I can testify that the hymn 'Abide with me' has been sung with perfect reverence; but with what amount of understanding is another matter. The words 'fast falls the eventide, the darkness deepens' seem out of place in broad daylight and sometimes in strong sunshine. The reverend father, of course, was thinking of his approaching death at all too young an age. But this sentiment is also out of place on the lips of people almost all of whom are young, and few beyond middle age.

The Rev H. W. R. Elsley might have found it out of place, but it was many years before the crowd could accept Queen Mary's choice drifting out of the programme.

Lord Wigram, with whom I worked so closely during the war, was the man who interested King George in football. It was a game he had played at school at Winchester and he transmitted his own enthusiasm

to the King when he was his aide. So Wembley became one of the great Royal occasions enriched by the Royal presence. Other sports envied us our good fortune and wished to share it. It was Lord Derby who came to see me on behalf of Rugby League. He wanted to ask the Queen and Prince Philip to attend a Rugby League final, but, as Derby was a Vice President of the FA, he did not wish to upset us in doing so. I was amused to be asked if rugby league could 'borrow' the Royal Family one year in five and had to agree that soccer had had more than its share of their interest.

And both the Queen and Prince Philip have taken a detailed interest. At the famous 'Stanley Matthews' Cup Final of 1953 the Queen talked with me on all the details of Stanley's career and was even aware of his birthday. Billy Wright, for so long England's captain, used to comment to me how surprised he was to find Prince Philip's detailed knowledge of each player to whom he was introduced.

The Earl of Athlone, like the Duke of Edinburgh, was an able and active President. He took trouble to influence the affairs of the FA during the period he presided and he too was in his element at Cup Finals. But these are evocative occasions and he startled me once by a flashback of memory to his Boer War days. We were watching the precision marching of the Guards band when he turned suddenly to me and said with great force and solemnity: 'Rous—Mafeking was a bad mistake.' There was no ready answer to that, nor indeed to a perceptive comment of the Queen's after one of the dullest post-war Cup Finals. Trying to gloss over the poor performance, I asked her who she thought had played well. 'The band' was the succinct reply.

The Queen and Prince Philip were always asked to sign the book kept ready in the tunnel as they left the Royal Box. Near the end of my time as Secretary the Prince turned suddenly to me and asked 'What will you do when we don't come any more?' 'I hope that is not a threat, sir,' I answered. 'The family is growing up and they will have to take their turn, you know.' And indeed they have. The sporting tradition—active as well as spectator—lives on and gives a welcome lead to sports enthusiasts throughout Britain.

Lord Montgomery of Alamein was never a man to take a passive role and as President of Portsmouth he was full of enthusiasm and theories for football. He revelled in his Club's success when Portsmouth celebrated their jubilee by winning the League two seasons in succession. But it was a different story when Portsmouth were relegated. At once he wrote to me demanding to know what corrective action should be taken. Should the manager go? And wonderful player and pleasant man as he was, had Jimmy Dickinson the *leader-ship* qualities to stay as captain? Defeat does not just happen. Someone has failed, was his theme. If he felt that was failure what would he have thought of Portsmouth's recent troubles!

But one player in whom he always took proprietary pride was Tom Finney. For Montgomery, as for so many of us, he was the greatest of them all. And since Finney had driven a lightly armoured Honey tank up Italy, Monty regarded him as one of his army, even though much of his service was under other commanders. 'How is my soldier-boy Finney doing?' he would enquire whenever we met, and I was happy to inform him of the latest achievements of a player whose sportsmanship was as unfailing as his skill.

Sir Harold Wilson, so good at judging the popular mood, was also the best forecaster of Cup Final results in my experience. When Leeds were leading Chelsea 2–1 in the 1972 Final he leant across to me and said it would end as a 2–2 draw with no further score in extra time. So it was, and he was right again in prophesying that Chelsea would win the replay 2–1. He was always good on publicity too: as Prime Minister in 1966 he appropriated the World Cup as if it was his own, or the Government's achievement. At the banquet after the match when the crowd outside the Royal Garden Hotel called for the players it was Harold Wilson who swept up the Cup and went out with them to wave the golden trophy.

Denis Howell might have been a more appropriate participant in that triumph. For as Minister of Sport he worked hard to ensure all went off smoothly, and it was he who arranged an interest-free loan of almost half a million pounds for clubs like Middlesbrough to bring their grounds up to the required World Cup standard. In preparation for those finals Denis Howell had taken a minute interest in every detail. When I accompanied him on an inspection of the stadiums to be used we took in even the ladies' rest rooms and toilets. Not many Ministers go that far!

There was a close association for me with the BBC as I was for twelve years a member of their Advisory Committee. This was a sounding board for them for our Committee was an entertaining mixture of people from the arts, from sport, from politics, and from the whole social spectrum. During my time there I never felt bold enough to venture outside my own field, but there were distinguished representatives of other walks of life who were ready to make informed comment on any subject including my own. The meetings themselves were impressively organised with the BBC Directors and Programme Controllers ranged at one end of the room answering our questions.

So far as football presentation was concerned there were two points I tried to impress. In the earlier days of TV the commentators tended to overdo the talking, distracting the viewer and talking down to him. The second point I stressed was that most of the talking ought to be an oblique teaching exercise explaining the subtler points of the game when they were visually illustrated for the viewer. The final development of this to the in-depth analysis which Jimmy Hill and Brian Moore so ably conduct, was most welcome to me. And though some complain that action replays put an unfair microscope on referees, the reverse seems to me to have happened. It has made viewers more conversant with the laws and the referee's problems, and has shown how often they are right when players and spectators are bitterly contesting a decision. And if players have to endure constant re-runs of some glaring miss, then referees can accept that inevitably they too will make the occasional mistake and it is not unfair for television to show this. On balance they have gained in respect, not lost it.

This Committee gave me further insight into the arts to which my own small contribution had been through the Arts Educational Schools. These were formerly known as the Cone/Ripley schools and I became a member in 1961. The schools consisted of a London day school, a boarding school at Tring Park, and at one time a teachers training college. They provided specialised training in all forms of dance, music, drama, and painting together with general education. From 1965 to 1972 I acted as Chairman of the schools at a time when I had to become heavily involved in their affairs. New premises had to be found for the London school, Tring Park had to be purchased off a member of the Rothschild family and a new principal appointed, a position the ballerina Beryl Grey held for some time. Once everything was running smoothly again I handed over to Sir William Hart. It had been a challenging experience and I was proud to be associated with schools whose ex-pupils number such distinguished stars as Julie Andrews, Lionel Blair, Claire Bloom, Anton Dolin, Leslie Crowther, Hughie Green, David Hemmings, Glynis Johns, Margaret Lockwood and so many others.

Another show-business personality to make an impression on me was Gracie Fields. She accepted an invitation to the FA's 75th anniversary banquet, where 'Our Gracie' had everyone joining in her songs. She captivated us all, but none more than Billy Heard, the elderly Secretary of the Middlesex FA. He was so struck by her performance that he left her some silver in his will. Gracie was always a warm, relaxed person, and it was a pleasure to see her in Capri on the few occasions I attended football meetings there. She was especially proud of her beautiful home there perched high above its series of terraces and commanding wonderful views of this lovely island. Gracie had a restaurant there which we used to visit. On one occasion we all had strawberries and Arthur Drewry's wife began sprinkling them with pepper. Dr Borassi intervened gallantly to save her from her mistake, but we had to tell him that this was just a strange Lincolnshire custom she always observed. Borassi still could not credit it, and whenever we afterwards had strawberries together he would pick up the pepper pot, look at it, and discard it with mock revulsion.

Politics inside or outside sport has never appealed to me, although back in 1945 I became a member of Paddington Borough Council. The approach was made because of various problems in the Borough which I could help them resolve. During the war most of their playing fields had been converted to allotments or pig farms as part of the 'Dig for Victory' campaign to make us self-sufficient in food. Once all the evacuated children returned there was a desperate need for sporting facilities to be swiftly restored. As soon as this was achieved I left the Council, having quickly become disenchanted with local government. As a non-political person looking for practical solutions I was frustrated to find how much delay and inefficiency is caused by political prejudice and posturing.

Much more rewarding was my work as a magistrate, which I undertook at the request of the Mayor. Because of the many other calls on my time my involvement was kept to a minimum, with the Clerk thoughtfully ensuring that the more straightforward duties and cases were passed to me. But there were still a number of interesting cases to deal with: sad, sordid, or humorous by turn. It was a humorous one which remains most vividly in memory. A barrow-boy was up before us for keeping his finger under the scales to give his customers short measure. Our Chairman that day was a Nonconformist minister of puritanical outlook who took an instant dislike to the defendant for his untidy clothes and disrespectful repartee. Finally, he reprimanded him sharply for his outlandish dress, his lack of a tie, and especially for his long-pointed shoes, and he concluded: 'It is ridiculous to have shoes in which your toes can't come anywhere near the toecap.' That drew an instant riposte: 'Wot abaht the coppers, then, Guv: do their 'eads come near the point of their bleeding 'elmets?' At which I laughed so loud that I was also rebuked by the Chairman.

It was in Paddington, too, that I became President of their Rotary Club. Rotary has always appealed to my gregarious instinct for its friendly fellowship and the chance it gives, nationally and internationally, to meet a variety of leading citizens in any town you visit. In Fiji recently I was invited by the High Commissioner to lunch with him only for him to apologise later that he had forgotten he was booked to attend a Rotary meeting instead. Once he found I was a Rotarian I was put on the guest list, and the speakers' as well. Since I have given hundreds of talks to Rotary meetings, I particularly appreciate that these are held at lunch-time and kept short. On one occasion when I was presiding at the Paddington and Marylebone Rotary a speaker droned on for almost twenty minutes without even reaching his main subject. At 2.20 pm he turned to me and enquired: 'How much longer may I talk?' I was happy to be able to reply, 'As long as you like, but we all go back to work at two-thirty.'

Professional footballers and the organisation of professional football have been my concern for much of my working life. But the amateur game has had as much fascination for me. Unless the enthusiasm is nurtured there, the rest falls apart. So I took a special interest in university football, in the Corinthian-Casuals, and in Pegasus, which gave such a stimulus to amateur football in the 1950s. That combined Oxford and Cambridge team, drawn from graduates as well as undergraduates, had such a fresh approach to the game that Wembley was filled to capacity for the two Amateur Cup Finals they won in 1951 and 1953.

One of those truly amateur players who has frequently crossed my path is Tony Pawson. He was in both those winning sides, and is the only person in the last forty years to have played as an amateur in both First Division football (for Charlton) and county cricket (for Kent). The crowds were always entertained by him, for in his day he was one of the swiftest runners between the wickets or down the wing, and was still quite fast when I watched him play in a Centenary celebration match against Charterhouse School in 1976. When the CCPR set up the Wolfenden Committee to review the structure of sport and recreation in the country he was one of those I recommended for the Committee. As a writer on sport he was called on to draft some of the chapters of that Report, which recommended many of the significant changes which have taken place in the organisation of British sport in the past twenty years.

Cricket was another of my interests, fostered at school and confirmed during the fund-raising activities in the war. For many years afterwards I brought a team to play a charity match against a strong club side, Eastcote in Middlesex. There were usually a few visiting Test players in my side and several cricketing footballers, such as Johnny Haynes. Tony played in many of those matches. On one occasion he was reporting a game down at Cardiff the day before, and then went fishing on a Welsh river until early morning, arriving just before the start time with a bootful of sea trout. Fortunately for him it had been raining hard, and it looked as if he might get an hour's sleep before having to open the innings. However, the umpires and captains were so keen to get the charity game started they went out to inspect the pitch even though there was still a pool or two of water on the outfield. When they reached the wicket, however, the sight of some apparently stranded fish changed their minds about starting. Tony then replaced his sea trout in the car and got in his nap before batting. And now I have cause to be grateful to him for the advice and assistance he has given me in writing this book.

Of all the players I have seen the two who have made the deepest impression on me have been Tom Finney and Pele. Both were complete footballers and perfect sportsmen, outstanding professional players yet in bearing the epitome of the amateur ideal. In Stockholm I watched Pele score two fine goals as a seventeen-year-old, which played a major part in winning the 1958 World Cup final against the host nation, Sweden. His maturity on the field had been remarkable and he was as self-possessed off it. As he came up for his medal he made a touching gesture of sympathy to King Gustav, putting his arm round the monarch's shoulders as if regretful to have defeated his country's team. And as he went from triumph to triumph he remained always a modest, likeable and immensely human individual. His innate courtesy was typified for me when, at the 1974 World Cup which he attended as a reporter, he sought me out to chat informally about soccer. He was its greatest star, but he had none of the aloofness or arrogance which affects many lesser players in their hour of glory.

He had a simple missionary zeal for soccer which brought him his greatest achievement of all. In his two years with Cosmos he made such an impact on America that he 'sold' them soccer far more effectively than any high-pressure publicity could have done. This was the breakthrough I had hoped for when I told American promoters earlier that they would have to show their public the real skills of the game before they would be hooked on it. No one but Pele could have made soccer so popular so quickly, and his final game became America's major sporting occasion of 1977. His quiet revolution there may well shape the future of world football, for America has been a sleeping giant as far as this game is concerned. Pele's genius has roused them at last. It was an American sporting journalist who coined that dreary phrase now used to justify every type of rough play: 'Nice guys don't win anything.' You cannot get two 'nicer guys' than Pele or Finney. They are both winners in every sense, as are so many other great footballers like Bobby Moore, Bobby Charlton, Stanley Matthews, Billy Wright, Johan Cruyff, Lev Yashin, Uwe Seeler, Jimmy Greaves, or Gordon Banks.

Pele's arrival with Cosmos for a $4¾ million contract paved the way to America for other world-class footballers, many of them, like Giorgio Chinaglia of Italy, and Franz Beckenbauer of West Germany, still in their prime. For his final games with Cosmos in New York, Pele was attracting 75,000 crowds and in his last League match there was a local record as 35,548 turned out to see him at Portland, Oregon. In 1977 the football crowds watching the American National Soccer League increased 31 per cent to an average of 13,599, with Cosmos averaging 34,142 and Minnesota Kicks 32,771. Such figures gave Phil Woosnam the confidence to claim without fear of ridicule, 'In as little as five years, this country could be the centre of soccer in the whole world.' It may indeed be.

Woosnam still rated the NASL as inferior to the other main League, the National Football League, but expected to overtake it in the same five-year period. 'Right now,' he said, 'the NFL is number one. You can't beat them for marketing and media coverage. But this League will overtake them before long.' Woosnam envisages a thirty-two-team 'Super-League' which might attract the top players in the world, apart from the stars America herself will produce. That is a pleasing prospect for the future of soccer, for this will be no 'pirate' circus, but a properly controlled league under the direction of USSFA and FIFA. And all this will stem directly from the magic of Pele's play.

In the higher reaches of the game in Britain there is so much talk these days of 'fear' and 'pressure', so little of fun, that it is refreshing to reflect on two such notable players who so obviously enjoyed their football, and who transmitted that enjoyment to millions. There was much the same spirit in many of the England teams with which I toured after the war. They seemed lively, yet relaxed, and with their share of humorists to lighten the tedium of journeys. The three main jokers in an engaging pack were Frank Swift, Stanley Mortensen, and Eddie Baily.

Once as we flew over Switzerland Stan Mortensen noticed that Harold Shentall was snoring, lying asleep with his mouth open. At once he snatched up Swift's lightweight jacket, which was large enough to look on him like a barber's coat, and went through the motions of lathering and shaving Shentall without actually touching him. It was an expert performance which had us all restraining our laughter so as not to wake the victim.

Another time we were flying over the snow-covered Alps which loomed menacingly close to the plane. Eddie Baily peered at the white wastes below then said straight-faced: 'Not many spectators on the terraces today, Sir Stanley.' Eddie was an even better mimic than Stan Mortensen and he may have suffered for his talent. Before a match in Spain we were waiting for Arthur Drewry, who was in charge of the party and the selection, to give his usual pep talk. Instead of Drewry it was Baily who came through the door, swaggering into the room with a paper under his arm, walking exactly as Drewry walked, left arm stiff, right arm swinging across his body. Everyone started laughing, the volume intensifying as, unnoticed by Baily, Drewry came in a few paces behind him exactly confirming the caricature. Drewry, unfortunately, was a sensitive man who didn't appreciate the joke, and Baily was never to play for England again.

15

Time for Reflection

●●●

Retirement from the world soccer stage crept up on me before I was quite ready for it. Shortly after our World Cup win in 1966 I was approached to stand as Chairman of the FA after the sad death of Joe Mears. I agreed with some diffidence, since it would be a heavy burden to undertake to be President of FIFA, and Chairman of the FA and CCPR at the same time. There was another problem in that I might not be eligible, as I was not a Council member. That appeared to have been resolved when the Council voted to let my name go forward. However, further legal advice was then taken and Counsel's opinion was that this was not a valid action under the existing Articles of Association.

A further proposal was then made and passed that a minor amend-ment to the existing articles be put to an extraordinary general meeting in January, which might allow me to stand. The meeting, however, decided not to change the articles, so I was unable to be a candidate in the election, which was narrowly won by Andrew Stephen. In one sense that was a relief, as I should have been hard put to give adequate attention to three such important jobs at the same time.

As the 1974 election for FIFA office approached I had to decide whether to stand again after thirteen years as President. Although I would be seventy-nine when the matter was decided in June at the Frankfurt Congress I let my name go forward. My mind seemed as active as before, my interest in soccer had flagged not at all; and physically I was still able to accept without undue fatigue the heavy schedule of travelling essential to an active President. If compromise was necessary, I hoped that at least I would be allowed a final two years in the job I so much enjoyed.

Partly of course that was a selfish wish because it was such mental fulfilment to me to remain involved in FIFA's work, and in planning the future of world football. Partly it was the conviction that I could still be an integrating force as football faced up to the growth pains of rapid expansion in developing soccer countries. Meeting their expectations without undermining the interests of the already powerful football nations was bound to put strains on the FIFA 'family'.

Indeed, those strains were already showing. For the FIFA Congress the China question was coming up again in its most acute form with a Kuwait resolution calling not just for China's readmission, but for them to expel Taiwan. At least one delegate was reported in the Press as saying that if the resolution was not carried there would 'soon be two FIFAs'. And before the FIFA meeting European fears had been voiced at the UEFA Congress in Edinburgh. There Louis Wouters of Belgium expressed anxiety at 'this inordinate ambition' of the Afro-Asians, while the President, Dr Artemio Franchi of Italy, declared: 'UEFA has no intention of surrendering its strong position in world football. No one shall ask us to abdicate.' In Britain, too, there were some fears in those pre-devolution days that FIFA might require the four British Associations to unite. So the pressures were clear enough, and I felt the diplomacy which had avoided any serious split in the past might still be of value to FIFA.

I was aware, however, that it was almost time for a change. For seventy years Europe had been the dominating influence in the administration of world soccer, as indeed had England for all our periodic aloofness. All my five predecessors as President had been Europeans, and I was already the third English President after Woolfall and Drewry. Yet South America had been for years a major and exciting power in the game, and it was important that their views of laws, of refereeing interpretations, and of attitudes to the game should frame its development as much as Europe's. England had suffered in the past from believing themselves still to be the 'masters' of the game and were too slow to adjust to the obvious fact that many of their 'pupils' had now outstripped them. Europe needed soon to face the same kind of re-evaluation as standards soared in other parts of the world.

I was in no way surprised, therefore, to be opposed by Brazil's Havelange. He had once promised not to stand against me, but the South American Federation (Conmebol) persuaded him to become a candidate. I had hoped, however, that South America would first elect him to a post within FIFA, so establishing his position for the future, and that I would be allowed a final period before he took over.

For I had no doubts that João Havelange should soon be FIFA President. He had made himself the driving force in Brazilian football and the embodiment of South American soccer ambition. He was an engaging personality and at fifty-eight was full of energy and ideas. As a multi-millionaire João was able to undertake an extensive and expensive campaign, and the papers soon recognised him as a possible winner. As the *Sunday Telegraph* put it: 'They do not come much more dynamic than the fifty-eight-year-old Havelange, lawyer, Director-President of six Brazilian companies, former swimming and water polo champion, high-powered sports administrator and, according to his glossy election campaign brochure, the holder of enough decorations to sink a ship.' So there was no doubt I had a battle on my hands!

This was one unlikely to be decided solely on personality, on my experience against João's dynamism. Politics inevitably came into it as well. And in a close struggle the opposition of Russia and her satellites was likely to be decisive. My failure to assist their political aims over Chile had made me *persona non grata* with Russia, and they blamed me for their withdrawal from the World Cup qualifying matches the previous year. There were in fact no grounds for this, as is made clear in the official FIFA report on the 1974 World Cup, extracts from which give this account of the incident:

> During the FIFA Organising Committee's session in Gelsenkirchen, Valentin Granatkin, FIFA's senior Vice President, made an application on behalf of the USSR Football Federation to play the return match in a neutral country and not Santiago, as had initially been decided upon, on account of the situation in Chile. In order to find out what the conditions there were like, the Committee sent a small delegation to Chile. Mr D'Almeida of Brazil and Dr Kaser came to the conclusion that, based on what they saw and heard in Santiago, life was back to normal and the guarantees given by the government were such that the World Cup preliminary match Chile *v* USSR could be played on November 21st 1973. It was proposed that the match take place in Santiago as scheduled. Thereupon Valentin Granatkin appealed verbally to FIFA President Sir Stanley Rous asking for the match to be played in another country.

I was naturally keen to resolve the problem if it was possible, and also to accommodate my old friend Valentin, if I could. But clearly this was a matter which the World Cup Organising Committee had to decide within their rules, and specifically within Articles 4 and 22 of the World Cup regulations. What I did to try and help was to have a cable sent to all members of the Committee: 'Despite investigating committee favourable report Granatkin still wishes Chile and USSR match to be played neutral country. Cable reply immediately whether you confirm committee's decision to play match in Santiago.'

There was an overwhelming majority—15 to 3—in favour of the game going ahead in Santiago. With the facts and opinions so heavily against them, there was no point in Moscow trying to blame me. As the FIFA report adds, the Chileans complained I had gone too far in support of Granatkin: 'Granatkin insisted persistently to the FIFA President, who *surprisingly* took the matter back to the Organising Committee' was their view of it. And we made one more attempt to satisfy Russia whose main complaint had been that they believed the National Stadium in Santiago had been used as a 'torture camp'. But when we suggested they might play on another ground in Chile, they immediately rejected any such compromise. So I could hardly be blamed for their elimination, which would probably have occurred anyway after they had been held to a 0–0 draw in Moscow. But that did not stop them indulging in a political vendetta and campaigning against me.

The Russian attitude may well have had repercussions outside Europe, since their political muscle extends so wide. And while a sitting President has certain advantages there were several 'political' issues militating against me, because I was not prepared to connive at FIFA ignoring its own statutes. The People's Republic of China would have been welcomed to FIFA any time if its application for readmittance had not been coupled to the demand for the simultaneous expulsion of Taiwan. I had to remind members that FIFA's statutes were quite explicit on the point. Membership could only be cancelled for three offences: non-payment of dues; infringement of the statutes or other dishonourable conduct; or ceasing to have the real standing of a national football association. Even in the case of such offence expulsion has to be by vote of three-quarters or more of those attending the Council meeting. Some, however, wanted Taiwan expelled regardless. It was made clear to me that some delegations would vote against me unless Taiwan was expelled, but I was not amenable to that sort of pressure. In the background also was the South African and Rhodesian question, raising emotive feelings even though they had been fairly dealt with and were suspended by FIFA.

Financially, I had no hope of competing with Havelange. All I could rely on was the support of those who knew my past work. The only counter I could make to Havelange's campaign was to produce a small pamphlet listing what I thought I had achieved at FIFA, and the future programme I hoped to implement. My comments on that future read: 'Some of the projects which I list below are already in hand. They cannot be rushed because it is necessary to make sure that all interests are being carefully examined, considered, and the appropriate committee consulted. A President cannot carry out a project by himself.' My projects included: 'The rules and regulations for the World Cup competition are always under review. There is a need to make modifications to the grouping and preliminary rounds as well as the number of teams admitted to the final. I have submitted five alternative proposals.'

The other projects listed covered the development of further coaching schemes, improved instruction for referees and better recruitment methods, better medical amenities for national Associations and proper instruction in sports medicine for coaches and trainers, a reorganisation of the Zurich headquarters designed to increase the scope and efficiency of FIFA's work, negotiations with the International Olympic Committee on the continuing basis for entering sixteen football teams in the Games, more financial aid to encourage youth and amateur football and promote more international matches for them, a wider information service to the Press and to members and the setting up of a reference library with a world-wide selection of technical football books, films and educational aids, the larger Confederations to be subdivided into zones each with a representative on the Executive, the Committee responsible for players' status to be fully briefed and able to advise on the changes in international law and contracts, sponsorship to be encouraged but controlled so that it did not take over the game, and the same approach to be adopted to Government aid to national Associations.

I ended my personal statement with the sentences which expressed my own position as I wished it to be considered: 'I can offer no special inducements to obtain support in my re-election, nor have I canvassed for votes except through this communication. I prefer to let the record speak for itself.' That was the best I could do, but predictably it was not enough.

The major disappointment for me was the African reaction. They had 38 votes compared to Europe's 33 and their influence was decisive in Havelange's election. The hurtful part of this was that I had done so much for the development of football in Africa during my term as

President. Indeed the Europeans who contribute the bulk of FIFA's money often criticised me for giving too much aid to African Associations. I could not expect that to be remembered, however, since the Associations are in many cases subject to government direction and when their officials change so frequently. Many of the delegates representing African and Asian Associations were indeed new to me, and when I checked the list afterwards some were members of embassies and it was a surprise to me that they had been properly accredited in time for the Congress. And they were to hold the key to a close contest.

The first vote was 62 to 56 against me; the decisive second vote 68 to 52.

In losing a contested election like this there is the danger of feeling rejected by old friends with whom one has worked closely, or disillusioned at the manner of one's defeat. And there was a trace of both in my immediate reaction. But that soon passed. I had been aware for some time of the odds against me, and on reflection could take personal pleasure in the heavy support there had still been for me in a close contest. Even more I was delighted to find that there were several who sought me out to assure me that they would still be seeking my advice and involving me in FIFA affairs in the years to come. These indeed were no idle assurances, for I am still invited to many parts of the world for conference courses and tournaments, travelling almost as much as when President. And the many expressions of friendship and appreciation soon erased any tinge of disappointment or bitterness.

In a way, too, there was in my defeat something symbolic of changing attitudes and standards. In football the talk was all of money, and my own lack of personal concern with it may have seemed outdated and amateurish. And while my whole inclination is to avoid politics becoming a dominant influence in football, the politically motivated are more and more using all sport to further their own aims. Politics had begun to seep into football, so an election with political undertones was not inapt.

More positively, it was very desirable that South America now took a leading part in administration. We had made great efforts to unify the interpretation of laws and development of the game within Europe. It was time a similar effort was made to have Europe and South America working in concert, and a Brazilian President was well placed to try and achieve this. Perhaps this was indeed the moment for a change in the old order of things in FIFA.

When the result of the election was announced in Frankfurt's Trade

Fair Hall I congratulated my successor and looked forward to FIFA's continuing success under him. Fortunately, my own involvement was still to continue for I was made a Président d'Honneur of FIFA, and the honorary post has allowed me to continue to work for it. The congratulations were sincere, too, for I did indeed respect Senhor Havelange: I had known him and his family for a long time, and if one had to be beaten it was best to be beaten by such an able and pleasant adversary. I already knew João as a generous man. A typical story of him was told to me by Jack Taylor after he had been refereeing in Brazil. Jack went bathing with a party, having been warned that they should not leave their clothes unattended on the beach. While Jack was bathing the man who should have been watching had his attention diverted, and some of Jack's clothes disappeared. As he had also been told not to leave his money in his hotel room, Jack had it all in his pocket, and over £100 was now missing. The police could do nothing. But as soon as João heard of it he made it up himself.

He was equally generous to me in victory, writing and speaking of me as the best President FIFA had had, and happy that I should continue to work for FIFA as Honorary President. He even proposed that I should be given a sizeable pension by FIFA. The Press picked that up as if it was accomplished fact and gave it headlines such as 'Rous to be soccer's highest paid pensioner'. There had been one precedent in the past when Jules Rimet was given a FIFA pension. But my view was known that it was inappropriate for an unpaid job like the presidency then to be pensioned. It is hardly right that you aren't paid when you are working and are when you aren't! So the suggestion was quietly dropped much as I appreciated the kind thought. No doubt it was Havelange too who prompted Brazil to offer a new World Cup to replace the one they won outright in Mexico and name it the Stanley Rous Cup. I was greatly moved by that gesture, but I asked the Executive Committee simply to call it the FIFA World Cup, as I do not believe such major trophies should bear individuals' names. Keeping that principle was not easy when it would have ensured some measure of immortality had my name been on the Cup!

At least the World Cup competition in Germany was a happy moment for me to take my farewell. In so many ways it expressed what I had hoped to achieve for football. Here was a spectacle which gave pleasure to millions worldwide. Every detail of the organisation was meticulously planned and executed from the colourful opening ceremony, the playing and refereeing arrangements, the continual Press briefings, to the complicated protocol of seating important visitors. Such was the fascination of the competition that 74 countries between them sent 4,616 accredited Press, radio, and TV representatives. And though they were not involved in the final round the United States had the fourth highest number of media men there, 138, to indicate that soccer was at last taking America by storm.

The finalists, West Germany and Holland, both excelled in attacking football which was a joy to watch, as did third place Poland who had so narrowly eliminated England. These three teams also disposed of the myth that it is the hard men who win. For all were in the top four of the Fair Play competition. I was particularly pleased that West Germany, whose team won both the World Cup and the Fair Play Trophy, was the country I had been at such pains to bring back into the family of football. To cap it all, the President of the Federal Republic, Herr Walter Scheel, recognised this contribution with the award of the Grand Cross of the Order of Merit of his country. In doing so he said: 'Since 1947, at a time when Germany had practically no friends left in the world, you made particular efforts on behalf of German football. Especially during the hard and difficult post-war period you have contributed essentially to the readmission of Germany into the International Football Organisation. Your endeavours to establish contacts and to bring about friendly matches between German teams and teams from developing countries have made it possible that the quality of German football became known far and wide. Through this and your close personal relations with German sports officials you have played a decisive part in gaining the present recognition for German football.'

For my part I was happy to recognise the quality of the West German organisation as well as their football. Hermann Neuberger, President of the Organising Committee, had indeed ensured a memorable final round with the able assistance of Hans Passlack, the General Secretary, Hermann Joch and his staff, and Dr Wilfried Gerhardt, the Press Officer. So I proposed Neuberger to succeed me as Chairman of the FIFA World Cup Organising Committee, knowing that would ensure the 1978 Competition was smoothly organised. The recommendation was readily accepted by the Argentine and by FIFA.

That experience in Germany was the perfect end to thirteen happy years as President. My chairmanship of the Central Council of Physical Recreation had ended two years before, when most of its staff and some of its functions were finally transferred to the Sports Council. When the Conservative Party was returned to power in June 1970 they had given a General Election pledge to 'make the Sports

Council an independent body and make it responsible for the grant-aiding functions at present exercised by Government'. Denis Howell, as the first Minister for Sport and Chairman since 1965 of the newly formed Sports Council, had been an easy and understanding man with whom to work and he had respected the separate role of the CCPR. Eldon Griffiths, who took over from him, also accepted that the CCPR had itself to decide its own future. But as the Sports Council's role was enlarged, and as Dr Roger Bannister was appointed as Chairman independent of the Government, amalgamation became a natural solution. At first, however, the Minister took his time studying the problem and held a rather different view.

At the Council's AGM in November 1970 I had to warn him of the dangers of delay: 'We are concerned about the uncertainty of the future and we hope that the staff will learn before long whether they are working for the CCPR or the Sports Council.' In reply, Eldon Griffiths praised the CCPR's work and added that it 'will and must continue' whatever the final organisation. As the new form of the Sports Council emerged, however, and as it became clear that all the staff were to be transferred, an even stronger case for integration was established. There were twelve months of negotiation with the Minister, the Department of the Environment, and the Sports Council, and I was fully involved with the protracted discussions. At the first meeting of the working party the D of E made it evident that they felt the CCPR should be wound up as a separate body and all its staff and assets be transferred once the new Sports Council received its Royal Charter. That of course was abhorrent to many in the CCPR, and I sympathised with their view. On reflection, however, I personally accepted that it might now be the logical solution. Looking back to our formation, I recalled that the 'vision' Miss Colson had originally had was one of the integration of diverse bodies with conflicting aims.

Prince Philip felt strongly that the CCPR still had an important separate role to play as the true voice of voluntary sport. I respected that view and admired the skilful way he achieved his aim. But I believed that the great achievements of the Central Council had been in the past and that the important thing now was to ensure that the Sports Council was fully effective. For in my opinion still, it is to the ultimate good of sport in this country that there is just one body to integrate all the effort, as was the original concept when the CCPR was formed; and so I was content to step quietly aside when the effective power was transferred to the Sports Council.

But I could look back in pride on much accomplished in the twenty-seven years I had chaired the Central Council. In particular I had been closely associated with the development of the network of Recreational Centres. It had been a dream of mine that there should be enough of these multi-sports centres to encourage sport in its widest sense, from cricket to camping. I always envisaged that they should be not just for the expert performer, but designed to interest the beginner or give the local some alternative to the week-end rush to the coast which jammed our southern roads. And to a degree they have filled all those hopes, with a wide selection of people using the Crystal Palace facilities, and even the England football team training at Lilleshall and the MCC holding its coaching examinations there.

Bisham Abbey was the first to open soon after the war, the direct result of a letter to *The Times* which drew a golden response. It was South African generosity which gave us our second. Their Government donated to Britain more than a million pounds to be used for sporting projects, in recognition of our efforts in the war. The plaque at the entrance to Lilleshall records our own gratitude that part of this magnificent gift from the South African people should have funded this Recreation Centre. We had searched the country for a suitable site, looking at an unused school in Scarborough and rejecting it along with a dozen other places before this splendid country house and grounds became available.

It was a bleak wintry day that Princess Elizabeth, as she then was, came to open the Centre. One side of the building was warmed by a pale sun, but where we waited there was only an icy wind playing on the shadowed entrance. The Princess was well briefed as always, and as I hurried her to the warmth of the house she stopped in the door and said 'Weren't you meant to show me the plaque, Sir Stanley?' 'I was too cold to think of it, ma'am,' was the best I could do in reply.

The Crystal Palace Centre was long contemplated and I was involved in lengthy debates with the GLC over the financing of the project. It was a relief when it finally opened to give the capital a true sports centre. By now we were supporting at great cost a real spread of such Centres, several of which provided specialist service, Plas-y-Brenin for mountaineering and fishing, Cowes for sailing, Holme Pierrepoint in Nottingham for water sports; this was a Centre capable of staging the world rowing championships. For me that was true progress.

Another development in which I took a particular interest was the setting up by the Central Council in 1957 of the Wolfenden Committee. The project was discussed in advance with Miss Colson, Justin Evans, the indefatigable and meticulously precise Secretary, Arthur Gem, Baroness Burton, and David Munrow. Sir John Wolfenden's Committee had a brief to look at the whole organisation and financing of sport in the country and, although the CCPR set it up, the Government had indicated they would take note of the recommendations. The report was to lead to many changes and to a closer involvement of the Government with the financing of sport. And if there was irony in the CCPR commissioning the report that was to lead in the long run to a strong Sports Council and an emasculated CCPR, their initiative was of benefit to the country as a whole.

As Chairman I was in daily touch with Phyllis Colson, who was the driving force of the Central Council and constantly maintained its impetus. Her dedication was total: she worked sixteen hours a day herself and stretched the staff to their limits. Even more remarkable, she never let herself be diminished by the ill-health which dogged her. Doctors had told her that rheumatoid arthritis would reduce her to a wheel chair at thirty, but she never accepted the possibility. Only when a new, undiagnosed illness attacked her was she temporarily thrown off balance. Then at times, when she was very low, I would get a midnight telephone call to say she was going down to the Embankment to end it all. And I would hurry round with her doctor to talk her back to her usual resolution. Once it was established that she was suffering from diabetes she was at ease in her mind, knowing just what she had to fight and tackling it with unflinching resolution. She adhered rigidly to her diet and her prescriptions, and refused to let diabetes interfere with her work any more than arthritis. The CCPR was her life, and it was also her life force with her absorption in it triumphing over all suffering. Only when she retired did illness overwhelm her at last.

Phyllis was one of the three most remarkable women I encountered, all with that same total dedication. The Dowager Marchioness of Reading (Stella), who ran the WVS in the war, was in the same mould. I had close contacts with her during the war, when her organisation helped with parcels of sports goods for the troops, and also as a fellow member of the King George VI Memorial Fund, the money from which was dispensed over five years on behalf of youth and the elderly. Lady Reading was as tireless a worker as Phyllis Colson, and with a nice sense of humour about herself. She would tell with relish the story of an American GI who got in the same railway carriage as herself and peered at her uniform. 'I see you are in the WVS,' he said. 'I've been told to go next Friday to see the old bitch who runs your outfit.' And, if she could be believed, when she was decorated for her work she received a cable from a WVS unit at Crewe station canteen: 'We earned it. You wear it.'

The third who greatly impressed me was Ellen Wilkinson. She had been a leader of the Jarrow march in the desperate days of unemployment in the 1930s, but she herself seemed capable of triumphing over any conditions. Ellen was chairman of the Civil Defence Benevolent Fund, and it was because of my involvement with the fund that I got to know and admire her.

There were others to admire in the Central Council staff who gave such splendid backing to Phyllis Colson, Walter Winterbottom, and myself. Justin Evans kept everything working smoothly. George McPartlin and Clinton Sayer brought a technical expertise that won respect from all sporting organisations, as did the dedicated work of the constantly expanding staff. And above all we were indebted to the personal interest of Prince Philip as President. He took a direct and active interest in our work and much was achieved through his initiative. He also had the ability to inspire those who worked for or with the Council.

The Duke of Edinburgh has a real facility for conversation which puts at ease the person he is addressing. It is not always appreciated how much detailed preparation that requires, as he must make most of the opening gambits. It needs technique too. One of his first television appearances was during the twenty-first anniversary celebrations of the CCPR in the Park Lane Hotel. For the programme it was arranged he should be 'plugged in' for conversations with boys and girls at the Bisham Abbey Sports Centre. My one concern was that, faced with both the Duke and a television appearance, the youngsters would be tongue-tied in awe, giving only monosyllabic answers. But Prince Philip got immediate response and had them chatting easily to him. When I asked how he did it, he told me had had two guiding principles: 'Never ask a question to which they can answer yes or no; and never ask a question to which they may not know the answer. Don't for instance ask "Do you like school?", but "What school do you go to?" Never ask "How many people are there in your school?", but "What games do you play and which do you like most?" Always make an opening for them to talk, and never say anything which might embarrass them into silence because they are not sure of the answer.' Those were useful hints, which I have tried to copy.

Prince Philip has been a vital force in the CCPR and no mere figurehead President. It was his determination which kept the Central Council a separate body, rather than merging with the newly formed Sports Council as the Government proposed. He had found the CCPR the authentic voice of sport and was determined that there should still be one voluntary body, free of any Government pressure, which could always express the real feelings of the ordinary sports enthusiast. And he had his way. The Annual General Meetings are occasions he enjoys and enlivens with his ready wit, which is never confined to his prepared speech. On Denis Howell's first appearance at the meeting as Minister of Sport his talk was interrupted by hammering on the roof. Urgent search parties failed to find the noisy workman. Suddenly there was silence. 'Splendid,' said Prince Philip, 'That must be his tea-break. We should have plenty of time to get through the business before he starts again.'

He was always intrigued by the performance of Sir Clarence Sadd, our Treasurer, who had a photographic memory for figures superior even to Roy Webber's 'memory man' efforts on the facts and figures of sport. Over the years a happy routine was established as we came to the usually dull matter of the balance sheet. 'Let's hear the Sadd story', Prince Philip would say, and Sir Clarence would reel off the four or so pages of figures without a note, and without pause, right to every last halfpenny of expenditure and income for the Council, all the individual Sports Centres, and all the other items embraced by the lengthy financial report. The performance was greeted with cheers and the final comment from Prince Philip, 'After that I imagine no one will dare to ask a question.'

With two such major interests of my life ending so quickly, the rest might have been anti-climax. Fortunately, there was no such abrupt end to my work for football or sport. As FIFA President I had made it a rule that I never visited a country without first being invited. Never would I impose on unwilling hosts. And it is satisfaction for me that invitations still flow in from organisations at home and countries abroad, so that my diary seems as full as ever and much of my year is spent travelling. UEFA made me an honorary member at their Stockholm Congress in 1976 and I still get appointments to inspect matches in their competitions and invitations to all their congresses, conferences and youth tournaments. With my other commitments as honorary President of FIFA there is welcome opportunity to maintain old friendships and make new ones as my football connection remains unbroken. There is also a steady stream of requests to give talks to clubs, schools, and referees' societies, and to write articles.

One which delighted me was an invitation to contribute to one of the American journals which is backing the surge of interest there in soccer. Chicago's *Soccer Unlimited* made me review for myself what football had meant to me by asking me to write on what I like about soccer. One extract sums up why I shall always be happy to help promote the game:

> Looking back to my boyhood days I think that soccer appealed to me because of its comparative simplicity. A lot of fun was forthcoming by just kicking a tennis or even a rag ball about. It did not require elaborate equipment and could be played on any open space without proper goalposts, or nets, or field markings. Improvised goals were made with any article available, such as coats, sticks, or stones.
>
> Games are intended to be recreation in its widest meaning. A relaxation from work in school, business or profession. The lessons are learnt incidentally without hard work, and if one learns to 'play the game' then one does so in daily life and becomes a law-abiding citizen. One of the most important lessons is to respect the authority of the referee by accepting his decisions without dissent. Later in life, when a man finds himself as a judge of situations in his daily work, he knows how to be fair to employees and colleagues.

The Americans wanted to know first about the game as fun, and clearly they have their priorities right. But I had thought that my view of the game might be only an administrator's or an average player's, not a professional's. So I was delighted to find the best of them all, Pele, expressing much the same opinions when interviewed at the end of his final match. He, too, stressed the game's simplicity, its availability to the poor, its universal appeal, its development of character and its fun. And if the faults of soccer are glaringly obvious at times—well, the faults are in the individuals who play, not in the game itself. For this is a sport which offers purpose and pleasure to uncounted millions.

Writing in 1970 for *Escape*, an inter-university magazine for Dutch students of English, I ended:

> For the moment professional football is flourishing. I believe it will continue to do so, but there are also real problems which have to be faced, studied and coped with. The game has developed through the years; it is passing through another phase of development now. The next five- and ten-year period should be very interesting and at the

end of that time, the game will still continue, and will still enjoy the crowd appeal and the popularity that it knows in 1970.

Despite all the forecasts of doom that optimistic assessment was clearly the right one. And while soccer is continually adjusting, its basic simplicity has to be preserved, for that is its greatest attraction.

'Crystal-gazing' was the derisive term applied in the past to those of us who thought it necessary to plan ahead by looking into the future. Now every big business has its five-year plan, its forward forecasts, and even its planning agreement with the Government, which at least makes the Government look beyond today's crisis and the next by-election. This forward planning was always an integral part of my own thinking, and it was a necessary drill to look at least five years ahead. That forced my imagination to go beyond the constraints of the present pattern, helping me to shape future developments as well as to adjust to them.

The 'Post-War Memorandum' which I drafted in 1942, and which was accepted unchanged by the FA Council, was a typical example. My mind was stretched to see how present structure could be improved. All the proposals were implemented within that time, except Sunday football, which took longer to gain popular acceptance but is now thriving. Thereafter, I continued to draw up five-year plans at the FA to chart the likely course of development. And at the CCPR there was even a twenty-one-year look ahead, which has proved a reasonably accurate forecast of the shape of things today.

These forward plans helped to keep us leaders in many fields, so that other national and sports associations were later to copy many of our developments. Since this proved a successful technique at the FA, I introduced the same methods to FIFA and UEFA. The problems of implementation are naturally more complex and more slowly resolved in dealing with a world organisation rather than a national one. So ten or more years was there the appropriate time-span of forward forecasts. And in some cases firm plans could be made on that time-scale to allow unhurried preparations. At the Congress in Tokyo in 1964, for instance, I persuaded FIFA to agree to a twelve-year location plan for the World Cup so that the countries concerned could plan at leisure. We confirmed not only England in 1966, but Mexico in 1970, West Germany in 1974, Argentina in 1978 and Spain in 1982. So there was never any danger of last-minute panics and unfinished facilities, as with the Canadian Olympic Games. Members readily accepted the advantages of knowing well in advance so that the host nation had years to study the 'blueprints' and look in detail at the actual organisation of the two previous finals. This way they were well prepared to accept their own responsibilities and had learnt in advance how to overcome likely problems, and formed early their own ideas for improving on the previous staging. So we continued to prepare well ahead, with Argentina having twelve years' notice of the last finals, Spain of the next, and Colombia of 1986.

Sadly, the long look ahead was then discontinued—I hope only temporarily. FIFA clearly had difficulty in knowing whether some African and Asian countries would be ready to stage the World Cup after 1986 and so delayed decisions. But desirable as it may be to give these countries the earliest opportunity of staging a Final, it is clearly much better to continue the long-range planning concentrating on those who already *know* they can. The delay will be insignificant in the perspective of the years, and when one country is ready to undertake the Finals, that country would have the opportunity of a long study and preparation period if the twelve-year plan is kept definite and rolled forward. It is also being argued that the world is so unstable politically it is unwise to fix firm arrangements so far ahead. The reverse is of course true. If three locations are known in advance, all will have at least done some planning. If a crisis then occurs it will be that much easier to make a late switch of venue to one or the other two already preparing.

There are other problems too about the finals which demand a long-term plan *now*. It is very desirable to help emergent football nations develop. But the present groupings are unsatisfactory. The finals should bring together more of the strongest teams and give a fair test between them. The present arrangements discriminate against Europe, where so many of the top soccer nations eliminate each other. Coupled with the arrangements for the finals, this also produces an unreal situation, with qualification in a group often depending on goal total against some outclassed country. It was unfair on Scotland, for instance, in 1974 that they should be eliminated without a play-off when they were unbeaten in their group and all turned on goal margins against the immature Zaire team.

There are growing problems, too, about the country which stages the finals, and very few have the facilities to cope with the high standards required of pitches and stadiums, Press and TV facilities, security and accommodation. FIFA should already be considering a long-term plan, and this should envisage zoning the Finals by splitting the games up between three or four countries. The soaring cost of one country staging the finals is going to limit severely the number of places where they can be held on present lines. Zoning the finals, with four teams playing off their zone in each of four different countries, would limit the cost and organisational problems of each, and cut down the present over-exacting programme of matches. The two winning sides going forward from each country to the finals could have a three-week break before the final knockout started in one of the capitals.

Such 'zones' should be more easily found. When I discussed this with Jugoslav officials they were interested in forming one with Austria, Hungary, and Czechoslovakia and there are other obvious groupings such as the Benelux countries or the Maghreb countries (Algeria, Tunisia, and Morocco).

Unless some such action is taken there may be splits within FIFA in the next decade. Europe might fall back on its own resources and give greater prominence to the European Nations Cup than the World Cup, as this would in some respects be a truer test of football ability. The same might happen in South America, while China would be only too ready to lead a secession of Asian and African countries. The strains are there which could lead to such dissolution, unless there is clear and sensible planning.

Europe in particular has felt aggrieved at making such a large contribution in terms of cash and player power, and yet having such small influence in the voting. A survey some years ago showed that the financial contribution through international matches came to FIFA 71 per cent from Europe; 12 per cent from South America; 7 per cent from Asia; 6 per cent from Concacaf; and 4 per cent from Africa. There was a similar breakdown for registered players with Europe providing 75 per cent; South America 16 per cent; Concacaf 4 per cent; Asia 3 per cent and Africa 2 per cent. Yet recently Africa had 40 votes, and Asia 34, and Europe also 34. With new emerging nations the voting balance tilts against Europe all the time, as they seek membership of FIFA almost before they apply to join the United Nations. As Chairman of UEFA Wiederkehr commented a few years ago 'either Europe will have to assert its dominance in world football or it will have to put up with anything'. Increasingly it looks as if it will have to put up with anything decided by others, as its own voting power bears no relation to its contribution. Even article 33, which takes away the vote from those associations which without valid reason do not take part in two successive World Cups or Olympic tournaments, is allowed to go by default now, so that those who make no contribution can still vote. In certain circumstances Europe might not put up with this situation for ever.

But on the brighter side, there has been an impressive and united step forward in youth football with the success of the first world youth tournament so efficiently organised by Harry Cavan in Tunis in 1977. With 94 nations entering for the next one in Japan this has instantly established itself as an exciting part of football's future.

It is, of course, easier to make predictions from the sidelines when without the responsibility, and the work, of fulfilling one's own prophesies. Peering ahead, there are many changes I would envisage, not all of which can I look forward to seeing in my own lifetime. So much has changed already while I have been concerned with the game—numbering of players, floodlights, lightweight equipment, improved stadiums, artificial grass pitches, substitutes, stricter and more difficult refereeing, more widespread competitions, incentives for winning, wages up to a hundred times higher than the old maximum, player unions and player dictation, sponsorship, broadcasts, television and so many new aspects which we take for granted, including the great growth of Sunday and women's football.

One innovation not yet with us, though I have anticipated it for years is the 'Super League' of only a dozem or so major clubs. The pressures towards it are growing all the time as inflation means that fewer and fewer Clubs can afford top facilities and top players. Freedom of contract will give a further push in this direction: it will discourage teams like Burnley from developing many high-grade apprentices only for other teams to buy them up; it will prevent small clubs from building large balances by selling players; and it will ensure the best players going to the highest bidders. The 'Super League' will be an opportunity for English football to halve the drain of players like Keegan to overseas Clubs; it will also cut down the number of League matches, which will give an England manager a chance again to develop a good English team.

We cling to the myth that our football League is the best in the world. There are others: the West German and South American Leagues for example are as good. But it *is* the toughest in its demands on players and it *is* destructive of national football in its drain of players' energy and in denying them time for national commitments. It has been obvious for years that the League ought to slim and revise its structure but, despite the work of forward thinkers like Alan Hardaker, it has obstinately defended the status quo. Indeed, when I first started airing the idea almost a quarter of a century ago (in an article in the *Daily Express*) the then President of the League, Arthur Oakley, threatened to have me sacked for suggesting it! I still think he was as blind to an inevitable development as to his own power to carry out the threat! Now I expect to see a greatly revised League structure within a decade.

Unless the league takes the right steps, another likely development is the formation of a 'Football Circus'. The price would be higher for the organiser, but so would the potential rewards, and the American experience with William Cox proved its practical possibility. The FA used to be well aware of the danger of such a development, and kept tight control of any teams being formed which were not affiliated to a national Association. That has been allowed to become a blurred area with scratch teams sanctioned: Bobby Charlton's XI is an example. I don't feel the football authorities are fully alert to this danger, which could creep up on them unawares despite the warning from cricket. Football is a world of financial impossibility, with English League clubs overdrawn by a total of over £16 million. Yet still they struggle on, buoyed by dreams, hope and individual ambition. If clubs can glide for a time over the financial deeps, kept floating by dreams of glory, so might a group of rich optimists with the dream of cornering the world's best, and the brashness and brass to do it. If Dubai can buy up the world's top athletes, may not other oil wealth buy up the top soccer players?

Certainly the game will have to become more and more commercialised, with the commercial manager as important to a club's survival as the playing manager. Success on the field will become the necessary adjunct to the financial operations, rather than the commercial ventures being the outcome of playing success. Sponsorships will increase, as will the range of advertising permitted, while clubs battle desperately to meet inflated playing fees, new ground safety regulations, and the whole range of soaring overhead costs from police protection to transport. That is the inevitable trend. But the authorities are right to slow down the development rather than hasten it. When money becomes the all-important consideration, football a secondary one, the game in general and the football supporter are likely to be the main sufferers.

These will be short-term expedients at best. The weak will still go to the wall in time, and the strong will get stronger, for they will have the commercial 'pull' as well as the playing power. Glasgow Rangers or Manchester United can attract over a third of a million pounds profit from their 'pools' and find endless other opportunities to exploit the fascination of their name. Stockport or Raith Rovers are hardly the magic names to make people reach for their cheque books. Commercialisation will not solve problems in the long term, and should therefore be kept in check as long as possible because it is the harmful aspect which will prove more lasting than the helpful ones. The League and FA have to move with the times in these respects, but it is good to see them drag their feet until need is proved.

I can foresee no need for, or likelihood of, significant changes in the laws in the next decade. That is not because I regard them as 'my' laws, as William Pickford did. It is because they continue to serve football so well, and over the past forty years have proved a strong and unifying base for the world's most entertaining and popular game. And those laws have held good at all levels of the game, and in all countries and climates. They are designed for the ordinary club player and still cater adequately for the top-class professionals. They hold good on muddy grounds or sun-baked pitches. They are simple and easily understood by the millions who play and watch. Changes of interpretation and application will always be needed as styles and fashions change. But one of soccer's great attractions is that it is easy for everyone to play and appreciate. Major changes are more likely to confuse than improve. That certainly has been the result in other sports. The more cricket legislators tinker with its complex laws, the less the response. It is so easy to think a change in laws can 'brighten' a game when what is wanted is a change of player attitudes. The dreary phase of defensive football at top level was ended not by new laws, but by the flair of forwards and the outlook of managers.

Most of the changes suggested to 'brighten' soccer have proved unnecessary or undesirable in practice. There was a trial match in Tunis recently to test out some proposals promoted by Prince Rainier and the Table Ronde Internationale as sensible improvements. The three main suggestions were kick-ins instead of throw-ins, mini corners from the edge of the penalty area, and temporary expulsion as in ice-hockey, where erring players can be sent for some minutes of repentance rather than be banished for good. The trial game had goals aplenty but none due to the innovations, which proved unacceptable. The kick-ins were going back to the game's origins and had been discarded for good reasons, not least because a casually won throw-in should not give the same advantage as a free kick awarded for a deliberate foul. The short corners were ineffective as they merely packed the penalty area too solid to penetrate. The 'sin-bin' idea reminded me of the time I allowed a sent-off player back for the second half. But it is impractical in climates like ours, where on wet or freezing days at the average club there are not the facilities to keep a player from stiffening up or catching cold as he waits to resume.

The most significant alteration in the past to the laws was the change in the offside rule to help goal-scoring, and that is the one law that has to be kept under close scrutiny. Had the dreary defensive tendencies in European football become a dominant theme of play, instead of a passing phase which principally afflicted Italy and England, then further change might have been needed. Until the 1925 alteration a player was offside unless there were three or more opponents between him and the goal when the pass was made. The reduction to two brought a scoring spree for a few years. Had the recent goal dearth become permanent, or if it returns in later years, a further reduction to one, or even none, would give another boost to the goal-scorers. But like the earlier change this would be only a temporary relief. If the tactical outlook continued defensive, new methods would soon be found to screen off the forwards, whatever the offside law. Only if the game became sick would the change be necessary, and then it would only be a temporary palliative rather than a cure.

There are two other aspects of offside which cause controversy and difficulty for referees. The fact that you can be 'played' onside by the ball touching an opponent raises queries about whether the offside was not in any case established in the fraction of time the ball was in flight before hitting the opponent. And the fact that you cannot be offside unless you are interfering with play raises problems in deciding what constitutes 'interfering with play'. The logic of the 'played onside' exception is that, as in most games, if you make a mistake you must expect the other side to benefit. So if you deflect the ball to an offside opponent, that is your error and your side's bad luck. My own rule in this case was simple enough. If I had not had time to blow my whistle *before* the ball touched the defending player then the forward was 'played onside', and free to run on. Minor differences in interpretation should not lead to the elimination of a part of the law that is basically sound.

The same applied to 'not interfering with play'. The difficulty for referees was vividly expressed in that famous—or infamous—incident which led to the Leeds United ground being closed for a number of games. The near-riot started as referee Ray Tinkler let Tony Brown run on while Leeds players pointed to another Albion player, Suggett, standing in the centre of the field in an offside position. A goal which probably cost Leeds the League championship followed Tinkler's decision that Suggett was 'not interfering with play'. Other referees might have viewed it differently, but there should have been no questioning of Tinkler's decision. Danny Blanchflower once said, 'If you are on the field and not interfering with play, what the hell are you doing?' But the logic of the law still seems sound: that a good goal should not be disallowed because of the position of someone quite un-involved in the action. In our own goal-starved game we should not look to further diminish them even if this law does give occasional difficulties.

As with the laws, it is important that refereeing methods are not changed for some passing whim. But I am not conceited enough to think that the diagonal system I introduced will remain the last word, incapable of improvement. Pressure on referees is growing, and their decisions become ever more vital as the money and prestige at stake in key games reaches frightening levels. And the referee is exposed now to the cold and critical after-judgements based on the television replay and a leisurely dissection of the incident. He may himself need more aids to guard against error.

A number of experiments in the past have not won instant approval. That expert Russian referee, Latyshev, showed us a new linear system just after the war when he officiated at Tottenham for the Dynamo match against Arsenal. A London fog made a farce of that game, and of the system which could not cope with such a limitation on vision. Latyshev could barely see the players on his side of the field, and never his two linesmen on the other.

More serious thought was given to a proposal that there should be two referees, as in hockey, each controlling one half of the field. I was myself quite impressed by experiments conducted shortly after the war in special trial games. After an Army XI had played Redhill with two referees officiating I arranged an FA trial in a North *v* South amateur match. E. Wood of Sheffield, a Football League referee, took charge of one half of the field while Dr A. Barton officiated in the other. The scheme was eventually abandoned as too complex and costly, and as leading to divided authority. But in a few years I think this idea will be revived, and may well lighten the load of referees in top-class competition.

With the referee now being judged by impersonal gadgetry, he should in future have electronics to aid him as well as to analyse him. Ever since Geoff Hurst's disputed goal in extra time proved decisive in our World Cup win over Germany in 1966 I have favoured the electronic recording of goals. I had no doubt Hurst's shot did bounce down over the line because Roger Hunt immediately turned away, arms upraised when he could so easily have headed the ball in had he been in any doubt. Yet but for the sharp-eyed Russian linesman, Bakhramov, that goal might not have been given. Had there been an electronic device registering when the ball crossed the line, as is the case already in ice-hockey and as is done for the 'touch' in swimming, there would have been no doubt and no controversy. The referee's only job then would be to decide whether the ball had *fairly* crossed the line.

Again in vital matches such as Internationals, World Cup finals, and the like, instant television replays should be available to referee as well as commentators. As it is, a referee will consult a linesman if he has doubt. It would be almost as quick for him to see a replay if he wished.

Whatever aids a referee may have in future, however, the crucial phrase in the laws will still be: 'If, in the opinion of the referee . . .' No electronic device will ever be an adequate substitute for that.

One of the most significant developments for football is the imitation grass all-weather pitch. It is one of the game's attractions that it can be played anywhere, even on the beach or in a back street. But only if pitches are good can standards be high. 'Tartan turf' and its successors will help develop the game fast in countries in Africa or the Middle East previously hampered by inadequate grounds.

We worry now about failing even to qualify for the finals of the World Cup. At least qualifying will not get harder for us, for the European nations have all developed their football already to the same high pitch of professionalism. But if we do reach the finals we will find a much higher overall standard. Not for much longer will the game be dominated by European and South American sides. There are countries in Africa, Asia, and the Middle East which will surprise us by their rapid improvement. And those two great sporting nations, America and Australia, will before long challenge the best in football as they do in other sports.

In cricket, women led the way by staging their own World Cup before the men. In football they are half a century behind. But now the standard of women's play has so improved a women's World Cup cannot be far off. England's women cricketers, led by Rachael Heyhoe-Flint, organised and won the first-ever cricket World Cup. Our women footballers cannot take a similar initiative as their football in most countries is controlled by the national association in membership of FIFA who would have to organise such a tournament. But UEFA has already set up a Committee to deal with women's football and Miss Gregory, Secretary of the English Women's FA, awaits their decision on an international tournament. With teams like Southampton showing the way our women footballers have a good chance of winning any such competition so good is their standard.

The main improvement in our sporting facilities will be an overdue recognition that multi-sports centres are a necessary provision for large communities. Football can lead the way. Abroad many major football grounds are the heart of sporting and social centres. The stadium complex caters for a number of sports and serves the community in other ways. It is a real club at all times, available as a club and as a centre of many recreational and community activities. In British sport only the Central Council of Physical Recreation has made any serious effort to meet this need. There are a few other isolated instances like the Sobell Leisure Centre at Islington, or Mr Lasteed's declared intention of converting Aintree into just such a complex, rather than merely the home of the Grand National. But football has been very slow to move in this direction, even when Clubs have had the money. Bristol City have their ten-pin bowling. Burnley called in Loughbrough College to study how best to build in a sporting or shopping complex to meet local needs as they rebuild one side of their ground. But they then delayed this progressive development for want of funds. And in general football has made little effort to use grounds all the time, instead of once or twice a week. A spread of such community clubs will be one way of reducing the hooliganism which plagues the game. If the young become part of their club they are more likely to behave well in it—a lesson Jimmy Hill taught with his work at Coventry, where the club set out to integrate spectators into all their activities.

We have been very dilatory in this country in such development, and need to make a major effort in the next decade when oil wealth may give us the financial strength for some ambitious leisure improvements for the community as a whole. It is a chance not to be missed. As expectations rise from improved education and living standards, sport has to adjust to meet them. All-weather pitches will become a must, and for football the playing season will need to be more flexible. Summer evenings are ideal for football matches. It is odd that we hold World Cup finals in June to ensure the best playing conditions and yet arrange our League season at the worst period for players and spectators. To split the season between autumn, spring and early summer would also give the players a welcome break from the long grind of League games. By resting them and making them more available for a national manager to train, this might help improve our national performance, which is a current cause of concern.

All footballing countries have their ups and down. Hungary was supreme in the 1950s then went into a long decline. Italy and Spain have had a similarly inconsistent performance, while Holland came from nowhere to produce a great team. Only West Germany and Brazil have been consistently successful, and *we* expect too much in thinking we have a divine right to be always up with the best. But we are right to be worried by the present fall in standards, which is due only in part to a dearth of outstanding players. We need to be more consistent in building a national team through the structure of youth and 'under-23' internationals, and in keeping together a pool of good players who learn to play together. Alf Ramsey made the best use of such opportunities, as did Walter Winterbottom when the selectors allowed him. If we are to improve as a national team, it is also essential that the national team Manager has a network of part-time assistants and the close co-operation of clubs. George Raynor was outstandingly successful as national Manager of Sweden because he had access to players even when with their Clubs, and was given some say in their training. When we get similar co-operation from our own League clubs, the national team Manager may achieve some improvement. Ron Greenwood is certainly a man who deserves such co-operation and has the sense to concentrate on a proper structure building to a consistent national team.

We have been leaders in the past in producing high-calibre referees, and there we can certainly maintain our standards. The appointment of a 'supremo' was a wise move. How successful he is depends on how well he organises and uses a central group of top-class referees as a basis for keeping up improving performance by a pooling of their knowledge and ideas, and as a nucleus for organising the training of a wide range of referees for all levels of the game.

Competition and rewards for leading professionals will grow apace. This will put additional strains on officials and administrators. It will require firm control from referees, and firm guidance from FIFA and national Associations. But the more the game changes the more we should strive to keep certain things the same. Players as well as administrators should appreciate the need to preserve sportsmanship, modesty in victory, goodwill in defeat. If it loses these virtues the game can soon destroy itself. If it changes its laws too abruptly it can lose its character as easily. In accommodating the future the best of the past must be preserved and there is much that is of permanent value in football's past.

It is said of some retired people that they are in their anecdotage, but that's only a half-truth for me. Fortunately, I am still only semi-retired, happily active in the present as well as looking back in pleasure at the past.

'To work that others may play' has been my guiding concept. But work for sport, and particularly for soccer, has in return given me a rich and rewarding life, bringing me friends in many countries and close contacts with the famous in many fields. For me football and living have indeed been fun, and given me a world of happiness. Long may sport and soccer give the same enjoyment to the world's millions.